DOING GOOD BE~~TTER~~

William MacAskill is an Associate Profe~~ssor~~ at Oxford University and the cofounder of ~~Giving What We Can~~ and 80,000 Hours. These non-profits have raised over $400 million in lifetime pledged donations to charity and helped to spark the effective altruism movement. He is a contributor to *Quartz*, the online business magazine of *The Atlantic*, and he and his organisations have been featured in the *New York Times*, the *Wall Street Journal*, NPR and TED, among other media outlets. He lives in Oxford, England.

Further praise for *Doing Good Better*:

'Groundbreaking . . . brilliant, smart and refreshing.' **Herald**

'Satisfyingly counterintuitive . . . a feel-good guide to getting good done.' **Amia Srinivasan, *London Review of Books***

'In this powerful and persuasive book, William MacAskill shows us how much we stand to gain from a little bit of thoughtfulness . . . If you care about the impact of the time or money you contribute to good causes, this book is a must-read.' **Dan Heath, co-author of the *New York Times* bestsellers *Made to Stick* and *Switch***

'Effective altruism – efforts that actually help people rather than making you feel good or helping you show off – is one of the great new ideas of the twenty-first century. *Doing Good Better* is the definitive guide to this exciting new movement.' **Steven Pinker, author of *The Better Angels of Our Nature***

'William MacAskill shows that we can make a surprisingly large life-changing difference to those in disadvantaged parts of the world – provided that our altruistic impulses are intelligently channelled. This fascinating and clearly-written book deserves wide readership.' **Lord Martin Rees**

'MacAskill tackles a monumental question: how can we make the biggest difference for the greatest number of people? His answer is a grand vision to make giving, volunteering, spending, and working more worthwhile.' **Adam Grant, Warton School of the University of Pennsylvania**

'Humanity currently spends more money on cigarette ads than on making sure that we as a species survive this century. We've got our priorities all wrong, and we need effective altruism to right them. If you want to make a real difference on the biggest issues of our time, you need to read *Doing Good Better*.' **Jaan Tallinn, co-founder of Skype**

'Take every preconceived idea you might have about what a head-in-the-clouds philosopher looks like, and bury them in a deep hole. MacAskill is warm, charismatic, and unrelentingly practical. His dedication to doing good is unparalleled, incorporating that ideal into every aspect of his life – his money, his research, and the charities he's founded. And if he can convince me, who has always thought of himself as a socialist, that working on Wall St might be an altruistic thing to do, then he can convince anyone.' **Charlie Bresler, Executive Director of The Life You Can Save**

'MacAskill leads his readers on a witty, incisive tour through the ideas and applications of effective altruism, which seems increasingly poised to become a dominant social movement of the twenty-first century.' **Julia Galef, co-founder of the Center for Applied Rationality**

'*Doing Good Better* has a rare combination of strikingly original ideas, effortless clarity of delivery and a thoroughgoing practicality that leaves the reader inspired to get out their chair and take on the world. Humanity faces some big challenges in the twenty-first century; this is a much-needed manifesto for social change, and MacAskill is the ideal ambassador.' **Dr Eric Drexler, The Oxford Martin School**

'The most valuable guide to charitable giving ever published. It lucidly explains key concepts – including randomised controlled experiments, cost/benefit and expected value analysis, and overhead costs – by applying them to real-world philanthropic choices. Even readers who disagree with MacAskill's conclusions about the value of particular charitable donations will make smarter decisions by learning from his analysis.' **Paul Brest, Stanford Law School**

DOING GOOD BETTER

Effective Altruism and a Radical New Way
to Make a Difference

WILLIAM MACASKILL

First published 2015
by Guardian Books, Kings Place, 90 York Way, London, N1 9GU
and Faber & Faber Ltd, Bloomsbury House,
74-77 Great Russell Street, London, WC1B 3DA

This paperback edition published in 2016

A CIP record for this book is available from the British Library
ISBN 978-1-78335-051-3

Typeset by K.DESIGN, Winscombe, Somerset
Printed and bound by CPI Group (UK) Ltd, Croydon CR0 4YY

8 10 9

To Toby Ord, Peter Singer and Stanislav Petrov
without whom this book would not have been written

CONTENTS

ABBREVIATIONS

AMF	Against Malaria Foundation
BFA	Books for Africa
CO_{2eq}	carbon dioxide equivalent
DALY	disability-adjusted life-years
DMI	Development Media International
DtWI	Deworm the World Initiative
GAIN-USI	Global Alliance for Improved Nutrition – Universal Salt Iodization
Gavi	Global Vaccine Alliance
ICS	Investing in Children and their Societies (previously International Christian Support)
IGN	Iodine Global Network
IPCC	Intergovernmental Panel on Climate Change
MIT	Massachusetts Institute of Technology
NGO	non-governmental organisation
OECD	Organisation for Economic Co-operation and Development
PHC	Project Healthy Children
PPE	Politics, Philosophy and Economics

QALY	quality-adjusted life-year
SCI	Schistosomiasis Control Initiative
SKAT	Swiss Resource Centre and Consultancies for Development
UN	United Nations
UNICEF	United Nations Children's Fund
WHO	World Health Organization

INTRODUCTION:
WORMS AND WATER PUMPS

How can you do the most good?

Until 1989, Trevor Field was a typical middle-aged South African man who had lived a fairly normal life. He enjoyed fresh steaks, cold beer, and fishing with his friends. Working in advertising for magazines like *TopCar* and *Penthouse*, he had never thought seriously about using his skills for the greater good. When he discovered the PlayPump, however, everything changed.

That year, Field and his father-in-law, a farmer, visited an agricultural fair in Pretoria. There he met a water engineer named Ronnie Stuiver, who was demonstrating a model for a new type of water pump. The demonstration reminded Field of a fishing trip he'd taken years before, during which he had watched the women of a rural village wait for hours next to a windmill-powered water pump. There had been no wind that day but the women, who had trekked for miles, still needed to bring water back to their homes. So they simply sat and waited for the water to flow. Field had been struck by how unfair this was. *There simply must be a better way to do this*, he'd thought. Now he was witnessing a potential solution.

Stuiver's invention seemed brilliant. Instead of the typical village hand pump or windmill pump found in many poor countries, Stuiver's doubled as a children's roundabout, which, as it spun, would pump clean water from deep underground up to a storage tank. No longer would the women of the village need to walk miles to draw water using a hand pump or wait in line next to a windmill on a still day. The PlayPump, as it was called, utilised the power of children at play to provide a sustainable water supply for the community. 'African girls have almost nothing – not even books in school let alone playground equipment – and access to water is a huge problem,' Field later told me. 'I thought it was just the best idea I've ever seen.'

Field bought the patent from Stuiver and worked in his spare time over the next five years to improve the design. His experience in advertising gave Field the idea of using the sides of the water tank as billboards that would generate revenue to pay for pump's maintenance. In 1995 he secured his first sponsor, Colgate Palmolive, installed the first PlayPump, and quit his job in order to focus full-time on the project, which by then was a registered charity called PlayPumps International. Progress was slow at first but he persevered, funding several pumps with his own money while developing connections with corporations and government bodies across South Africa to provide more. By the turn of the millennium he had installed fifty pumps across the country.

His first major breakthrough came in 2000, when he beat 3,000 other applicants to win a World Bank Development Marketplace Award, given to 'innovative, early stage development projects that are scalable and/or replicable, while also having high potential for development impact'. That award attracted funding and attention, which culminated in a site visit from Steve Case, CEO of internet service provider AOL, and his wife Jean. 'They thought the PlayPump was incredible,' Field said. 'As soon as they saw it in action, they were sold.' In 2005 the Cases agreed to fund the project and worked with Field to set up an American arm of PlayPumps International. Their aim was to roll out thousands of new PlayPumps across Africa.

The PlayPump became the centre of a massive marketing campaign. Steve Case used his internet expertise to pioneer new forms of online fundraising. The One Foundation, a British fundraising charity, launched a bottled-water brand called One Water and donated the profits to PlayPumps International. It was a huge success, and became the official bottled water of the Live8 concerts and the Make Poverty History campaign. The PlayPump became the darling of the international media, who leapt at the opportunity to come up with punning headlines like 'Pumping water is child's play' and 'The magic roundabout'. In an article for *Time* magazine in 2006, Bill Clinton called the PlayPump a 'wonderful innovation'.

Celebrities, too, jumped on the bandwagon. Rapper Jay-Z raised tens of thousands of dollars through his 'Water for Life' concert tour in 2006. Soon after, PlayPumps International secured its biggest win: a $16.4 million grant awarded by then First Lady Laura Bush, launching a campaign designed to raise $60 million to fund 4,000 PlayPumps across Africa by 2010. By 2007, the PlayPump was the hottest thing in international development, and Trevor Field was at the centre of it all – a rock star of the charity world.

'It has just gone berserk! . . . When I first looked at this water pump . . . I could never imagine that this is something that could possibly change the world . . .' Field said in 2008, reflecting on PlayPump International's startling success. 'It really rocks me to know we're making a difference to a lot of people who are nowhere near as privileged as I am or my family is.' By 2009 his charity had installed 1,800 PlayPumps across South Africa, Mozambique, Swaziland and Zambia.

Then things went sour. Two damning reports were released, one by UNICEF and one by the Swiss Resource Centre and Consultancies for Development (SKAT). It turned out that, despite the hype and the awards and the millions of dollars spent, no one had really considered the practicalities of the PlayPump. Most playground roundabouts spin freely once they've gained sufficient momentum – that's what makes them fun. But in order to pump water, PlayPumps need constant force, and children playing on them would quickly become exhausted.

According to the UNICEF report, children sometimes fell off and broke limbs, and the spinning motion made some of them vomit. In one village local children were paid to 'play' on the pump. Much of the time, women of the village ended up pushing the roundabout themselves – a task they found tiring, undignified and demeaning.

What's more, no one had asked the local communities if they wanted a PlayPump in the first place. When the investigators from SKAT asked the community what they thought about the new PlayPump, many said they preferred the hand pumps that were previously installed. With less effort, a Zimbabwe Bush hand pump of the same cylinder size as a PlayPump provided 1,300 litres of water per hour – five times the amount of the PlayPump. A woman in Mozambique said, 'From 5 a.m., we are in the fields, working for six hours. Then we come to this pump and have to turn it. From this, your arms start to hurt. The old hand pump was much easier.' One reporter estimated that, in order to provide a typical village's water needs, the round-about would have to spin for twenty-seven hours per day.

Even when communities welcomed the pumps, they didn't do so for long. The pumps often broke down within months, but, unlike the Zimbabwe Bush Pump, the mechanism was encased in a metal shell and could not be repaired by the community. The locals were supposed to be given a phone number to call for maintenance, but most communities never received one, and calls from those who did were rarely answered. The billboards on the storage tanks lay bare: the rural communities were too poor for companies to be interested in paying for advertising. The PlayPump was inferior in almost every way to the unsexy but functional hand pumps it competed with. Yet, at $14,000 per unit, it cost four times as much.

Soon, the media turned on its golden child. PBS ran a documentary exposing the PlayPump's many shortcomings. (One thing that didn't change was the media's love of puns: the documentary was called 'Troubled Water'; the *Guardian* repeatedly referred to the PlayPump as 'money down the drain'.) In an admirable response to this criticism, the US arm of PlayPumps International shut down and its sponsor, the Case Foundation, publicly acknowledged that the programme had been a failure. Yet, despite its fall from grace, the PlayPump lives on. Under the name Roundabout Water Solutions, Field's non-profit organisation continues to install the same model of PlayPumps across South Africa, with backing from corporations including Ford Motor Company and Colgate Palmolive.

Many people want their lives to make a difference and, if you're reading this book, you're probably one of them. As Trevor Field's story illustrates, however, good intentions can all too easily lead to bad outcomes. The challenge for us is this: how can we ensure that, when we try to help others, we do so as effectively as possible? How can we ensure that we avoid inadvertently causing harm and have the greatest positive impact we can?

This book tries to help answer these questions. I believe that by combining the heart and the head – by applying data and reason to altruistic acts – we can turn our good intentions into astonishingly good outcomes. To illustrate, let's look at a story with a very different ending from the one you just read.

In 2007, at the peak of the PlayPump's popularity, Michael Kremer and Rachel Glennerster launched an organisation of their own, the culmination of decades of research into how to improve the lives of the poorest people in the world.

Glennerster had studied economics at the University of Oxford, graduating in 1988. She was interested in learning about poverty relief so she decided to live in a developing country and spent a summer in Kenya. She spoke to people working in development, many of whom were deeply disillusioned. When she asked why, they told her to look at some of the ways development projects had backfired.

'I got sent down to big projects that had failed,' Glennerster told me. 'I went to Lake Turkana, up in the north of Kenya. The Turkana people are basically nomadic, and various development projects had hoped to improve their quality of life by settling them on the lake, so they built a big factory for fish. They managed to get them to settle and fish in the lake, but then the lake got over-fished, and the fish stock collapsed . . . It was depressing.' Disenchanted about the potential to have an impact in global development, she moved into domestic policy, taking a job at the British Treasury.

Michael Kremer also spent some of his young adult-hood in Kenya, living there for a year after finishing his undergraduate degree. Like Glennerster, he was concerned by extreme poverty and wanted to learn more, so he lived with a local family and taught English at a secondary school. He also saw some dramatic ways in which attempts to improve conditions there were failing. When he returned to university, he decided to figure out how things could be done better.

Kremer and Glennerster met at Harvard University in 1990. Kremer was a PhD student and Glennerster was visiting on a Kennedy Scholarship, having taken a sabbatical from her work at the Treasury. By the time Kremer became a professor at MIT in 1993, he and Glennerster were married. As a vacation, they returned to Kenya to visit the family Kremer had lived with several years prior.

While there, Kremer spoke to Paul Lipeyah, a friend who worked for the Dutch charity International Christian Support (now called Investing in Children and Their Societies, or ICS). ICS's main programme was child sponsorship, in which a donor paid a regular amount to help an individual child or a small community. ICS had been trying to improve school attendance and test scores. They provided a mixed package: new textbooks, additional teachers, school uniforms and so on. ICS had received new funding, and Paul Lipeyah was about to roll out the programme to seven new schools.

Kremer urged Lipeyah to test his programme using a method known as a randomised controlled trial: he would monitor and collect data for fourteen local schools, implementing the programme in seven of them, while leaving the other seven to go about their business as usual. By comparing data from the two groups he could find out whether his programme actually worked.

In hindsight, Kremer's idea seems obvious. Randomised controlled trials are the gold-standard method of testing ideas in other sciences, and for decades pharmaceutical companies have used them to test new drugs. In fact, because it's so important not to sell people ineffective or harmful medicines, it's illegal to market a drug that hasn't gone through extensive randomised controlled trials. But before Kremer suggested it, the idea was almost unheard of in the development arena.

With the help of collaborators, Kremer tested the different ICS programmes one by one. First, he looked at the efficacy of providing schools with additional textbooks. Classrooms would often have only one textbook for a class of thirty, so it seemed obvious that providing more textbooks would help students learn. However, when Kremer tested this theory by comparing test scores between schools that received books and those that didn't, he found no effect for all but the most high-achieving students. (He suggests the textbooks were written at too high a level for the children, especially considering they were in English, the pupils' third language after Swahili and their local languages.)

Next, Kremer looked at providing flipcharts. The schoolchildren couldn't understand the textbooks, but having flipcharts would allow teachers to tailor lessons to the specific needs of the students. Perhaps these would work better? Again, however, no effect.

Undaunted, he took a different approach. If providing additional materials didn't work, maybe increasing the number of teachers would? After all, most schools had only one teacher, catering to a large class. But, again, he found no discernible improvement from decreasing class sizes.

Over and over again, Kremer found that seemingly obvious programmes to improve education just weren't working. But he persisted. He refused to believe there was simply no way to improve the education of children in Kenya. At that point a friend at the World Bank suggested he test deworming.

Few people in developed countries know about intestinal worms: parasitic infections that affect more than a billion people worldwide. They aren't as dramatic as AIDS or cancer or malaria because they don't kill nearly as many people as those other conditions. But they do make children sick, and can be cured for pennies: off-patent drugs, developed in the fifties, can be distributed through schools and administered by teachers, and will cure children of intestinal worms for a year.

Kremer did an experiment to see whether treating children for these intestinal worms had an impact on education. The results were striking. 'We didn't expect deworming to be as effective as it was,' Kremer told me. 'It turned out to be one of the most cost-effective ways of increasing school participation.'

Absenteeism is a chronic problem in schools in Kenya, and deworming reduced it by 25%. In fact, every child treated spent an extra two weeks in school, and every $100 spent on the programme provided a total of ten years of additional school attendance among all students. Enabling a child to spend an extra day in school therefore cost just 5¢. It wasn't merely that deworming children 'worked' at getting children into school. It worked incredibly well.

What's more, deworming didn't merely have educational benefits. It had health and economic benefits, too. Intestinal worms can cause a variety of maladies, including anaemia, intestinal obstruction and a suppressed immune system that can increase the likelihood of contracting other diseases like malaria. Deworming decreases all these risks. Moreover, when Kremer's colleagues followed up with the children ten years later, those who had been dewormed were working on average an extra 3.4 hours per week and earning an extra 20% of income compared to those who had not been dewormed. In fact, deworming was such a powerful programme that it paid for itself through increased tax revenue.

By the time his work on deworming was published, Kremer's revolutionary new approach to development had spawned a following, with dozens of the brightest young economists running hundreds of trials of different development programmes. Meanwhile, Glennerster had quit her job and become the executive director of the newly founded Poverty Action Lab at MIT, where she used her knowledge of policy to ensure the research Kremer and his colleagues were conducting would have real-world impact.

In 2007, on the basis of this research, Kremer and Glennerster co-founded the non-profit Deworm the

World Initiative, which provides technical assistance to the governments of developing countries, enabling them to launch their own deworming programmes. The charity has provided over 40 million deworming treatments, and the independent charity evaluator GiveWell regards them as one of the most cost-effective development charities.

When it comes to helping others, being unreflective often means being ineffective.

The PlayPump is the perfect example. Trevor Field and everyone who supported him were driven by emotions – the appeal of seeing happy children provide their communities with clean water through the simple act of playing – rather than facts. The Case Foundation, Laura Bush and the Clinton Global Initiative supported the PlayPump not because there was good evidence that it would help people but because it had the thrill of a revolutionary technology. Even critics of the campaign would stop short of accusing Field and his supporters of bad intentions – they of course genuinely wanted to help the people of rural Africa. But this is an excellent example of how relying on good intentions alone to inform your decisions can be potentially disastrous.

It would be nice if the PlayPump were an isolated example of unreflective altruism, but sadly it's just an extreme example of a much more general trend. We very often fail to think as carefully about helping others as we could, mistakenly believing that applying data and rationality to a charitable endeavour robs the act of virtue. And that means we pass up opportunities to make a tremendous difference.

Imagine, for example, that you're walking down your local high street. An attractive and frighteningly enthusiastic young woman leaps in front of you, barring your way. She clasps a tablet and wears a T-shirt that says 'Dazzling Cosmetics'. You agree to speak to her and she explains that she represents a beauty products company that is looking for investment. She tells you how big the market for beauty products is, and how wonderful the products they sell are, and how, because the company spends over 90% of its money on making the products, and less than 10% on staff, distribution and marketing, the company is extremely efficient and therefore able to generate an impressive return on investment. Would you invest?

Of course you wouldn't. If you wanted to invest in a company, you would consult experts or investigate different companies and compare Dazzling Cosmetics' performance with the rest of them. Either way, you would look at the best available evidence in order to work out where you will get most bang for your buck. In fact, almost no one is foolish enough to invest in a company that is pitched to them on the street – which is why the imaginary situation just described above never occurs. Yet, every year, hundreds of thousands of people donate to charities they haven't heard of simply because a well-spoken stranger asks them to, or even simply shakes a bucket at them. And they usually have no way of knowing what happens to the money they donate.

One difference between investing in a company and donating to a charity is that the charity world often lacks appropriate feedback mechanisms. Invest in a bad company and you lose money, but give money to a bad charity and you probably won't hear about its failings. Buy a shirt that's advertised as silk when it's really polyester and you'll realise you've been duped pretty quickly, but if you buy coffee that has a Fairtrade stamp on it you'll never know whether doing so has helped people, harmed them, or had no effect whatsoever. If it weren't for the independent investigations by UNICEF and SKAT, PlayPumps International would have looked like a terrific success to those who supported it. Because we don't get useful feedback when we try to help others, we often don't get a meaningful sense of whether we're really making a difference.

Kremer and Glennerster succeeded in part because they didn't assume they knew what the most effective way of helping people was. Instead, they tested their ideas before putting them into action. They were willing to revise their beliefs about what worked in light of the evidence they received and then go out and do what the evidence suggested they should. In contrast with the PlayPump, the most effective programme turned out to be remarkably boring: Grace Hollister, now the director of Deworm the World Initiative, told me that, 'deworming is probably the least sexy development programme there is'. But by focusing on what was effective rather than what was emotionally appealing, they produced outstanding results, significantly improving the lives of millions.

Kremer and Glennerster exemplify a way of thinking I call *effective altruism*. Effective altruism is about asking

'How can I make the biggest difference I can?' and using evidence and careful reasoning to try to find an answer. It takes a scientific approach to doing good. Just as science consists of the honest and impartial attempt to work out what's true, and a commitment to believe the truth whatever that turns out to be, effective altruism consists of the honest and impartial attempt to work out what's best for the world, and a commitment to do what's best, whatever that turns out to be.

As the phrase suggests, effective altruism has two parts, and I want to be clear on what each part means. As I use the term, *altruism* simply means improving the lives of others. Many people believe that altruism should necessarily denote sacrifice, but if you can do good while maintaining a comfortable life for yourself, that's a bonus, and I'm very happy to call that altruism. The second part is *effectiveness*, by which I mean doing the most good with whatever resources you have. Importantly, effective altruism is not just about making *a* difference, or doing *some* amount of good. It's about trying to make the *most* difference you can. Determining whether something is effective means recognising that some ways of doing good are better than others. The point of this isn't to lay blame, or to claim that some ways of doing good are 'unworthy'. Rather, it's simply to work out which ways of doing good are best, and to do those first. This project is crucial because, as we'll see, the best ways of doing good are very good indeed.

I helped to develop the idea of effective altruism while a graduate student at Oxford University. I had begun donating to charity and wanted to ensure that my donations did as much to help others as possible. Along with Toby Ord, a postdoctoral researcher at Oxford, I began to investigate the cost-effectiveness of charities that fight poverty in the developing world. The results were remarkable. We discovered that the best charities are hundreds of times more effective at improving lives than merely 'good' charities. In 2009 Toby and I co-founded Giving What We Can, an organisation that encourages people to donate at least 10% of their income to these most cost-effective charities. Around the same time, two New York hedge-fund analysts, Holden Karnofsky and Elie Hassenfeld, quit their jobs to start GiveWell, an organisation that conducts extraordinarily in-depth research to calculate which charities do the most good with every dollar they receive.

From there, a community developed. I and others in this community realised that effective altruism could be applied to all areas of our lives – choosing a charity, certainly, but also choosing a career, volunteering, and choosing what we buy and don't buy. On the basis of this, in 2011 I co-founded 80,000 Hours (a name that refers to the number of hours you typically work in your life), which provides advice and coaching on how to choose a career that will allow you to make the most difference.

In this book I'll present in more depth effective altruism's approach to making a difference. What I hope to convey is not a series of facts, but a new way of thinking about helping others which you can take with you and apply in your own life. Part I outlines effective altruism's way of thinking, enabling us, in Part II, to apply that way of thinking to specific issues.

Part I comprises five chapters, each exploring one of effective altruism's five key questions:

1. How many people benefit, and by how much?
2. Is this the most effective thing you can do?
3. Is this area neglected?
4. What would have happened otherwise?
5. What are the chances of success, and how good would success be?

In each case, asking the question can help us to avoid a common pitfall when thinking about doing good:

Question 1 (Chapter 2) helps us to think concretely about how different actions improve people's lives, so that we don't squander our time or money on activities that don't, ultimately, make people better off.

Question 2 (Chapter 3) ensures we try to spend our efforts not on 'merely good' activities, but on the *very best* activities.

Question 3 (Chapter 4) directs us to focus on those areas which receive comparatively little attention, and for which others haven't taken the outstanding opportunities to make a difference.

Question 4 (Chapter 5) helps us to ensure that we're not trying to do good works that would happen with or without our involvement.

Question 5 (Chapter 6) helps us to think about uncertainty correctly, so that we can know when to pursue activities that have low odds of success but large potential payoffs instead of activities with guaranteed smaller benefits.

Taken together, these five questions help us to answer the guiding question of effective altruism: 'How can I do the most good?' They form the core of effective altruism's approach to making a difference.

In Part II I apply these questions to specific considerations: How can I figure out which charities will use my donations to do the most good? How can I choose a career or volunteering opportunity with the biggest impact? How much of a difference can I make through ethical consumption? Of the many problems in the world, how can I decide which to focus on? In each case, I provide a framework for thinking about the issue, and a checklist of questions to help you ensure that you think through all the most important issues. In this second part I hope to show how effective altruism can help us to have a greater impact in all aspects of our lives. For ease of reference, the frameworks and the five key questions are all restated in an appendix.

Before we begin, let me emphasise why these considerations are so important. In the next chapter, I'll explain why each and every one of us has the power, if we so choose, to do extraordinary things.

1

YOU ARE THE 1%

Just how much can you achieve?

When the Occupy Wall Street movement gained traction in late 2011, disaffected citizens of the Western world quickly adopted the term 'the 1%' to refer to the top 1% of income earners in wealthy nations, primarily the United States. The term came from a popular statistic that the richest 1% of the population receives 24% of total income; that's over $340,000 per person per year, twelve times the $28,000 earned by the typical American worker. References to the 1% versus the 99% – i.e. the rest of the population – quickly became shorthand for the income gap in America.

Inequality in America is getting starker over time: while typical household income grew by less than 40% between 1979 and 2007, the income of the richest 1% grew by 275% in that same time period. The French economist Thomas Piketty, who gained international fame for his 2014 book *Capital in the Twenty-First Century*, has suggested that the level of income inequality in the US is 'probably higher than in any other society at any time in the past, anywhere in the world'.

These facts can lead those of us who aren't in that 1% to feel powerless, but this focus on the top income earners in the United States neglects just how much power almost any member of an affluent country has. If people focus exclusively on American inequality, they're missing an important part of the bigger picture.

Consider the graph of global income distribution shown in Figure 1. This graph lines up everyone in the world, ordered in terms of their income. The space between 0% and 25% represents the 25% of the world with the smallest incomes; the space between 75% and 100% represents the 25% of the world with the largest incomes. If everyone had the same income, the line would be flat, forming a neat rectangle under it. But they don't. The poorest people in the world barely even register on the graph. Income soars when you hit the top 10%. And the richest 1%? That spike goes off the chart. If I wanted to draw the whole of this graph, so that you could see where the spike ends, this book would have to be as tall as a 23-storey building, taller than the original Godzilla.

Where do you fall on this graph? You obviously won't know for sure since I've deliberately left the vertical axis unlabelled, but have a guess. What percentage of the world's population is above you in income, and what percentage is below?

When I ask residents of the US or UK this question, they typically guess they fall into the 70th or 80th percentile. They know they're from an affluent country, but they

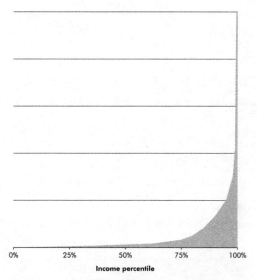

Figure 1: Global income distribution by percentile

Sources: Milanovic, *The Haves and the Have-Nots*; PovcalNet
(http://iresearch.worldbank.org/PovcalNet/index.htm?1),
Numbeo (www.numbeo.com/cost-of-living/)

also know they're not like those bankers and CEOs who make up the global elite. They therefore guess that they're at the corner of the curve, peering up at the mega-rich who sit atop that spike. That's what I used to think, too.

Figure 2 shows the same graph but with the vertical axis labelled. If you earn above $52,000 (£34,000) per year, then, speaking globally, you are part of the 1%. If you earn at least $28,000 (£18,200) – that's the typical income for working individuals in the US – you're in the richest 5% of the world's population. Even someone living below the US poverty line, earning just $11,000 (£7,000) per year, is

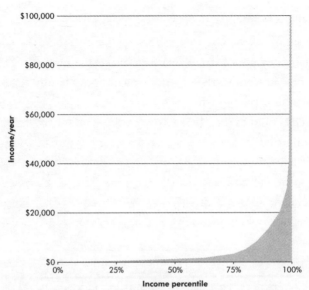

Figure 2: Global income distribution by percentile and income

Sources: As Figure 1

still richer than 85% of people in the world. Because we're used to judging ourselves in comparison with our peers, it's easy to underestimate just how well off those of us in rich countries are.

You might be feeling sceptical at this point. I certainly was when I first heard these facts. 'Sure,' you might say, 'the poor in developing countries might not have much money, but that money can pay for so much more because the cost of living in those places is cheaper.'

It's true that money goes further overseas. When I was in Ethiopia, I ate at one of Addis Ababa's fanciest restaurants, and the bill came to about $10. I even once stayed in a hotel room (albeit a nasty one) for a night for $1. However, that graph of income inequality has already taken the fact that money goes further overseas into account. Let's look at that bottom 20% of the world's population: that's 1.22 billion people who earn less than $1.50 per day, and thereby count as members of the 'extreme poor'. You might assume that '$1.50/day' means that every day the extreme poor live on the equivalent of $1.50 in their local currency. But it actually means they live on an amount of money equivalent to what $1.50 could buy in the US in 2014. What can $1.50 buy you in the United States? A candy bar? A bag of rice?

You might still be sceptical. Perhaps, you think, people in poor countries can live on less than $1.50 a day because they produce a lot of their own goods. They don't have much money but they don't need that much money because they farm their own land and mainly live off what they grow. Again, however, this has already been taken into account in that graph. Suppose Annette is a farmer who earns $1.20 per day from selling her produce, but who also eats 40¢ worth of what she grows per day. According to the way these figures are calculated, she lives on $1.60/day, and is therefore above the $1.50/day poverty line.

You might wonder how anyone can live on so little money. Surely they'd die? And the answer is . . . they do. At least, they die much more regularly than those of us who live in developed countries. Even though average life expectancy in developing countries has skyrocketed over the last few decades, in poor countries in sub-Saharan Africa it is only fifty-six years, compared to over seventy-eight years in the USA. In other dimensions, their lives are just as lacking as you'd expect, given their earnings. In order to get a full picture of what life is like for the extreme poor, Professors Abhijit Banerjee and Esther Duflo, economists at MIT, conducted a survey of thirteen countries. They found that the extreme poor consume an average of 1,400 calories per day – about half of what is recommended for a physically active man or a very physically active woman – while spending most of their income on food. The majority are underweight and anaemic. Most households own radios but lack electricity, toilets or tap water. Less than 10% of households possess a chair or a table.

There is, however, one way in which the $1.50 per day figure can't quite be cashed out as 'what $1.50 could buy in the US in 2014'. In the US, because there is no extreme poverty, there is no market for extremely cheap goods. The lowest quality rice you can buy in the US is far better than what you could buy in Ethiopia or India. The room I rented in Ethiopia for $1 a night was far worse than anything I could rent in the US. (Trust me on this.) The very worst housing you can buy in the US is *far* better than the mud-brick houses typical for those living below the $1.50/day extreme poverty line. This explains how someone living in extreme poverty can still have a 'home', but it doesn't do much, if anything, to improve life in extreme poverty.

The fact that we've found ourselves at the top of the heap, globally speaking, provides us with a tremendous opportunity to make a difference. Because we are comparatively so rich, the amount by which we can benefit others is vastly greater than the amount by which we can benefit ourselves. We can therefore do a huge amount of good at relatively little real cost.

Just how much good should we expect to be able to do? Let's very simplistically suppose that by some social action – giving to a development charity, buying Fairtrade goods, or something else – we make ourselves $1 poorer and thereby make an Indian farmer living in extreme poverty $1 richer. How much more would that $1 benefit the poor Indian farmer than ourselves? It's a basic rule of economics that money is less valuable to you the more you have of it. We should therefore expect $1 to provide a larger benefit for an extremely poor Indian farmer than it would for you or me. But how much larger?

Economists have sought to answer this question through a variety of methods. We'll look at some of these in the next chapter, but for now I'll just discuss one, which is to ask people directly about their wellbeing. (Estimates via other methods would support my conclusion at least as well as this one does.)

In order to work out the relationship between level of income and level of subjective wellbeing, economists have conducted large-scale surveys of income levels and the subjective wellbeing of people in each of them. Their results are given in Figure 3, which shows the relationship between income and subjective wellbeing both within a country and across countries.

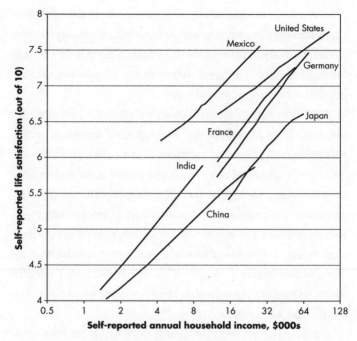

Figure 3: Life satisfaction and income

Source: Stevenson and Justin Wolfers, 'Subjective well-being and income'

The vertical axis of Figure 3 represents self-reported wellbeing. Those interviewed had to say how satisfied they were with their lives on a scale from 0 to 10. Rating yourself at 10 means you consider yourself maximally happy: you think that, realistically, life couldn't get any better. Rating yourself at 0 means you consider yourself maximally unhappy: you think that, realistically, life couldn't get any worse. Most people fall in the middle of this range. The horizontal axis represents annual income.

What's interesting about this graph is that a doubling of income will always increase reported subjective wellbeing by the same amount (note that the $ amounts double at each division). For someone earning $1,000 per year, a $1,000 pay rise generates the same increase in happiness as a $2,000 pay rise for someone earning $2,000 per year, or an $80,000 pay rise for someone already earning $80,000 per year. And so on.

This graph allows us to determine just how much greater a benefit the extreme poor receive from $1 than you or I do. Imagine if your boss called you in and told you your salary would double for the next year. You'd be pretty pleased, right? What the conclusions from the economic studies suggest is that the benefit you would get from having your salary doubled is the same as the benefit an extremely poor Indian farmer earning $220 a year would get from an additional $220.

As noted earlier, the typical US wage is $28,000 (£18,200), so there is good theoretical reason for thinking that the same amount of money can be of at least one hundred times as much benefit to the very poorest people in the world as it can be to typical citizens of the West. Anyone earning this much is one hundred times as rich as the very poorest people in the world, which means one additional unit of income can do a hundred times as much to benefit the extreme poor as it can to benefit you or I. This isn't to say that income is all that matters to wellbeing – of course other factors such as safety and political freedom are involved. But income certainly plays a critical role in how enjoyable, long, and healthy your life is. Looking at how much we can benefit people via increasing their income gives us a particularly robust way of assessing how much we can benefit others compared to ourselves.

It's not often you have two options, one of which is a hundred times better than the other. Imagine a happy hour where you could either buy yourself a beer for $5 or buy someone else a beer for 5¢. If that were the case, we'd probably be pretty generous – next round's on me! But that's effectively the situation we're in all the time. It's like a 99% off sale, or buy one, get ninety-nine free. It might be the most amazing deal you'll see in your life.

This idea is important enough that I've given it a name. I call it The 100x Multiplier. For those of us living in rich countries, you should expect to be able to do *at least* one hundred times as much to benefit other people as you can to benefit yourself.

The 100x Multiplier should surprise us. We shouldn't expect to be able to do so much to benefit others at such little cost to ourselves. But we live in an unusual place during an unusual time.

It's an unusual place because, if you're reading this book then, like me, you're probably lucky enough to be earning $16,000 (£10,500) per year or more, putting you in the richest 10% of the world's population. That's a remarkable situation to be in.

It's an unusual time because it comes after a period of extraordinary economic progress that has led to some of the world experiencing what is, historically, fabulous wealth.

In 1800 the gross domestic product per person per year in America was only $1,400 (in today's money), whereas now it's over $42,000. In a mere 200 years, we've become thirty times richer. But it is a time following remarkably *unequal* economic progress. Despite the riches of people like us, there are still billions living in abject poverty. This is highly unintuitive, as can be seen by the graph of gross domestic product per person, over the last 2000 years, shown in Figure 4.

For almost all of human history – from the evolution of *Homo sapiens* 200,000 years ago until the Industrial Revolution 250 years ago – the average income across all countries was the equivalent of $2 per day or less. Even now, over half of the world still lives on $4 per day or

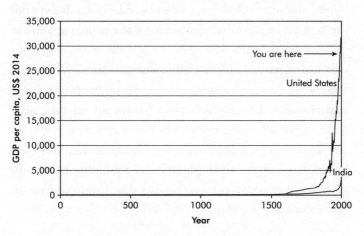

Figure 4: GDP over time

Source: Angus Maddison, *Contours of the World Economy 1–2030 AD*

less (see Figure 2). Yet, through some outstanding stroke of luck, we in the developed world have found ourselves the inheritors of the most astonishing period of economic growth the planet has ever seen, while a significant proportion of people stay as poor as they have ever been.

Moreover, because of that economic progress, we live at a time in which we have the technology easily to gather information about people thousands of miles away, the ability to significantly influence their lives, and the scientific knowledge to work out what the most effective ways of helping are. For these reasons, few people who have ever existed have had so much power to help others as we have today.

Sometimes we look at the size of the problems in the world and think, 'Anything I do would be just a drop in the bucket. So why bother?' But, in light of the research shown in these graphs, that reasoning doesn't make any sense. It's the size of the drop that matters, not the size of the bucket, and, if we choose, we can create an enormous splash. We've already seen that we have the opportunity to provide a benefit for others that is one hundred times greater than the benefit we could provide for ourselves. That we can't solve all the problems in the world doesn't alter in any way the fact that, if we choose, we can transform the lives of thousands of people.

PART I

THE FIVE KEY QUESTIONS
OF EFFECTIVE ALTRUISM

2

HARD TRADE-OFFS

Key question 1:
How many people benefit, and by how much?

June 21st 1994. Kigali, Rwanda. Two months into one of the most horrific genocides the world has ever witnessed, James Orbinski manned a small Red Cross hospital, a tiny wellspring amid a moral wasteland.

The problems in Rwanda had begun to build up decades earlier, when the early Belgian colonialists had decreed that, of the native population, the minority Tutsi were racially superior to the more numerous Hutu. Under this regime, the Tutsi assisted the colonial rulers while Hutu were used as forced labour. This situation changed radically in 1959 when the Tutsi monarchy was overthrown and replaced with a Hutu republic and Rwanda became independent of Belgium. But things did not get better. The country's new leaders imposed dictatorial military rule and harvested the little wealth the country had for their own ends. Many of Rwanda's Tutsi fled to neighbouring countries as refugees, and the nation soon became one of the poorest in the world.

As prosperity declined, Hutu resentment towards the Tutsi grew. Over time, the extremist ideology known as Hutu Power, explicitly based around racist anti-Tutsi principles, gained popularity. By 1990 Rwanda's leaders had begun arming Hutu citizens with machetes, razor blades, saws and scissors; a new radio station had been set up to broadcast propaganda and hate speech; and attacks from the Tutsi refugee army, the Rwandan Patriotic Front, were being used to catalyse fear among the Hutu populace. In 1994 anti-Tutsi sentiment reached its zenith when, on 6 April, the Rwandan president was assassinated. Extremist Hutu blamed the Rwandan Patriotic Front, giving them the perfect opportunity to initiate their long-planned genocide.

By the time Orbinski found himself at that Red Cross hospital, hundreds of thousands of Tutsi had been killed. The UN was stalling, not wanting to admit that a genocide was in progress, and had provided almost no support. Only a handful of non-profit workers remained in the country. Later in his life, Orbinski would become the president of Médecins Sans Frontières and accept the Nobel Peace Prize on its behalf, but at this time his role was simply to provide care for those who needed it, and with so many casualties, what could he do? He later recalled:

> There were so many, and they kept coming. Patients were taped with a 1, 2 or 3 on their foreheads: 1 meant treat now, 2 meant treat within twenty-four hours, and

3 meant irretrievable. The 3s were moved to the small hill by the roadside opposite the emergency room and left to die in as much comfort as could be mustered for them. They were covered with blankets to stay warm and given water and whatever morphine we had. The 1s were carried by stretcher to the emergency room or to the entrance area around it. The 2s were placed in groups behind the 1s.

I cannot comprehend what it was like for James Orbinski to see so many in pain at once and know he could help so few of them. I can only be thankful that I will never witness suffering of that magnitude. I imagine you feel the same.

However, there is a way in which Orbinski's situation is similar to ours. With so many casualties coming in, Orbinski knew he could not save everyone, and that meant he had to make tough choices: who did he save, and who did he leave to die? Not all could be helped, so he prioritised and engaged in triage. If it were not for that cold, calculating, yet utterly necessary allocation of 1s, 2s and 3s, how many more lives would have been lost? If he had made no choice – if he had put his hands in the air and claimed defeat, or if he had simply tried to treat whoever came in first – he would have made the worst choice of all.

The reality of our world is such that, if we want to make the world a better place, we must make choices similar to those Orbinski had to make.

Suppose you have money you want to donate to charity. If you donate to Haiti earthquake relief, you help disaster victims. That means you have less money to fund antiret-rovirals to fight HIV in Uganda, or to help the homeless in your local area. As a result of your choices, someone is made better off and someone else misses out. Confronted with the choice, you might be inclined to give to all these causes: make more room in your budget for increased char-itable giving or divide your donation among several causes. But your time and money are limited and you cannot solve all the problems in the world. This means you need to make some hard decisions: whom do you choose to help?

Exactly the same problem arises for our use of time. If you have a spare couple of hours per week that you're happy to dedicate to helping others, how should you use them? Should you work at a soup kitchen? Join a mentor-ship programme for troubled youth? Organise fundraisers for your favourite charity? Again, there are far too many problems in the world and not enough time to solve them all. We need to prioritise.

Orbinski's situation was more salient than ours since the potential beneficiaries were there in front of him, crying out for help. The fact that he *had* to make a choice, and that not-choosing would itself be a decision, was inescapable. That we are not directly confronted with the competing beneficiaries of our charitable efforts and donations may lead us to take our situation less seriously than we would if we were in Orbinski's shoes, but it makes the situation no less real. There are literally billions of potential recipi-ents of our help. Each one is a worthy beneficiary, someone who has real problems and whose life could be made better by our actions. We therefore need to make decisions about whom we choose to help, because failure to decide is the worst decision of all.

Effective altruism, at its core, is about confronting Orbinski's dilemma and trying our best to make hard trade-offs. Of all the ways in which we could make the world a better place, which will do the *most* good? Which problems should we tackle immediately, and which should we leave for another time? Valuing one action over another is difficult both psychologically and practically, but it is not impossible. In order to make comparisons between actions, we need to ask: how many people benefit, and by how much? This is the first key question of effective altruism.

To begin to answer this question, we need to know the consequences of our actions. To illustrate, let's think about choosing which charity to give to. In order to assess your potential impact by donating to a charity, you need to know what exactly that charity will do with your donation.

For many charities, it's not clear what the answer is. For example on the Salvation Army website you can read about the many programmes they run, including soup kitchens, community support for veterans, emergency shelters for the homeless, and summer camps and after-school programmes for children from low-income families. If you dig further you can learn how their spending is divided among broad categories such as 'rehabilitation', 'corps community centre' and 'other social services'. Nowhere, however, is it stated how much any of their programmes cost, and therefore exactly what you give would achieve.

This is such a typical state of affairs that you might not have thought about how astonishing it is. But imagine going into a shop where none of the products had prices on them. Instead, the proprietor asks: 'How much would you like to spend today?' You hand over some money and receive in return a selection of goods chosen by an assistant.

This, of course, is absurd. If this was how things worked, how could we ever do our shopping? One store could charge ten times the amount for the same product and we wouldn't be able to tell until after we'd paid.

If it would be absurd to shop this way, why is donating to charity any different? In the case of charity, you're buying things for other people rather than yourself, but if you're interested in using your money most effectively, that shouldn't make a difference.

Sometimes, charities do tell you what you're buying with your money. For example, on its 'Donate Now' webpage, the New York City branch of the United Way tells you that a donation of $50 is enough to provide five books with parent guides to a family. This is a step in the right direction. But, even assuming that the '$50 for five books' figure is accurate, it's still not that useful because we don't know what benefits those books provide. We care about providing books only if doing so will lead to things that really are of value. Do the books help children do better in school? Do they enrich families' lives through a better understanding of the world? If those extra books don't actually improve anyone's lives, then your $50 donation is worthless.

We can overcome this problem by thinking in terms of *improving lives*, rather than in terms of intermediate metrics like number of schoolbooks provided. In order to truly make comparisons between different actions, we need to measure impact in terms of the size of the benefits we confer through those actions.

In some cases, it's relatively clear which action will provide a larger benefit. Let's think about Orbinski again. Saving someone from dying provides a larger benefit than saving someone from losing a limb, so if Orbinski had to choose between one or the other, he should save the life. Similarly, he would provide a larger benefit by saving five lives than by saving one. So, if, for example, he could provide five simple life-saving surgeries in the time it would take to provide one more complicated life-saving surgery, it's clear he should opt to perform the simpler surgeries.

However, there are many harder cases: if you can prevent the death of a five-year-old or a twenty-year-old, which should you do? What if you can prevent ten people from suffering from AIDS or one hundred people from suffering from severe arthritis? What about preventing one woman from being domestically abused versus enabling one child to go to school?

For health benefits, economists have spent decades conducting research in order to answer questions like these. They have developed a metric called the quality-adjusted life-year, or QALY (pronounced 'kwalee') in order to help make decisions about how to prioritise among different health programmes.

The idea behind the QALY is that there are two ways you can give a health benefit to someone. First, you can 'save someone's life'. (I use quotes here because 'saving' a life, of course, only ever means extending someone's life.) The second way to benefit someone is to improve the quality of their life during the time they are alive. Migraines don't kill people but, as someone who occasionally suffers from them, I know that life is better without them.

The QALY combines these two benefits into one metric, using survey data about the trade-offs people are willing to make in order to assess how bad different sorts of illnesses or disabilities are. For example, on average people rate a life with untreated AIDS as 50% as good as life at full health; people on average rate life after a stroke as 75% as good as life at full health; and people on average rate life with moderate depression as only 30% as good as life in full health.

We can illustrate the QALY metric using graphs. Figure 5 illustrates a fairly typical representation of how well a

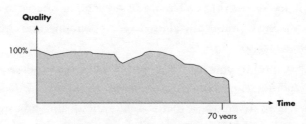

Figure 5: Typical quality of life over time

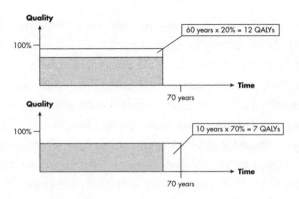

Figure 6: Two ways to improve quality of life

person's life goes over time. This graph shows a person who lives most of his life very healthy, who has some mild health troubles at age thirty-five but then gets better. His health begins to deteriorate as he enters old age, until his death at seventy-two.

Figure 6 shows the two ways you can benefit someone's quality of life. The upper panel illustrates improving the quality of someone's life by 20% for the sixty years they are alive. That would amount to 12 QALYs in total (60 × 20%=12). The lower panel illustrates extending the life of someone who is currently at 70% health by ten years. That amounts to 7 QALYs overall. The QALY metric therefore allows us to measure the size of benefits that different people receive.

If you want, you can come up with your own personal quality weights. Think of an ailment that you have suffered from at some point in your life. Suppose you suffer from back pain, as I sometimes do. You could think to yourself: if 10 represents how good my life is when I'm perfectly healthy, how good is my life on a day when I'm suffering from back pain? This can be difficult to answer, so a way to make your judgements more precise is to ask yourself about what sorts of trade-offs you'd make. If you could live one extra day at perfect health or a certain larger number of days living with back pain, at what point would you be indifferent? In my own case, I'd be indifferent between living an extra four days perfectly healthy, or an extra five days with back pain. That suggests that I think life with back pain is 80% as good as life pain-free. In the endnotes, I link to some official lists of quality-of-life estimates, to help you assess the severity of different conditions yourself.

Economists have used the QALY metric to assess the cost-effectiveness of different health treatments. They test a certain programme, assess how much it costs and what health improvements it provides, and then translate those health improvements into QALYs. After doing this for a number of different programmes, they can work out which programme provides the largest benefit for a given amount of money. If you have limited resources, then, other things being equal, you should spend those resources in whatever way will provide the most QALYs.

To illustrate, consider a simple hypothetical example. Suppose that you have $10,000 and with that money you could pay for antiretroviral therapy for a forty-year-old who has AIDS, or a surgery to prevent blindness in a twenty-year-old, but not both. Without the antiretroviral therapy, the forty-year-old will die in five years' time; with the anti-retroviral therapy, the forty-year-old will die in ten years' time. The twenty-year-old will live to the age of seventy whether or not the blindness-preventing surgery is carried out. (Of course, in the real world we can never know exactly how long people will live, so to perform this calculation we'd have to use average life expectancy.) Should you pay for the antiretroviral therapy or for the surgery? QALYs can help us to make that decision. First, we assess the size of the benefit from the antiretroviral therapy. People rate the quality of life with AIDS while not receiving antiretroviral therapy at 50%, and rate the quality of life with AIDS while receiving antiretroviral therapy at 90%. By providing antiretroviral therapy to the forty-year-old, you'd therefore increase quality of life by forty percentage points (from 50% to 90%) for five years, and give an extra five years of life at 90% health. That equals 6.5 QALYs ((40% × 5) + (90% × 5) = 6.5).

Second, we assess the size of the benefit from the blindness-preventing surgery. People rate the quality of life while blind at 40%. By preventing the blindness of the twenty-year-old, you'd therefore increase quality of life by 60% (from 40% to 100%) for fifty years. That equals 30 QALYs (60% × 50 = 30). This tells us that you'd provide a larger benefit by paying for the surgery than for paying for the antiretroviral therapy. All else equal, the surgery is the better option.

QALYs are imperfect, as any measure of health benefit will be. For example, people who have never been on dialysis typically estimate that, if they were on dialysis, their health-related quality of life would be 39%, whereas people who actually are on dialysis on average rate their health-related quality of life at 56%. The same is true for other medical conditions: patients tend to regard their conditions as less bad than non-sufferers do. Is this because the general public doesn't really understand what life with the medical condition is like and overestimates how bad it is? Or is it because patients have subconsciously lowered the standard for what they regard as 100% health? It's difficult to know, and academics continue to debate the topic. Similarly, some people think that we should give special importance to preventing the deaths of younger people, or give special weight to those who are particularly disadvantaged. These are contested issues, and they are unlikely to be resolved any time soon.

For our purposes, however, it's often not important for us to have precise numbers on how good or bad different conditions are. As we'll see in the next chapter, programmes differ dramatically in how great an impact they have, so even a rough idea of how many people are affected, and by how much, is often enough to show that one programme has a much larger impact than another.

In this book I'll talk about QALYs quite a lot. That's not because I think the only way to make a difference is to improve someone's health. Rather, it's because, as I'll explain in the coming chapters, many of the best, most concrete and easy-to-measure ways of doing good involve improving global health. We've also got much better data for health programmes than for many other sorts of activity.

Since the goal of effective altruism is to do the most good we can, health is a good place to start.

Moreover, in principle the same methods that were used to create the QALY could be used to measure the costs and benefits of pretty much anything. We could use these methods to estimate the degree to which your wellbeing is affected by stubbing your toe, or by going through a divorce, or by losing your job. We could call them 'well-being-adjusted life-years' instead. (Unfortunately, the acronym for this would be 'WALY', which might explain why it hasn't yet taken off.) The idea would be that being dead is at 0% wellbeing; being as well off as you realistically can be is at 100% wellbeing. You can compare the impact of different activities in terms of how much and for how long they increase people's wellbeing. In Chapter 1 we saw that doubling someone's income gives a 5% increase in reported subjective wellbeing. On this measure, doubling someone's income for twenty years would provide one WALY.

Thinking in terms of wellbeing improvements allows us to compare very different outcomes, at least in principle. For example suppose you were unsure about whether to donate to the United Way of New York City or to Guide Dogs of America. You find out that it costs Guide Dogs of America approximately $50,000 to train and provide one guide dog for one blind person. Which is a better use of $50: providing five books, or a 1/1,000th contribution to a guide dog? It might initially appear that such a comparison is impossible, but if we know the impact of each of these activities on people's wellbeing, then we can compare them.

Suppose, hypothetically, we found that providing one guide dog (at a cost of $50,000) would give a 10% increase in reported wellbeing for one person's life over nine years (the working life of the dog). That would be 0.9 WALYs. And suppose that providing 5,000 books (at a cost of $50,000) provided a 0.001% increase in quality of life for 500 people for forty years. That would be 2 WALYs. If we knew this, then we'd know that spending $50,000 on schoolbooks provided a greater benefit than spending $50,000 on one guide dog.

The difficulty of comparing different sorts of altruistic activity is therefore ultimately due to a lack of knowledge about what will happen as a result of that activity, or a lack of knowledge about how different activities translate into improvements to people's lives. It's not that different sorts of benefits are *in principle* incomparable.

Not everyone agrees with this. For example in 2013 the CEO of Charity Navigator (a charity evaluation service that I'll discuss in Chapter 7), Ken Berger, and his colleague Robert M. Penna wrote a critical piece on effective altruism for the *Stanford Social Innovation Review* blog. They objected that the comparing of one cause to another, 'amounts to little more than charitable imperialism, whereby "my cause" is just, and yours is – to one degree or another – a waste of precious resources'. As they clarified in correspondence, Berger and Penna believe 'it's impossible to weigh one person's interests against another's'. They therefore think it's futile to try to determine which causes are most effective.

However, their view surely cannot be correct. If Berger and Penna were right then we couldn't say that giving someone an extra dessert is a smaller benefit than saving someone's life. Nor could we say that you do more good by saving a million lives than by saving ten. We would have to conclude that nurses who engage in triage – ensuring that doctors don't spend their time treating mild coughs when they could be treating heart attacks – have no basis for their decisions. But that would be absurd. It might be difficult, both emotionally and practically, to weigh different people's interests against each other, but it's not impossible either in principle or, I believe, in practice.

Let's consider a different objection. Doesn't the focus on trying to benefit others as much as possible neglect the fact that you might have a closer personal connection to some causes than others? If a family member died of cancer, isn't it natural to want to direct your energies to fighting cancer? Shouldn't you focus on that cause, even if you could theoretically do more good elsewhere?

I feel the pull of this objection. For example in 2009, when setting up Giving What We Can, I was trying to find those charities that do the most good with every dollar they receive. In the course of doing this I came across the Fistula Foundation. Obstetric fistulas are truly awful conditions: a hole between a woman's vagina and bladder or rectum, through which urine or faeces leak uncontrollably. They are generally caused by prolonged labour during childbirth, though they can be caused by rape or sexual abuse. They occur almost entirely in poor countries, where malnutrition results in women having an underdeveloped pelvis, and where there are insufficient medical resources available to perform a caesarean. The fistula causes incontinence, and the women who suffer from them often end up ostracised from their local communities, unable to get work.

The primary recipient of the Fistula Foundation's revenue is the Hamlin Fistula Hospital in Addis Ababa, Ethiopia. Fistulas are treated there with surgery and follow-up care, counselling and education are provided. This was clearly a highly worthy cause, doing a huge amount of good. Ultimately, however, I concluded that an even bigger impact on people's lives could be made by donating elsewhere. (I'll discuss what causes I believe to be most effective later in the book.)

But there was a problem. When I'd been in Ethiopia several years before, I'd visited this hospital. I'd hugged the women who suffered from this condition, and they'd thanked me for visiting them. It had been an important experience for me: a vivid first-hand demonstration of the severity of the problems in the world. This was a cause I had a personal connection with.

Should I have donated to the Fistula Foundation, even knowing I could do more to help people if I donated elsewhere? I do not think so. If I were to give to the Fistula Foundation rather than to charities I thought were more effective, I would be privileging the needs of some people over others for emotional rather than moral reasons. That would be unfair to those I could have helped more. If I'd visited some other shelter in Ethiopia, or in any other country, I would have had a different set of personal connections. It was arbitrary that I'd seen this particular problem at close quarters.

Similar considerations apply to deciding what cause to focus on more generally. As already noted, if an uncle dies of cancer, you might naturally want to raise money for cancer research. Responding to bereavement by trying to make a difference is certainly both understandable and admirable, but it doesn't give you good reason to raise money for one specific cause of death rather than any other. If that person had died in different circumstances it would have been no less tragic. What we care most about when we lose someone close to us is that they suffered or died before their time, not that they died from a specific cause. By all means, the sadness we feel at the loss of a loved one should be harnessed in order to make the world a better place. But we should focus that motivation on preventing death and improving lives per se, rather than preventing death and improving lives in one very specific way. Any other decision would be unfair on those we could have helped more.

If we want to do as much good as we can, we need to think about what consequences our actions will have. Moreover, we need to think about how our actions will eventually improve people's lives. When making decisions, whether that's where to volunteer, what career to pursue, or whether to buy 'ethical' produce, we should therefore consider (1) the cost of the activity, in terms of time or money, (2) the number of people it benefits and, crucially, (3) how much it improves people's lives.

This is the first step towards addressing the hard question of how to allocate our limited time and money. The crucial second step is to realise the importance of focusing on the *best* activities. Let's turn to that.

3

HOW YOU CAN SAVE HUNDREDS
OF LIVES

*Key question 2: Is this the most
effective thing you can do?*

In 2009 a Zambian-born economist, Dambisa Moyo, published a book called *Dead Aid: Why Aid Is Not Working and How There Is a Better Way for Africa*, in which she argued that 'aid is malignant', and should stop. She summed up her views early on in the book: 'So there we have it: sixty years, over US$1 trillion of African aid, and not much good to show for it.' Her message rang true for many, and her book was a bestseller.

She's not alone in her anti-aid sentiment. In 2006 William Easterly, an economist at New York University, wrote a book entitled *The White Man's Burden*. Easterly's book, which popularises the view that aid has been ineffective at best and harmful at worst, has become a bible for aid sceptics – those who believe international aid efforts have been a waste of time and energy. He writes:

the other tragedy of the world's poor . . . is the tragedy in which the West spent $2.3 trillion on foreign aid over the last five decades and still had not managed to get twelve-cent medicines to children to prevent half of all malaria deaths. The West spent $2.3 trillion and still had not managed to get four-dollar bed nets to poor families. The West spent $2.3 trillion and had still not managed to get three dollars to each new mother to prevent five million child deaths.

I endorsed something like aid scepticism for quite a long time. After I graduated from college, I decided against applying for jobs at non-profits partly because of stories I'd heard about food aid being stolen and sold by corrupt governments, and assumed there was no way I could have an impact under these conditions. I donated to development charities, but I always felt uneasy about whether I was actually helping others or merely alleviating my own sense of guilt about being born privileged in a world with so much need.

I've since realised that I was thinking about development in entirely the wrong way. The picture that aid sceptics paint is highly misleading and, even more importantly, isn't particularly relevant for people who want to do good.

One error sceptics make in their critiques is emphasising the amount of money spent. A trillion dollars of aid spending, which Moyo appealed to in her book, sounds like a lot of money, but, to the average person, it's too great a sum to comprehend, so we need to put it into context. The total annual economic output of the world is $87 trillion; the US spends about $800 billion on social security every year; a decade of cosmetics sales amounts to $1.7 trillion; and in 2001, Donald Rumsfeld mentioned that the US military had simply *lost track* of $2.3 trillion. In global terms, therefore, $1 trillion is not very much money. We can see this even more clearly once we translate this figure into more meaningful terms. Over sixty years of aid spending, $1 trillion is slightly under $17 billion per year. Divided by 412 million people – the average population of sub-Saharan Africa in that time – that's only $40 per recipient per year. When we take into account the fact that the $1 trillion in aid spending must be divided among a very large number of people over many decades, we see that the amount of aid spent per recipient is very small indeed.

Second, the claim that there is 'not much to show for it' is simply false. Even among the 'bottom billion' – the population of countries that have experienced the weakest economic growth over the last few decades – quality of life has increased dramatically. In 1950, life expectancy in sub-Saharan Africa was just 36.7 years. Now it's 56 years, a gain of almost 50%. The picture that Dambisa Moyo paints is inaccurate. In reality, a tiny amount of aid has been spent, and there have been dramatic increases in the welfare of the world's poorest people.

Of course correlation does not prove causation. Merely showing that the people's welfare has improved at the same time the West has been offering aid does not prove that aid *caused* the improvement. It could be that aid is entirely incidental, or even harmful, holding back still greater progress that would have happened anyway or otherwise. But in fact there's good reason to think that, on average, international aid spending has been incredibly beneficial. Moyo points to aid's inefficiencies by focusing on *typical* aid programmes. But to get a true picture of how much benefit the developing world has received from aid, one needs to focus instead on the *best* aid programmes.

A good contender for the best aid programme ever is the eradication of smallpox. Smallpox was a horrific disease. The infection would present itself initially like the flu, resulting in fever, muscle pain, malaise and headaches. After two weeks, small lesions appeared on the mouth, tongue and throat. Soon afterwards, fluid-filled blisters developed on the skin: first the forehead, then the face, then the rest of the body. Everyone who was infected would be badly disfigured for the rest of their lives and about 30% would die. In the twentieth century alone, smallpox killed over 300 million people. In 1977, it was finally eradicated.

It's difficult to comprehend just how great an achievement this was, so let's make a comparison. Suppose we'd achieved world peace in 1973. How many deaths would have been prevented? That timescale includes the killings by Cambodia's Khmer Rouge, the Rwandan genocide, the two Congo wars, the 9/11 attacks and the wars in Afghanistan and Iraq. If you add up all the wars, genocides and terrorist acts that have occurred since 1973, the death toll is a staggering 12 million. Prior to its eradication, smallpox killed 1.5 to 3 million people every year, so by preventing these deaths for over forty years, its eradication has effectively saved somewhere between 60 and 120 million lives. The eradication of smallpox is one success story from aid, saving five times as many lives as world peace would have done.

Just for the sake of argument, let's be generous to the aid sceptics. Let's suppose that, over the last six decades, foreign aid achieved absolutely nothing except eradicating smallpox. A simple calculation shows that *even if this were true*, foreign aid would still be a bargain. The total aid spending of all countries over the last five decades is $2.3 trillion (Moyo's $1 trillion figure was aid just to Africa). That means that, using the low estimate of the benefits of eradicating smallpox, at 60 million lives saved, foreign aid has saved a life with every $40,000 spent. In comparison, government departments in the US will pay for infrastructure to improve safety if doing so costs less than about $7 million per life saved: the precise figures are $9.1 million for the Environmental Protection Agency, $7.9 million for the Food and Drug Administration, and $6 million for the Department of Transportation. This means that, even if aid had achieved absolutely nothing except eradicating smallpox, it still would have prevented a death for 1/150th of the cost that the US is currently willing to spend to save the lives of its own citizens.

This calculation not only shows that aid has 'worked', but also that it's been cost-effective on average. Moreover, this calculation significantly underestimates the positive impact of aid. Thanks to immunisation, annual deaths from preventable illnesses have declined from 5 million in 1960 to 1.4 million in 2001, despite world population doubling in that time. Annual malaria deaths have declined from

3.8 million to about 0.7 million. Annual diarrhoeal deaths have declined from 4.6 million to 1.6 million. Aid isn't responsible for all these reductions, but it is responsible for a proportion of them, and that's despite the fact that the amount of money spent on aid is tiny in global terms.

Indeed, even aid sceptics agree that the best sorts of development programmes, especially those within global health, are very effective. For example, William Easterly (the author of *The White Man's Burden*) notes, 'There are well known and striking donor success stories, like the elimination of smallpox, the near-eradication of river blindness and Guinea worm, the spread of oral rehydration therapy for treating infant diarrheal diseases, DDT campaigns against malarial mosquitoes (although later halted for environmental reasons), and the success of WHO vaccination programmes against measles and other childhood diseases.' He summarises his view by commenting that 'even those of us labeled as "aid critics" do not believe aid has been a universal failure. If we give you aid agencies grief on failures, it is because we have seen some successes, and we would like to see more!'

There are certainly many examples of attempts to help that do little good: PlayPumps is just one example. But when evaluating whether aid has worked *on average*, it's not enough to look at *typical* cases of aid; you also need to look at the *best* cases. In the context of doing good, this is vital because the best activities are often far superior to typical ones, which can make the average benefits of aid spending very high, even if typical benefits are small.

We're used to thinking of what's typical and what's average as being the same. For example if you measured the height of all women in North America and plotted those heights on a graph, the result would be something like Figure 7.

The height of a typical woman in North America (that is, a woman who is taller than 50% of people and shorter than 50% of people) is 5 feet 5 inches; the height of the average woman (which is equal to the total height of all women divided by the number of women) is also 5 feet 5 inches. In the case of height, what is typical and what is average is the same. This sort of distribution is what we're most familiar with, so it's aptly called a *normal* distribution.

But this isn't true in every situation. Look at Figure 8, which uses data from the graph in Chapter 1 representing global income distribution. This graph shows how many people live in various income brackets. Notice how different this is from the distribution of height. In this graph, the

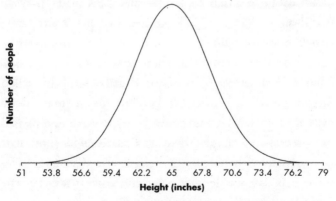

Figure 7: Height of North American women

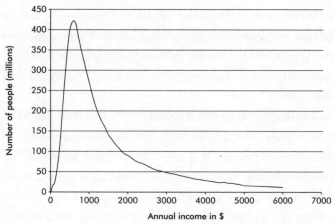

Figure 8: Global income distribution

Sources: See Figure 1

right-hand 'tail' of the curve just keeps going. In fact, in order to make the shape of the curve visible on the page, I had to cut off the graph at $6,000 per year, even though 20% of the world earns more than that.

Distributions that look like this are called *fat-tailed* distributions. (You might have heard of the '80/20' rule: that 80% of the value of an entire set of activities can be achieved by performing the best 20% of those activities. That rule describes a fat-tailed distribution.) Fat-tailed distributions are interesting because they're marked by extreme events. Whereas there are very few extremely small or extremely tall people, there are a relatively large number of extremely rich people. (If height were distributed like income is, we would regularly see people towering 270 feet tall, peering over skyscrapers.) That's why the world's average income, which is $10,000 per year, is so much higher than the typical income, which is only $1,400 per year: the richest people bring up the average.

For this reason, fat-tailed distributions are unintuitive. That's partly why it's so difficult to understand income inequality. We don't realise that we're extreme outliers. In fact, fat-tailed distributions are fairly common. For example most people live in a small number of cities; most people who have died in an earthquake died in one of the relatively rare catastrophic ones; a small number of words make up the majority of most printed text (which means that, if you want to learn a language, you're better off learning the thousand or so most common words first). When it comes to doing good, fat-tailed distributions seem to be everywhere. It's not always true that exactly 80% of the value comes from the top 20% of activities – sometimes things are even more extreme than that, and sometimes less. But the general rule that most of the value generated comes from the very best activities is very common.

The effectiveness of different aid activities forms a fat-tailed distribution, and this fact is very important if we want to make a difference. In response to Dambisa Moyo, I pointed out that, because the best programmes are so good, they make aid very effective on average. But we don't need to fund programmes of merely average effectiveness. We can deliberately choose to fund only the very best programmes, which allows us to do a *tremendous* amount of good.

To see how this plays out, let's consider two types of aid programmes. First, developing-world education (see

Figure 9). All the programmes listed in this graph are programmes that 'work', in the sense that they have a measurable positive impact. But the differences between these four estimates are enormous. Providing cash rewards to girls who stay in school yields an additional 0.2 years of school attendance with every $1,000 spent. Providing free primary school uniforms does ten times better, resulting in 7.1 additional years of school attendance for every $1,000 spent. But deworming schoolchildren does fifteen times better than that, with 139 total years of school per $1,000.

In the context of helping others, the difference between a good use of money and a great use of money is huge. We shouldn't just ask: 'Is this programme a good use of money?' We need to ask: 'Is this programme the *best* use of money?'

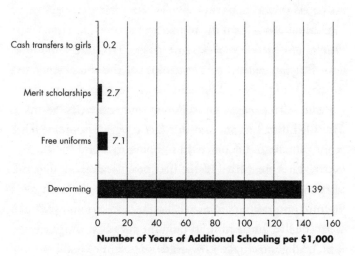

Figure 9: Improving school attendance

Source: Abdul Latif Jameel Poverty Action Lab

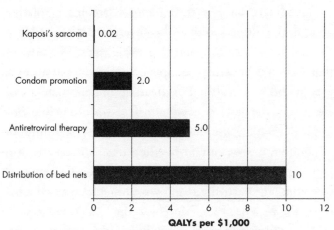

Figure 10: Health programme effectiveness

Sources: Jamison et al. (eds.), *Disease Control Priorities*; Galárraga et al., 'HIV prevention cost-effectiveness'; www.givewell.org

The same phenomenon occurs with respect to developing-world health. Figure 10 lists the estimated cost-effectiveness of different health programmes, measured in QALYs (where one QALY, remember, represents a benefit equivalent to giving one person one year of life in perfect health). These results are even more amazing than those for school attendance. Consider Kaposi's sarcoma, a cancer that occurs in those with HIV and typically causes disfiguring purple tumours on the skin and in the mouth. Kaposi's sarcoma can cause painful swelling of the legs and feet and it can be life threatening if the tumours occur in the lungs, liver, or digestive tract. One estimate puts the cost-effectiveness of surgery to remove Kaposi's sarcoma, which produces mainly cosmetic benefit, at about $50,000 per QALY.

Spending money to treat Kaposi's sarcoma is clearly a good deal, costing less than the governments of the US or the UK are willing to spend to provide one QALY and less than I would be willing to spend to give myself an extra year of perfect health. But treating Kaposi's sarcoma is clearly not the best use of money if we wish to help people in the developing world. On these estimates, by promotion of condom use we can do one hundred times as much to benefit people than we can by treating Kaposi's sarcoma; by providing antiretroviral therapy we provide two and a half times the benefit again. Moreover, the QALY allows us to make comparisons across very different programmes that combat very different illnesses. By donating to the Against Malaria Foundation, who buy and distribute long-lasting insecticide-treated bed nets, you would, by this estimate, provide five hundred times the benefit that you would by spending the same amount of money treating Kaposi's sarcoma.

Once again, we see the importance of focusing on the very best activities. We need to ensure we're making not just *a* difference but the *most* difference we can.

Importantly, the cost-effectiveness estimates given above are just that: estimates. The figures for Kaposi's sarcoma, condom distribution and antiretroviral therapy are individual estimates based on specific contexts and may therefore be optimistic. The figure for bed-net distribution is more robust – the calculation behind it tries to correct for biases in favour of optimism, and takes into account the specific context in which the charities work – but even this estimate should not be taken as gospel. However, in the context of fat-tailed distributions, even rough estimates are vitally important for decision-making. In Figure 10, the best healthcare programme is estimated to be five hundred times more effective than the worst (which, remember, is still a good programme). Even if the highest estimates were too optimistic by a factor of fifty, it would still be vitally important to focus on the best programmes rather than merely good ones.

What we've seen is that thinking carefully about how you can do the most to benefit others doesn't just allow you to do a *bit* more good – it enables you to do vastly more than you might have done otherwise.

Imagine saving a single person's life: you pass a burning building, kick the door down, rush through the smoke and flames and drag a young child to safety. If you did that, it would stay with you for the rest of your life. If you saved several people's lives – running into a burning building one week, rescuing someone from drowning the next week, and diving in front of a bullet the week after – you'd think your life was really special. You'd be in the news. You'd be a hero.

But we can do *far* more than that.

According to the most rigorous estimates, the cost to save a life in the developing world is about $3,400 (or $100 for one QALY). $3,400 is a small enough amount that most of us in affluent countries could donate that amount every year while maintaining about the same quality of life. Rather than just saving one life, we could save a life every working year of our lives. Donating to charity is not nearly as glamorous as kicking down the door of a burning building, but the benefits are just as great. Through the simple act of donating to the most effective charities, we have the power to save dozens of lives. That's pretty amazing.

In this chapter, we've seen the importance of focusing on the best charitable programmes, and we've seen just how good those programmes can be. In the next, we'll look at one rule of thumb to help us find those very most effective programmes, and we'll begin to look at how we can best use our time as well as our money.

4

WHY YOU SHOULDN'T DONATE TO DISASTER RELIEF

Key question 3: Is this area neglected?

Greg Lewis was fourteen when he decided to become a doctor. Born and raised in the rural city of Salisbury in Wiltshire, his reasons were typical of countless others who decide to pursue medicine. 'I want to study medicine because of a desire I have to help others,' he wrote in his university application.

Indeed, medicine is the banner career for people who want to make a difference. Every year about 20,000 people in the US and 8,000 people in the UK go to medical school, and the number is growing year on year. Even for those for whom medicine isn't a good fit, the desire to pursue a career that makes a difference is widespread. According to one study, 70% of young people regard ethical considerations as 'crucial' in their choice of employer. Enterprises like Teach for America have grown dramatically, explicitly targeting students who care more about making a difference than about making a high salary. Organisations such as Net Impact, Idealist and ethicalcareers.org all offer advice on choosing a vocation that does good. Even Oprah Winfrey, on her website, provides examples of 'jobs that make a difference'.

But since effective altruism holds that we should test our assumptions about how to do good before putting them into action, we should look at this more critically. Are the most popular ways to make a difference through one's work really the most effective ones?

If anyone was going to make a big difference through medicine, it was Greg Lewis. After acing his high school classes and representing his country in the Biology Olympiad, he pursued his dream and went to Cambridge to study medicine. He excelled there, too, publishing his first paper at the age of twenty-one. But as Greg began life as a doctor, he started to wonder what impact he was really having.

Wasn't it obvious? He was on the ward, in the midst of the action, saving lives and healing the sick on a daily basis. He could see the beneficiaries of his actions – they were right there in front of him!

It wasn't obvious enough for Greg, though, and he started to use the research skills he'd honed in the lab to analyse a new question: how much good was he really doing by choosing medicine as a career rather than some other? As a result of that research, he developed a different view on how he could best make a difference in the world. To explain the reasoning behind that view, we need to look at the third of effective altruism's key questions: Is this area neglected?

Which is more valuable: water or diamonds?

I imagine this question has divided my readership into two camps. Team Water will say: *Obviously* water is more valuable. If we didn't have water, we'd all be dead. If we didn't have diamonds, we'd just have slightly less attractive jewellery. No big loss. In contrast, Team Diamonds will say: *Obviously* diamonds are more valuable. If you think water is more valuable, then how about we make a little trade? I'll give you a gallon of water and you give me a 20-carat diamond. Sound fair?

So which team is right? They both are, depending on what exactly we mean. Drinkable water is in one sense extremely valuable because it's necessary for us to keep living. This makes the *average* value of drinkable water high. But we've already got a lot of water, so the value of an *additional* gallon of water (in developed countries) is very low. If I, a citizen of a developed Western nation, have one additional gallon of water, that means I may simply have a slightly deeper bath one evening. This is why the cost of a gallon of water from the tap in New York City, where I'm writing these lines, is just $0.015 – less than two cents.

In contrast, even though the average value of diamonds is much lower than that of water, the value of an additional (or 'marginal') diamond is much higher. The reason, simply, is that there aren't that many diamonds available on the market: they are therefore scarce in the way that water isn't. If I had no possessions at all, and couldn't sell what I gained, I'd rather have a gallon of water than a 20-carat diamond. In contrast, given the easy access to water that I currently have, I'd prefer the diamond if given the choice.

This 'water and diamonds' paradox shows the importance of what economists call *thinking at the margin*: assessing the value of an additional thing – what is known in economics as its *marginal utility* – rather than thinking about the average value of that thing.

We think on the margin all the time. Suppose you receive a new sweater for Christmas. How good is that sweater? The answer depends on how many sweaters you already have. If it's winter, you're homeless, and you have no warm clothes, that sweater might prevent you from getting hypothermia so an additional sweater would be extremely valuable. If you've got a place to live but are low on sweaters, that extra cable-knit might give you something new to wear on a cold day and would therefore still be pretty valuable. If you already have too many sweaters, though, one more might just be a nuisance – one extra thing to pack when you move – and therefore be bad overall.

The value of a new sweater decreases the more sweaters you already have. The value can even become negative if you already have lots of sweaters. In fact, it's true of most good things (though not all of them all the time), that their value diminishes as their quantity increases. The first slice of cake is delicious, but by the third, you're feeling a little sick. Having one copy of this book might provide you with an interesting and entertaining experience, but having a second might just provide you with a makeshift doorstop. This is what economists call the law of diminishing returns.

So far we've only compared different sorts of programmes within a specific cause – like developing-world education, or developing-world health. If we want to do as much good as we can, we've also got to ask which cause to focus on. The law of diminishing returns provides a useful rule of thumb for comparing causes. If a specific area has already received a great deal of funding and attention, then we should expect it to be difficult for us to do a lot of good by devoting additional resources to that area. In contrast, within causes that are comparatively neglected, the most effective opportunities for doing good have probably not been taken.

Consider disaster relief. On 11 March 2011 the Tōhoku region of Japan was hit by the fourth most powerful earthquake since records began in 1900. Tsunamis reached heights of 130 feet and travelled six miles inland. The earthquake was so large that the entire main island of Japan was moved 2.4 metres east. Millions of people were left without electricity or water. Thousands died.

On 12 January 2010, just one year before, an earthquake hit Haiti. The epicentre was near Léogâne, sixteen miles west of the country's capital, Port-au-Prince; 280,000 buildings collapsed, including the Presidential Palace, the National Assembly, Port-au-Prince Cathedral, and the main jail. Cholera broke out. Thousands died.

In both cases there was massive international media attention and a huge humanitarian relief effort. The disasters dominated the news. Aid agencies were mobilised and individuals around the world reached for their wallets. In each case the total international aid raised in the immediate aftermath came to about $5 billion.

The two disasters seem very similar. Both were caused by earthquakes. Both resulted in destruction on a massive scale. But in two ways they were very different, which should make us wonder why the international aid response was so similar. First, the human scale of the two disasters differed dramatically. In total, the Japanese earthquake caused 15,000 deaths; the Haitian earthquake, by comparison, caused 150,000. Second, Japan is the fourth richest country in the world and had the resources to deal with a disaster on that scale. Haiti didn't. Per person, Japan was thirty times richer than Haiti. As a whole, the country was 1,000 times richer. For that reason, on 15 March, just four days after the earthquake hit, the Japanese Red Cross made the following statement:

> The Japanese Red Cross Society, with the support of the International Federation of Red Cross and Red Crescent Societies, has determined that external assistance is not required, and is therefore not seeking funding or other assistance from donors at this time.

If the international response to natural disasters was rational, we would expect a greater amount of funding to be provided to larger disasters and to disasters that occur in poorer countries, which are less able to cope. But that's not what happens. Funding seems to be allocated in proportion with how evocative and widely publicised the disaster is, rather than on the basis of its scale and severity.

I'm using this example because it illustrates why, if we want to have an impact, we should donate to less widely publicised disasters rather than to the ones that make the news. For example, in 2008 an earthquake hit Sichuan, China. You probably haven't heard of it: I hadn't before I started writing this book. This earthquake struck fifty miles north-west of Chengdu, right in the centre of China. It killed 87,000 people: five times as many as the Japanese earthquake, and half as many as the Haitian earthquake. Yet it raised only $500 million in international aid – one tenth that of Haiti or Japan. For some reason, it wasn't as widely publicised as these other earthquakes, so it received less funding. Because it received so much less, donations would have probably made a bigger impact.

The law of diminishing returns also explains why, *in general*, it makes less sense to donate to disaster relief than it does to donate to the best charities that fight poverty. Every day people die from easily preventable diseases like AIDS, malaria, or tuberculosis. This is a disaster far beyond that of Haiti, or Tōhoku, or Sichuan. Every day over 18,000 children – more than the number of people who perished in Tōhoku – die from preventable causes. For every death the Japanese earthquake caused, aid organisations received $330,000 in donations. In contrast, for every person that dies from poverty-related causes worldwide, only $15,000 on average is spent in foreign aid and philanthropy. Partly for this reason, experts from the World Health Organization and World Bank concluded: 'Emergency health interventions are more costly and less effective than time-tested health activities.'

Our response to natural disasters is one of the clearest cases of how, when it comes to charity, most people follow their gut and respond to new events rather than ongoing problems. When a disaster strikes, the emotional centres of our brain flare up: we think – *emergency!* We forget there is an emergency happening all the time because we've grown accustomed to everyday emergencies like disease and poverty and oppression. Because disasters are new and dramatic events, they inspire deeper and more urgent emotions, causing our subconscious to mistakenly assess them as more important or worthy of attention.

Ironically, the law of diminishing returns suggests that, if you feel a strong emotional reaction to a story and want to help, you should probably resist this inclination because there are probably many others like you who are also donating. By all means, you should harness the emotion you feel when a natural disaster strikes, but remind yourself that a similar disaster is happening all the time – and then consider donating to wherever will help the most rather than what is getting the most attention.

Diminishing returns also provides a powerful argument for focusing your altruistic efforts on people in poor countries rather than those in rich countries.

For example, it costs about $50,000 to train and provide one guide dog for one blind person, something that would significantly improve that person's quality of life. However, if we could use that $50,000 to completely cure someone of blindness, that would be an even better use of money since it provides a larger benefit for the same cost. Not only is $50,000 enough to cure one person of blindness in the developing world, it's enough to cure 500 people of blindness if spent on surgery to prevent blindness caused by trachoma (a bacterial infection that causes the eyelids to turn inwards, causing the eyelashes to scratch the cornea). Any programme that can cure blindness at a cost of $100 would have been fully funded in rich countries decades ago. The same is not true in poor countries, which means we can do so much more to help people than we can at home.

Similar considerations apply to which sorts of health treatments do the most good with additional funding. Every year cancer kills 8.2 million people and is responsible for 7.6% of all deaths and ill health worldwide (measured in terms of QALYs lost). $217 billion per year is spent on cancer treatment. Malaria is responsible for 3.3% of QALYs lost worldwide. In terms of its health impacts, cancer is about twice as bad as malaria, so if medical spending were in proportion to the scale of the problem, we would expect malaria treatment to receive about $100 billion per year. In reality only $1.6 billion per year is spent on malaria treatment: about sixty times less than we would expect.

Cancer treatment receives so much more funding than malaria treatment because malaria is such a cheap problem to solve that rich countries no longer suffer from it. (It was eliminated from the US in 1951.) The fact that cancer treatment receives so much more funding than malaria treatment means that, on the margin, each of us can provide a far greater benefit for other people by funding the most effective malaria treatments in the developing world than we can by funding the most effective cancer treatments in the developed world. In the United States, public health experts regard any programme that provides one QALY for less than $50,000 as good value, and health programmes will often be funded even if the cost per QALY is much higher than $50,000. In contrast, providing the same benefit in poor countries (such as by distributing insecticide-treated bed nets to prevent the spread of malaria) can cost as little as $100. That means that, with a given amount of money, you can benefit people in poor countries 500 times more than people in rich countries.

Again, we see The 100x Multiplier at work. We're about one hundred times richer than the poorest billion people in the world, and we can do several hundred times more to help them than we can to help others in the rich countries we live in.

So far we've looked at how money diminishes in value, but similar reasoning applies to time. One subtle implication of the principle of diminishing returns is how it applies to career choice. Let's come back to Greg Lewis, the idealistic medical student we encountered at the beginning of this chapter, and consider the question: how much good does a doctor do?

'I had hoped that this question would already be extensively researched,' Greg told me. 'Because you'd think that if you were trying to run a health service, you'd really want to know what the returns are on having more doctors. So

I was quite surprised to find that no one had really looked at this question at all.'

You might think this is easy to work out, and that's why no one had needed to research it. To ascertain how many lives a doctor saves, all you have to do is add up how many life-saving surgeries they perform and life-saving treatments they administer over the course of their careers. To figure out how much sickness they heal, you add up all the occasions when they've done something to improve a patient's life. Add up the benefits of both activities and that tells you how much good they've done. Easy, right?

This is what Greg did initially. He looked at the data for a large number of countries. For the US, he divided the total benefit of American healthcare by the number of doctors in the United States. The National Area Health Education Organization estimated there to be 878,194 doctors in the US, and Greg found work by an epidemiologist named John Bunker, who estimated that the total benefits from medicine in the US is about 7 QALYs per person, or 2.2 billion QALYs in total. (Remember that a QALY is equivalent to providing someone with one additional year of healthy life.) On this calculation, each doctor is estimated to provide 2,500 QALYs (2.2 billion/878,194). That includes both benefits through saving lives and benefits through improving quality of life. It can be hard to get an intuitive sense of that, so we could think of this in terms of the equivalent number of 'lives saved'. Health economists estimate that, on average, the benefit of 'saving a life' is the same as the benefit of providing 36.5 QALYs.

Based on this calculation, a doctor provides health benefits equivalent to saving seventy lives over the course of his or her career. Greg knew this was an overestimate insofar as it didn't account for the impact of nurses, hospital administrators, and so on, so he scaled down that number, thinking the real figure might be something like twenty-five or thirty lives saved per doctor. Still, pretty impressive.

Let's call this the Simple View. Greg realised that, even though this was the view most people intuitively held, it wasn't the right way to think about things because it made the mistake of assessing the *average* value of a doctor. As we've discussed throughout this chapter, this is the wrong calculation to consider when trying to determine how much impact you can have. Instead, young people wanting to make a difference through their career should determine the *marginal* value they would provide by becoming a doctor.

To see why the Simple View doesn't work, imagine you're in a small town, isolated from the rest of the country. That town has the resources to employ in its hospital three doctors – Alice, Bob and Charlotte. There are three categories of activities that they do: (i) life-saving operations and treatments, like heart surgery; (ii) major health improvements, like anxiety treatments; (iii) treating minor ailments, like coughs and colds. In this hospital, Alice, Bob and Charlotte each spend about one-third of their time on each of these categories, and the healthcare needs of the town are met. Each doctor performs a hundred life-saving surgeries per year, so, according to the Simple View, each saves approximately a hundred lives per year.

Now let's suppose that the clinic loses resources and can no longer afford to employ Charlotte. How bad would that be for the residents of the town? According to the Simple View, it's a disaster because Charlotte will not be available to perform those hundred life-saving operations, which means a hundred people will die.

However, when we think about this realistically, we realise this is not what would happen. If Charlotte was no longer employed, Alice and Bob would do some reprioritising. They'd neglect or delegate to other healthcare personnel all the minor ailments they could have treated so they can focus solely on major health improvements and life-saving operations and treatments. In Charlotte's absence, Alice and Bob now each save 150 lives per year. So, even though Charlotte was performing life-saving operations, the difference she made by working for that clinic was really in treating minor ailments like coughs and colds that could not have been treated with fewer doctors.

Saving lives is the most important task a doctor can do – and it's a task that would be taken care of in the absence of almost any individual doctor we could point to. As we saw earlier, there are an estimated 878,194 doctors in the US. Suppose you become the 878,195th doctor. What's the difference you make as a result? Well, those 878,194 will have already plucked all the low hanging fruit in terms of easy ways to save lives, so you, as the 878,195th doctor, will have only hard-to-realise opportunities to improve health. That's unlikely to include performing heart surgeries and more likely to involve treating minor ailments.

Using this idea, we can revise our estimates of how much good a doctor really does. The good that you would do by becoming a doctor (effectively becoming the 878,195th doctor in the US) is the difference between the total benefit provided by US healthcare given that the US has 878,194 doctors as against 878,195 doctors. How big is that difference?

Greg used statistics to work out the answer. He looked at both how good the quality of health is in many different countries and how many doctors there are in each of those countries, and then plotted the relationship between those two factors (while also taking into account the effect of things like wealth and education). This enabled him to answer his question. He worked out that adding one doctor to the US adds about four QALYs per year to the population as a whole. Over a forty-year career, that's 160 QALYs. Once we take into account the fact that nurses and other healthcare workers also generate some of this benefit, we get the conclusion that one additional doctor in the US provides a benefit equivalent to about four lives saved over the course of their career. That is still awesome. But it's also less than you probably thought before, all because of diminishing returns. Of course, the good that a doctor does will vary from speciality to speciality; this estimate is an average across all specialities. Unless some specialities do far more good than others, however, this won't make much difference to our assessment of the good that doctors do.

If you aim to become a doctor in a rich country, you're only adding your labour to the already very large pool of doctors who are working in that country. That means that becoming a doctor probably does less good than you'd intuitively think. The same consideration explains why doctors have a much bigger impact if they work in poor countries than in rich ones. Greg used some more statistics to work out how much good he'd do if he upped roots and went to work in a very poor country such as Ethiopia. He found that he'd make a much larger difference, providing an extra 300 QALYs per year, or about 300 lives over a forty-year career. That's more than one hundred times as big an impact than if he worked in the UK. Once again, we see The 100x Multiplier in effect: because far less is spent on healthcare in poor countries, Greg could do far more good working in a poor country than in a rich one.

Asking 'Is this area neglected?' and trying to focus only on those areas that truly are neglected can be counterintuitive. It means that the most popular causes are, precisely for that reason, the ones where it will be difficult to have a big impact. Because of diminishing returns, we can make a much bigger difference if we focus our efforts on areas that have received comparatively fewer resources, such as less-publicised disasters or global rather than domestic poverty.

You might be wondering what Greg ultimately decided to do with his career: did he move to work in a poor country? In fact, he concluded that he should continue to work in the UK. We'll find out why in the next chapter.

5

THE BEST PERSON WHO EVER LIVED IS AN UNKNOWN UKRAINIAN MAN

Key question 4: What would have happened otherwise?

Out of everyone who ever existed, who has done the most good? In researching this question, I came across a list that *Esquire* had published, called 'The 75 Best People in the World'. The writers suggested that the number 1 spot should go to . . . Matt Damon. Which seems unlikely.

In Chapter 3 I suggested that smallpox eradication was one of humanity's greatest achievements. If we're looking for the Best Person Ever, we could start by looking at those who helped in this effort. In fact, much of the credit for smallpox eradication can be attributed to just one man.

In 1966 Ohio-born doctor D. A. Henderson became the leader of the WHO's Global Smallpox Eradication Campaign. At only thirty-eight years old, and with only ten years' clinical experience, he was fifteen years younger than everyone else in the programme, but he excelled at what he did. When he took charge of the campaign, he proposed an ambitious goal: to completely wipe smallpox off the face of the planet within ten years. Astoundingly, the campaign succeeded and between 1967 and 1971 the number of smallpox endemic countries plummeted from thirty-one to five. Henderson pioneered the novel technique of ring-vaccination in which, rather than vaccinating an entire population – a costly and time-consuming procedure – his team used large-scale reporting to identify outbreaks of the disease, contain those who had it, and vaccinate everyone else within a certain radius. The results exceeded everyone's expectations, and in 1977 the last naturally occurring case of smallpox was diagnosed in Somalia. Smallpox was the first disease that humans have ever eradicated.

Henderson's success resulted in a string of accolades. He won more than a dozen major awards, including the Public Welfare Medal, the National Medal of Science and the Presidential Medal of Freedom – the highest civilian award in the United States. He received honorary degrees from seventeen different universities. Immediately after 9/11, he became President George W. Bush's lead expert on bioterrorism. He was even knighted by the King of Thailand.

But D. A. Henderson is not the person I'm talking about.

By the time Henderson was hired, the political will to eradicate smallpox already existed. There was a job opening – a job he didn't even want initially – and Henderson filled it. This isn't to say he didn't rise to the challenge or that he wasn't a hero, but if he had never existed, someone else would have been in his shoes and eradicated smallpox eventually. This person might not have been as good or as quick as Henderson, but as long as they were good enough, smallpox would have been eradicated.

Instead, we should look to a much more unlikely hero: Viktor Zhdanov, a Ukrainian virologist who died in 1987. At the time of this writing, he has a mere four-paragraph Wikipedia page, and there are only a few grainy black-and-white photos of him available online. I'm not aware of any major accolades for his work.

In 1958, Zhdanov was a deputy minister of health for the Soviet Union. In May of that year, at the Eleventh World Health Assembly meeting in Minneapolis, Minnesota, during the Soviet Union's first appearance in the assembly after a nine-year absence, Zhdanov described a visionary plan to eradicate smallpox. At the time, no disease had ever before been eradicated. No one knew if it could even be done. And no one expected such a suggestion to come from the USSR. But he conveyed his message with passion, conviction and optimism, boldly suggesting that the disease could be eradicated within ten years. Since smallpox was an exclusively human disease, he argued, it would be easier to eradicate than mosquito-borne infections such as malaria. He pointed to the Soviet Union's success at eliminating smallpox, despite its vast territory and poor transportation networks. He referenced Thomas Jefferson's letter to the inventor of the smallpox vaccine, Edward Jenner: 'I avail myself of this occasion of rendering you a portion of the tribute of gratitude due to you from the whole human family. Medicine has never before produced any single improvement of such utility . . . Future nations will know by history only that the loathsome small-pox has existed and by you has been extirpated.'

By the force of his arguments, Zhdanov was successful. For the first time in its history, the WHO agreed to form a campaign to completely eradicate a disease.

To assess how much good Zhdanov did, we should bear in mind that, even if he had not lobbied the WHO, smallpox would probably have been eradicated anyway. The problem was serious enough that someone would have started a campaign to fix it. Many of those 120 million lives that have been saved by smallpox eradication would therefore have been saved anyway. But there would probably have been a considerable delay in the smallpox eradication campaign. Suppose, therefore, that Zhdanov moved forward the eradication of smallpox by a decade. If so, then he alone prevented between 10 and 20 million deaths – about as much as if he'd achieved three decades of world peace.

We don't usually think of achievements in terms of what would have happened otherwise, but we should. What matters is not *who* does good, but whether good is done; and the measure of how much good you achieve is the difference between what happens as a result of your actions and what would have happened anyway.

Suppose, for example, that I see a woman collapse on the ground. She's had a heart attack. There's no one else around, so I run up to her and start performing CPR.

Suppose I've never performed CPR before, but I manage to restart the woman's heart. She recovers, but as a result of the poor quality CPR, is left with a disability. Even so it's clear that I have done a great thing.

Now suppose there had been a paramedic around when the woman collapsed. This paramedic would have surely restarted her heart without causing injury, but, while I was running toward the woman, I pushed the paramedic out of the way and started performing CPR myself. In this case, I still saved her life, but if I hadn't, the paramedic would have been able to do the same thing without causing damage. In this case, how should I feel about my actions? Am I a hero? After all, I 'saved a life'!

Of course I'm not a hero. The good I do is not a matter of the direct benefits I *cause*. Rather, it is the *difference* I make. Even though I technically saved this woman's life, I actually did harm overall.

Looking at what would have happened otherwise is a fundamental piece of scientific reasoning, referred to as 'assessing the counterfactual'. But the mistake of neglecting the counterfactual is rife within the world of altruism, and this mistake can have terrible consequences.

Sixteen-year-old Brandon lived in the north-west of Detroit. He had already been in trouble with the law for armed robbery, home invasion and drug-related offences, and he was being brought into Oakland County Jail so he could see how awful prison life was. The goal was to make him reconsider his life choices before he ended up in jail for good. Brandon is the central character in an episode of *Beyond Scared Straight*.

Scared Straight! began in 1978 as a documentary by Arnold Shapiro. It told the true story of a group of teenage delinquents who were taken by correctional officers to spend three hours at a prison. The inmates screamed at, intimidated and threatened the juveniles, telling stories of the horrors of life in prison, of rapes and beatings, in order to scare them out of a life of crime. The documentary ends by revealing that most of the juveniles have turned away from their troubled paths, though acknowledging that some did go on to reoffend. The film was highly successful, wining an Oscar and eight Emmys, and begat a succession of TV follow-ups: *Scared Straight! Another Story, Scared Straight! 10 Years Later, Scared Straight! 20 Years Later*. The latest incarnation, *Beyond Scared Straight*, broadcast on A&E in the US, is as of this writing in its eighth season, airing weekly and attracting millions of viewers.

In this episode, when Brandon enters the prison, he's cocky and defiant. He faces a wall of inmates through the bars. They taunt him, yelling, 'We got a hard ass?! Let's do this!' and 'You want to be a real fucking tough guy, is that it?' They threaten him, they jeer, and the guards emphasise the seriousness of their threats.

Through all this, Brandon smiles. He thinks it's funny. When he gets taken aside by a correctional officer, he continues to play the tough guy: 'I ain't tripping. I ain't scared of none of these shitheads . . . they breathe just like

I breathe and they bleed just like I bleed.' Time and again, he shrugs off the intimidation.

Things change when he sees an 'extraction': a prisoner tasered, bound to a chair, and forcibly sedated. Out in the corridor he breaks down, tears in his eyes. The guards tell him they are on his side. They don't want him to end up in here.

At the end of the show, we visit Brandon one month later. He's smiling again, but this time there's hope in his eyes, not defiance. He's got a personal tutor, and he's stopped hanging out with the friends who got him into trouble. He goes back to the prison to apologise to the guards he stood up to. Brandon says he now recognises he was wrong. 'I'm happy I went to the jail tour because it changed my life and made me a better person,' he says. 'And it made me realise that some of the stuff I was doing wasn't good . . . the future look[s] bright now.'

Beyond Scared Straight introduces us to a world most of us will never experience. It's a mix of pop entertainment and uplifting coming-of-age narrative. The producers say it's a highly effective social programme, with cases like Brandon's, in which a once-troubled teen turns his or her life around, being the norm rather than the exception. Since the original release of *Scared Straight!*, hundreds of prisons across the US have adopted similar programmes. The programme seems to be a win–win: It reduces the recidivism rate among juvenile offenders, and it makes for great TV.

But, as you've probably guessed based on my discussion of it in this chapter, there's a darker side to *Scared*

Straight. Those who tout the programme's effectiveness are wrong. Not only is the programme ineffective, it's down-right *harmful.*

Nine high-quality studies have been done on the programme, assessing the progress of one thousand juveniles overall. The Cochrane Collaboration, a non-profit institute that rigorously assesses the evidence behind health and social programmes, looked at these studies and found that two of them had no significant effect, while the remaining seven showed *increased* rates of criminality among juveniles. The authors of the review estimated that the Scared Straight programmes that had been studied increased the odds of offending by about 60%. 'The analyses show the intervention to be more harmful than doing nothing,' they concluded. 'The programme effect, whether assuming a fixed or random effects model, was nearly identical and negative in direction, regardless of the meta-analytic strategy.' In the jargon of academia, that's just about as harsh a criticism as you can get, claiming that, no matter how they looked at it, Scared Straight caused more crime than it prevented. In a separate study, the Washington State Institute for Public Policy estimated the value for society, per dollar invested, of a range of preventative social policies, such as psychotherapy and anger management. Of the sixty interventions studied, the vast majority were shown to produce more value then they cost. Only three were harmful and only one of these egregiously so – the Scared Straight programme. The researchers concluded that, because Scared Straight was increasing rates of crime, with associated penitentiary costs and costs to the local community, every $1 spent on Scared Straight cost society $203.

Yet Scared Straight programmes still continue and are still touted as effective. How can a programme that has been proven to cause harm thrive?

The problem is that those who tout its effectiveness aren't thinking in terms of what would have happened otherwise. They see delinquent kids come to the Scared Straight programme, they see them go on to commit fewer crimes than they'd been committing in the past (only one third of kids who go through the programme go on to commit a crime in the following year), and they conclude it's a success. But you can't conclude a certain programme *causes* things to get better based solely on the fact that they *have* gotten better. In the case of Scared Straight, studies show that rates of delinquency would have decreased even without the Scared Straight programme. In fact, they show that rates of delinquency would have decreased by a greater amount if the Scared Straight programme had never been run. Scared Straight actually impedes progress that is happening anyway.

I suspect the apparent effectiveness of Scared Straight can be explained by a phenomenon called regression to the mean. If you play a truly excellent round of golf one day, you'll probably play worse the next time you play because that excellent round was statistically unlikely and you should expect to see a more typical performance the next time. Similarly, people who are undergoing a bout of particularly severe depression will on average be happier three months later, because they are likely closer to their average level of happiness. And, similarly, if you select a group of juveniles to go through a reform programme because they've committed an unusually high number of misdemeanours in a given time period, they're likely to exhibit something closer to typical behaviour in the following months.

But that only explains why Scared Straight can appear to be effective when it really does nothing. Why, then, does the programme increase rates of criminality? No one knows for sure, but one hypothesis is that the inmates – who play up how tough they are for surviving life in prison – act as role models rather than deterrents for the delinquents. The delinquents identify with the inmates and then imitate their behaviours. Watching the show again, this hypothesis seems plausible. The inmates tell the kids they should try to avoid prison not because it's an awful place to be, or because it's shameful to have broken the law, but because they're not tough enough for life inside.

The example of Scared Straight shows the import-ance of ensuring, wherever possible, that large-scale social programmes undergo rigorous testing through controlled trials before they are put into practice. If an amateur chemist created a pill he claimed would reduce crime, we would never administer it to thousands of children without rigorous testing because it would be dangerous, not to mention illegal, to do so. Yet new social programmes like Scared Straight can be rolled out without any good evidence behind them. Without rigorous testing, we can't know whether a social programme is making things better, making things worse, or achieving nothing at all. Of course, sometimes programmes are too small in scale for testing to be a good use of money, and sometimes rigorous trials are impossible. But our default attitude should be that, if a social programme is going to be rolled out on a large scale, then it should have been proven to be effective first.

The most subtle and interesting way in which we neglect to think about what would have happened otherwise is when we think about career choice. This takes us back to Greg Lewis, our statistically inclined doctor from the previous chapter, and his estimate of how much good doctors do.

In the previous chapter, we estimated the benefit of one additional doctor in the United States at four lives saved per doctor. But that doesn't yet measure how good becoming a doctor is, because, by becoming a doctor, you aren't simply adding one extra doctor to the supply of doctors. There is usually competition for places at medical school, so if you decide not to go, someone else will take your place and become a doctor in your stead. Thus, by becoming a doctor, you're really just changing who works as a doctor, not how many doctors there are. The difference you make isn't equal to the difference between your country having X doctors and $X + 1$ doctors (which is how we analysed it in the previous chapter). It's the difference you make by becoming a doctor as compared to the difference someone else would make if they took your place.

This consideration means that our previous estimate that each doctor saves approximately four lives over the course of a career is too high. There are still benefits to becoming a doctor: if you get into medical school then you increase the average quality of doctors (assuming the selection process selects the best applicants); and adding yourself to the labour pool may decrease doctors' wages slightly, allowing more doctors to be employed. But the contribution won't be as much as we suggested earlier. Factoring this consideration into his calculations, Greg estimated that, rather than saving four lives over the course of his career, he might actually only save an additional one or two that would not have been saved otherwise. This is still a very valuable contribution to society, but less than we might expect.

This consideration is widely applicable. For example in my teenage years I used to work as a care assistant at a nursing home. How great an impact was I making? When I initially considered this, I thought about the direct benefits of the work: the improvements in the lives of the people who were living at that nursing home. Instead, I should have thought about whether I was doing a better job than whoever would have taken my place. Though enthusiastic, I was slow and inexperienced, and I probably needed the money I was paid less than whoever would have been employed in that position instead of me, who might have had a family to support. So it's not clear that, on balance, I was doing any good at all.

This explains, in part, why Greg didn't go to Africa. If he took a job in a non-profit, he'd be taking the place of someone else who wanted to do the same. The impact of an additional doctor in a developing country is about 300 QALYs per year, which is very large, but the difference he'd make by taking someone else's position would be less than that. He therefore chose a different path, one that brings together many of the considerations we've covered so far. I call it earning to give.

Earning to give means exactly what it sounds like: rather than trying to maximise the good you do directly via your job, you instead try to increase your earnings so you can donate more, improving people's lives through your giving rather than your day-to-day work. Most people don't consider this option when choosing a career that 'makes a difference'. But time and money are usually interchangeable – money can pay for people's time, and your time can be used to earn money – so there's no reason to assume the best careers are only those that benefit people directly through the work itself. If we're serious about doing good, earning to give is a path we should consider.

Let's look at Greg Lewis's options. If he worked as a doctor in a rich country and didn't donate a portion of his income, he would do an amount of good equivalent to saving two lives over the course of his career. If he went to work as a doctor in a very poor country, he would do an amount of good equivalent to saving four lives every year, or 140 lives over a thirty-five year career. But how many lives could he save if he stayed home and donated his earnings?

The average salary of a doctor in the UK is about £70,000 per year before tax. In dollars, that's about $110,000 or $4.6 million over a forty-two-year career. By pursuing a particularly lucrative speciality – medical oncology – Greg could earn almost double that one day: about $200,000 per year. Earlier I said that one of the most cost-effective ways to save lives is by distributing antimalarial bed nets, which saves one life for every $3,400 spent. By pursuing medical oncology, Greg could therefore eventually donate 50% of a $200,000 annual salary while still drawing a very comfortable $100,000 per year pre-tax (donations are tax-deductible). His donations would save dozens of lives each year, considerably more than would have been the case if he'd worked directly in a poor country.

Because of this, Greg decided to earn to give, planning to specialise in medical oncology. 'I found it pretty humbling, when I looked at the difference. I'd save a few lives through my direct impact as a doctor,' Greg told me. 'Which was less than I thought, but still great. But through my donations, I could save hundreds of lives.' For Greg, the same reasons that made him want to go into medicine made it clear to him that he should start donating, too. 'I started out giving around 10%. But I've gradually been increasing that, as I found that I really didn't miss the money. Now I'm donating about 50% and my life is, if anything, better than it was. I feel that I'm doing justice to my seventeen-year-old self who wanted to make the world a better place.' In 2014, Greg donated $30,000, enough to save ten lives.

Importantly, by earning to give Greg is making a difference that wouldn't have happened otherwise. If he weren't a doctor, someone else would take his place, but that doctor would probably donate very little (the average is about 2%). In contrast, by working for a non-governmental organisation (NGO) in a poor country Greg would be using money from the NGO that would otherwise have been spent on a different doctor's salary, or on medical supplies. Because he's making a difference that wouldn't have happened anyway, Greg will do even more good by earning to give than he would have done if he'd worked directly in poor countries. And he can do so without having to give up the comforts of home.

It's worth reflecting on this. In 2007 Louis Theroux, a British documentary filmmaker, released a documentary called *Under the Knife* in which he explored the world of cosmetic surgery in Beverly Hills. In the culmination of the show, he accused the cosmetic surgeon he'd been interviewing of wasting his talent and skills to make wannabe movie stars more attractive, rather than saving lives. What we've seen so far shows that Louis Theroux's sentiment, while understandable, is misplaced. It's the cosmetic surgeon's decision about how to spend his money that really matters.

Earning to give seems to be an enormously powerful way of doing good. It exploits the fact that even typical workers in developed countries are among the top income earners in the world, and that there are some charities that do huge amounts to help the world's poorest people for relatively little money. Moreover, unlike the conventional 'ethical' careers guidance, earning to give is a path that's open to everyone. The conventional advice is that if you want to make a difference you should work in the non-profit or public sector or work in corporate social responsibility. But many people struggle to get *a* job, let alone find a job in a specific sector. However, many more people have the option to work overtime in order to earn more, or to work harder in order to get a pay increase or a promotion, or to move towards a higher-paying career, or just to live on less. By doing this, and being smart about where you give, almost anyone in a rich country can do a tremendous amount to help others.

There is plenty more to be said about doing good through your career, and the whole of Chapter 9 will be devoted to it. But before we can address this question properly, and before we can see why earning to give is merely one path, and not always the most effective career choice, we need to look at the fifth and final key question of effective altruism.

6

WHY VOTING IS LIKE DONATING THOUSANDS OF DOLLARS TO CHARITY

Key question 5: What are the chances of success,
and how good would success be?

'The possibility of a severe accident occurring is so small that from an engineering standpoint, it is practically unthinkable.' This is a quote from the comprehensive accident management plan of the Fukushima Daiichi nuclear power plant, and it helps us see the importance of thinking correctly about risk.

Fukushima Daiichi was located seventy kilometres from the epicentre of the massive earthquake that hit Japan in March 2011. All operating nuclear reactors shut down automatically following the earthquake, a safety precaution designed to prevent a meltdown, which would result in hazardous radioactive material leaking out into the environment. However, an ensuing tsunami hit and disabled the plant's cooling system, causing the meltdown of three of its reactors. Although no one died from radiation exposure,

WHY VOTING IS LIKE DONATING

about 160,000 people had to be evacuated from their homes, and 1,600 people died during the evacuation because of conditions such as hospital closures. The Fukushima disaster remains the worst nuclear accident since Chernobyl.

Four months after the disaster, the Japanese government formed an Investigation Committee, made up of a panel of ten independent experts in fields including radiation protection, medicine and law, which presented a 450-page report to Prime Minister Yoshihiko Noda. Panel chairman Yotaro Hatamura, an emeritus professor of engineering at the University of Tokyo, told a news conference that 'the root cause of the Fukushima crisis is that [the regulatory bodies and the Tokyo Electric Power Company] selfishly assumed that natural disasters that are beyond their imagination would not occur'. In a closing note, Hatamura wrote that Japan, 'should take the accident as a reminder from nature that humans' way of thinking can be defective'.

So far in this book we have focused on measurable, concrete ways of helping others. The real world, unfortunately, is not always so simple. Often we don't know whether our actions will be successful, and, given the difficulty of knowing what would have happened otherwise, we will usually never know whether our actions really make a difference. When it comes to effecting political change, this problem becomes particularly severe. Even if you run a campaign and the policy you've campaigned for is put into place, there are usually other forces at work, making it difficult to measure your individual impact.

We shouldn't dismiss more speculative or high-risk activities out of hand, though, because, when successful, they can have an enormous impact. We therefore need a way to compare higher-risk but higher-upside actions with actions that are certain to have an impact.

Within economics and decision theory the standard way to do this is to look at an action's *expected value*. To take a simple example, suppose I offer you a bet. I'll flip a coin and if the coin lands heads, I'll give you $2, if the coin lands tails, you give me $1. Should you take the bet? According to the idea of expected value, you should.

To calculate the expected monetary value of each bet, you look at all the possible outcomes of that bet. For each outcome, you take the monetary gain or loss and multiply it by the probability of the outcome. In this case, there are two possible outcomes, Heads and Tails. Each has a 50% chance of occurring. The expected monetary value of taking the bet is therefore (50% × +$2) + (50% × −$1) = $0.50. The expected monetary value of refusing the bet is $0. Taking the bet has the higher expected value, so you should take the bet.

Maximising expected value is generally regarded as the best strategy for making decisions when you know the value and the probability of each option. It's the strategy used by economists, statisticians, poker players, risk management experts and pretty much anyone else who regularly needs to deal with uncertain outcomes. To see why, suppose that I offer you the same bet over and over again. In the long run, you're almost guaranteed to make more money if you accept my bets than if you don't: in fact, on average you'll make $0.50 for every bet that you take.

In the flipping a coin example we talked about expected monetary value. When thinking about buying things for yourself, however, expected monetary value isn't always what you care about. Most people would prefer to keep $1,000 than to bet it on a one-in-a-hundred chance of receiving $100,001, even though the expected monetary value of the bet is positive. That's rational because money has diminishing returns: if you're like most people, the improvements you'd make to your life by spending the first $1,000 of your $100,001 lottery winnings will bring you more joy than the improvements you make to your life by spending the last $1,000. The same isn't true, however, when we're thinking about philanthropy. If you donate $1,000 to the Against Malaria Foundation, they will buy and distribute 200 bed nets. If you donate $100,000 to the Against Malaria Foundation, they will buy and distribute 20,000 bed nets. Because the social problems in the world are so big, additional resources directed to them diminish in value very slowly. Additional resources do diminish in value *somewhat* – if the Against Malaria Foundation received $50 million (several times its current budget), it would struggle to spend all that money as quickly or as well as it has spent money so far. And after spending billions of dollars on bed nets, spending more money on bed nets wouldn't be effective because everyone who needed a bed net would have one. And, as we've seen, it's more effective to spend money on malaria treatment than cancer treatment in part because malaria treatment receives a tiny fraction of the resources that cancer treatment receives. But when thinking 'merely' in terms of millions of dollars, one can often assume the altruistic value of money stays the same no matter how much of it you have.

To see how useful the idea of expected value is, let's consider a morbid but important application: assessing the risk of death from different activities. Smoking, riding a motorbike, scuba diving, taking ecstasy, eating peanut butter: all these things increase your risk of death. How much should you worry about each of them? Public health experts use the concept of a 'micromort' to compare the risks, where one micromort equals a one-in-a-million chance of dying, equivalent to thirty minutes of expected life lost if you're aged twenty, or fifteen minutes of expected life lost if you're aged fifty. By comparing different activities in terms of micromorts, we can easily assess their relative dangers. The results can be surprising. Based on reported cases of deaths from these activities, one ecstasy session (two tablets) is only about one micromort, whereas going scuba diving is five micromorts and going skydiving is nine micromorts. Flying in a space shuttle is 17,000 micromorts, or a 1.7% chance of dying, which is about as dangerous as attempting to climb Mount Everest beyond base camp, at 13,000 micromorts, or a 1.3% chance of dying.

The same concept can be applied to things that increase risk of death later in life as well. Eating forty tablespoons of peanut butter gives you one micromort because you risk ingesting aflatoxin, a fungal toxin that increases your risk of liver cancer later in life. Smoking a single cigarette gives you 0.7 micromorts, increasing your chance of dying of lung cancer many years down the line. Taking this into account, smoking one cigarette reduces life expectancy by five minutes – about the same length of time it takes to smoke it.

When thinking about risk from transport, you can think directly in terms of minutes of life lost per hour of travel. Each time you travel, you face a slight risk of getting into a fatal accident, but the chance of getting into a fatal accident varies dramatically depending on the mode of transport. For example, the risk of a fatal car crash while driving for an hour is about 1 in 10 million (so 0.1 micromorts). For a twenty-year-old, that's a 1 in 10 million chance of losing sixty years. The expected life lost from driving for one hour is therefore three minutes. Looking at expected minutes lost shows just how great a discrepancy there is between risks from different sorts of transport. Whereas an hour on a train costs you only twenty expected seconds of life, an hour on a motorbike costs you an expected three hours and forty-five minutes.

In addition to giving us a way to compare the risks of different activities, the concept of expected value helps us choose which risks are worth taking. Would you be willing to spend an hour on a motorbike if it was perfectly safe but caused you to be unconscious later for three hours and forty-five minutes? If your answer is 'no', but you're otherwise happy to ride motorbikes in your day-to-day life, you're probably not fully appreciating the risk of death.

Thinking explicitly about expected value is important because humans are often terrible at assessing low-probability high-value events. Psychologists have found that people either give too much weight to low-probability events (as, perhaps, when people choose to play the lottery), or they simply ignore them altogether.

This takes us back to the Fukushima safety report.

The authors of the comprehensive accident management plan were correct that the probability of a catastrophe occurring was very small. However, they didn't think correctly about how they should deal with that probability. They assimilated 'very small' to zero, and promptly forgot all about it. Their mistake was failing to consider that *if* a catastrophe happens at a nuclear power plant, the costs are huge – in this case, more than a thousand deaths. Even though the chance of this catastrophe was small, it was clearly worth taking substantial safety precautions.

The Fukushima safety engineers were trying to prevent harm with their safety assessment, and they failed by ignoring an important but low-probability event. In just the same way, when trying to do good, we need to be sensitive *both* to the likelihood of success *and* to the value of that success. This means that low-probability, high-payoff activities can take priority over sure bets of more modest impact. It also shows that people are often confused when they say that 'one person can't make a difference'. Voting provides a vivid illustration.

Most people believe you should vote in government elections. But many economists argue that, if your concern is to actually affect the outcome, it's a waste of time. Steven Levitt, Professor of Economics at the University of Chicago and co-author of *Freakonomics*, wrote a blog post reiterating a sentiment he'd previously expressed in the *New York Times*:

> Nobody in their right mind votes because they think they're going to affect the outcome of an election. If you look over the last hundred years of, say, elections for the U.S. House of Representatives, I think there's been maybe one [very close] election that's been decided by votes . . . The reasons for voting have to be something very different: it's fun, your wife will love you more if you do it, it makes you feel like a proud American – but never should anyone delude themselves into thinking that the vote they cast will ever decide an election . . . . Just about anything you do with your time would be more productive.

Given the concept of expected value, however, Levitt's reasoning is too quick. We can't just say that the chance of affecting the outcome by voting is so small as to be negligible. We need to work out how large the benefit would be if we did indeed affect the outcome.

For the US two-party system, some statisticians have done the hard work for us, including political pundit extraordinaire Nate Silver, who correctly predicted the winner of the 2012 election in all fifty states and the District of Columbia. Along with Columbia University Professor of Statistics Andrew Gelman and Berkeley Professor of Law Aaron Edlin, Silver calculated the odds of an individual vote swaying the outcome of the 2008 presidential election and found that, on average, a voter had approximately a 1-in-60-million chance of affecting the outcome – small odds to be sure.

Next, we have to work out what the stakes are. This will necessarily involve some guesstimation. Voters should start by asking themselves how much they personally expect to gain by having their preferred party in power. If their preferred party is the Republicans, then they might expect to benefit because they'll pay fewer taxes. Democrat voters might expect to benefit from more government-funded public services. Suppose for the sake of argument the value to an individual voter of his or her preferred party getting into power is $1,000. Although this $1,000 per citizen figure is hypothetical, it seems plausible to me. The total spending of the US government is $3.5 trillion per year: that's $14 trillion over four years, or $44,000 per person. If that money is spent 2.5% more effectively, then the benefits amount to $1,000 per person. The government also, of course, makes people better or worse off in other ways, such as through regulation.

An economist like Levitt might say that the expected value to an individual of voting is only 1 in 60 million times $1,000, which equals 0.0016¢. With such a low expected value, it's clearly not worthwhile to vote.

But this line of reasoning assumes that the value of voting is only the value to the individual. Instead, we should think about the *total* benefit of the better party being in power. Let's keep using this hypothetical $1,000 figure of the benefit per person of the better party being in power. If so, the total benefit to all Americans is $1,000 multiplied by the US population of 314 million, so $314 billion. The average expected value of voting for the better party, therefore, is the probability of success (1 in 60 million) multiplied by the benefit to Americans (which I'm supposing to be $314 billion), which equals about $5,200 of value to the people of the US. That's the sense in which voting is like donating thousands of dollars to (developed-world) charities. For all but the ultra-rich, that's a much better use of time than you could get, for example, by working the hour it takes you to vote and donating your earnings.

Some caveats on this conclusion are required. First, the total benefit per American was a purely hypothetical number, so it should be taken with a grain of salt. If you're uncertain about which party is really better, you might reasonably think that it's an overestimate: your expected value of voting will be lower due to a greater chance of voting for the worse party; and if you're completely unsure which party is better, the expected value of voting drops to $0. If so, that's fine: you should make your own estimate of the benefits of your preferred party getting into power, and then run the calculation. Only if you think the expected benefit of one party over another is very small (perhaps less than $20 of benefit per person) will you conclude that voting isn't a reasonable altruistic activity.

A more important caveat is that the probability of swinging the election varies dramatically by state. In swing-states such as Colorado, New Hampshire, New Mexico and Virginia, the probability goes as low as 1 in 10 million, which makes the case for voting much stronger. Using my hypothetical number of $1,000 of benefit per person, the value of the benefit to the people of the US of an individual voting for the better party is $30,000. However, in safe states the probability of a single vote making a difference is much less. In Massachusetts, for example, the probability is only 1 in 1 billion. Given my estimate of the benefit of the better party being in power, that would still mean that voting has an expected value of $300, which seems well worth it. In the District of Columbia, however, the probability of your vote making a difference is less than 1 in 100 billion, giving an expected value of voting of only $3.

We used the idea of expected value to show why voting for the better party is often a high (expected) impact altruistic activity. The same sort of reasoning, however, can be applied to other areas. On many issues, I find that people hold the following two views:

- If *many* people did this thing, then change would happen.
- But any *individual* person doesn't make a difference.

Holding that combination of views is usually a mistake when we consider expected value.

Consider ethical consumption, like switching to Fairtrade coffee, or reducing how much meat you buy. Suppose someone stops buying chicken breasts, instead choosing vegetarian options, in order to reduce the amount of animal suffering on factory farms. Does that person make a difference? You might think not. If one person decides against buying chicken breast one day but the rest of the meat-eaters on the planet continue to buy chicken, how could that possibly affect how many chickens are killed for human consumption? When a supermarket decides how much chicken to buy, they don't care that one fewer breast was purchased on a given day. However, if thousands or millions of people stopped buying chicken breasts, the number of chickens raised for food would decrease – supply would fall to meet demand. We're then left with a paradox: individuals alone can't make a difference; millions of them acting together can; but the action of millions is simply the combined actions of many individuals. Moreover, an iron law of economics is that, in a well-functioning market, if demand for a product decreases, the quantity of the product that's supplied decreases. How, then, can we reconcile these thoughts?

The answer lies with expected value. If you decline to buy some chicken breast then most of the time you'll make no difference: the supermarket will buy the same amount of chicken in the future. Sometimes, however, you will make a difference. Occasionally the meat buyer will assess chicken-breast sales and decide to decrease stocks, even though they wouldn't have done so had the number of chicken breasts sold been one higher. (Perhaps they follow a rule like: 'If monthly sales fall below 5,000, decrease stock intake by 20%.') And when that buyer does decide to decrease their order, they will decrease it by far more than your single non-purchase. Perhaps your decision will have an effect only 1 in 1,000 times, but it will spare around 1,000 chickens when it does.

This isn't just a theoretical argument. Economists have studied this issue and worked out how, on average, a consumer affects total sales by declining to buy one unit of a product. They estimate that, on average, if you give up one egg, total production ultimately falls by 0.91 eggs; if you give up one gallon of milk, total production falls by 0.56 gallons. Other products are somewhere in between: if you give up one pound of beef, beef production falls by 0.68lb; a pound of pork: 0.74lb; a pound of chicken: 0.76lb.

This same reasoning can be applied when considering the value of participating in political rallies. Suppose there's some policy that a group of people want to see implemented. Suppose everyone agrees that, if no one attends a rally on this policy, the policy won't go through, but if 1 million people show up, the policy will go through. What difference do *you* make by showing up at this rally? You're just one body among thousands of others – surely the difference you make is negligible? Again, the solution is to think in terms of expected value. The chance of you being the person who makes the difference is very small, but if you do make the difference, it will be very large indeed. Again, this isn't just a speculative model. Professors of political science at Harvard and Stockholm Universities analysed Tea Party rallies held on Tax Day, 15 April 2009. They used the weather in different constituencies as a natural experiment: if the weather was bad on the day of a rally, fewer people would show up. This allowed them to assess whether or not increased numbers of people at a rally made a difference to how influential the rally was. They found that policy was significantly influenced by those rallies that attracted more people, and that the larger the rally, the greater the degree to which those protestors' representatives in Congress voted conservatively.

For our purposes, the most important use of expected value reasoning is in comparing concrete, measurable ways of doing good with more speculative but potentially higher-payoff strategies. One example of this concerns how to compare different careers. Whereas earning to give in order to donate to charities like the Deworm the World Initiative provide a reliable way of doing good, others, like politics, are much less certain. How should we compare these?

'I expect to fail,' Laura Brown told me while putting down her cup of coffee. We were sitting at the Grand Café in Oxford, the oldest coffee house in the UK, and I was there to discuss Laura's career plans. A second-year student of Philosophy, Politics, and Economics (PPE), Laura had recently read a newspaper article discussing the chances of a PPE student being elected to Parliament. Intrigued, she traced the original source, finding work by my organisation 80,000 Hours, and studied the calculations carefully. The research persuaded her to pursue a career in politics. 'I'm most likely going to fail to become a high-flying politician. But I could do so much good if I did succeed that I think it's worth taking the chance,' Laura told me.

Before making her decision, Laura had been unsure about whether to go into politics or whether to enter a lucrative career and earn to give, but she knew she wanted to pursue whichever would make the bigger difference. You might think it would be impossible to make this comparison, and it is certainly very difficult to do so. However, the idea of expected value allows us to come up with a reasonable answer. At 80,000 Hours we did a very rough calculation to see whether entering politics could plausibly be competitive with earning to give.

First, we must calculate the odds of success. The most naïve estimate of the odds of becoming an MP would be to work out how many people alive in the UK today will ever serve as an MP (which we estimated at about 3,100, five of whom would become prime minister), and divide by the total population of the UK (64 million), giving a 1 in 20,000 chance of becoming an MP, and a 1 in 12 million chance of becoming prime minister. However, most people don't try to enter politics, and the representation of politicians in the UK is highly skewed towards people of certain backgrounds. In particular, graduates of Oxford are dramatically over-represented within UK politics, with graduates of PPE especially over-represented. For example, both David Cameron and Ed Miliband earned a degree in PPE from Oxford. Of the 650 members of Parliament, over a hundred studied at Oxford (despite there being only 3,000 graduates every year), of which thirty-five studied PPE (despite there being only 200 PPE graduates each year). Of Cabinet ministers (those MPs who hold executive power) 32% studied PPE at Oxford, and of the thirteen prime ministers since 1945, nine studied at Oxford and three of those studied PPE.

These statistics represent some disappointing facts about political mobility and equal representation in the UK. However, for someone who is altruistically minded and happened to study PPE at Oxford, they also represent a powerful opportunity. Laura was such a person. We worked out that a graduate in PPE from Oxford who chooses to enter politics had a historical chance of 1 in 30 of becoming an MP and 1 in 3,000 of becoming prime minister. Laura's background gave her remarkably good odds of entering Parliament, but, it was nonetheless still far more likely that she would fail, so entering politics as a means of doing good was still a high-risk stratagem.

In order to determine the expected value of her pursuing politics, we next need to work out how great an impact she would have as an MP.

This is very difficult to estimate so we'll use what I call lower-bound reasoning: given that it's impossible to calculate precisely her potential impact in politics, we'll try to create a value that we feel confident is an underestimate (or a 'lower bound'). Then we can say that, even though we don't know how much influence she'll have, it will be *at least* as much as the lower-bound estimate. If Laura's expected impact from going into politics is greater than that through earning to give, even based on this lower-bound estimate, then we can be confident that her expected impact really will be greater through politics than through earning to give.

In the spirit of being conservative, therefore, we'll first assume that Laura will have zero impact if she fails at least to become an MP, even if she were to secure a political position such as special advisor to an MP, or working at a think tank. Second, we'll assume that the impact of being an MP comes only through government expenditure, and not at all through legislation, or through other forms of influence via the public platform that a political position would give her. Both of these assumptions are false, of course, but they help to ensure that we can be reasonably confident that the number we end up with is an underestimate of her expected impact.

We're therefore only trying to estimate her potential influence over governmental spending as an MP. The way we do this is to think on an annual basis: how much influence do PPE-graduate MPs have, and how many people who read PPE at Oxford try to enter politics? Again, we'll try to remain conservative throughout.

First, the annual influence that all MPs have (including the Cabinet and the prime minister). Total UK government spending in 2014–2015 was £732 billion. Legally speaking, MPs and ministers decide government policy and spending, though in practice they are restricted in how they can allocate that spending by other political actors, international bodies and the views of the electorate. We want to be conservative, so we'll assume that each of these reduce MPs and ministers' influence by a half. Using these assumptions, we conclude that MPs and ministers influence one-eighth of government spending. However, it is civil servants who actually implement the policies that

MPs and ministers decide upon. This reduces the MPs and ministers' effective influence yet again. We'll estimate that this again decreases their influence by half, giving us our final estimate of the annual influence of all MPs at one-sixteenth of government expenditure, or approximately £45 billion.

Next, we estimate what proportion of that is influenced by PPE graduates. Currently, 5% of MPs and 32% of Cabinet ministers studied PPE at Oxford. We'll assume that the influence of all 628 non-Cabinet MPs is the same as the influence of the 22 MPs in the Cabinet (including the PM): so each group influences 50% of the approximately £45 billion that MPs in total influence. (Again this seems conservative: PPE has even higher representation at Cabinet and PM level than it does at MP level, and we suspect that the Cabinet and PM really have even more influence than the other MPs combined.) We therefore estimate that people who studied PPE at Oxford influence 5% × £22.5 billion + 32% × £22.5 billion = £8 billion annually. Every year, 200 people graduate from Oxford in PPE; however only about a quarter of them pursue a career relevant to party politics. Therefore, fifty graduates are responsible for that £8 billion of influence. The expected influence of each of those graduates (such as Laura Brown) is therefore 1/50 × £8 billion = £160 million. That expected influence might come, for example, from the chance of causing a change in allocation of spending between defence and overseas development aid; or it might come from the chance of improving the effectiveness of money spent on healthcare.

That's her expected financial influence, but how much is that influence worth? Because she will be restricted in how that money is used, it won't be worth as much as if she simply had £160 million that she could target to the most effective causes. Moreover, we must compare how much good that money would do, given she is the person influencing it, compared to how much good that money would do if someone else were in her shoes. Again being conservative, let's assume that the money she can influence will only do 2% as much good as money that was donated directly to the most effective causes. If so, then our estimate of Laura's expected impact of entering politics is as great as £8 million donated to the most effective causes.

In coming up with this number, we made conservative assumptions at every stage, assuming no impact if she didn't become an MP or Cabinet minister, and assuming that her impact as an MP would come only through government expenditure rather than through legislation. We should therefore think that the £8 million figure is an underestimate of her expected impact. However, £8 million is considerably more than she could donate if she earned to give. Even given our pessimistic assumptions, for Laura politics therefore seems to have a greater expected impact than earning to give. She wanted to have as big an impact as she could so, in part on the basis of this reasoning, she chose to enter a political career.

The conclusion that earning to give isn't always the highest-impact career path isn't a conclusion that's unique to Oxford PPE graduates. In Chapter 9 I'll discuss several other career paths, such as research and entrepreneurship, that have a low probability of success but a very high upside when success occurs and that seem highly competitive with earning to give.

As well as assessing careers, the concept of expected value can be used to assess efforts to effect political change. Donating to highly effective charities provides a comparatively concrete, reliable and measurable way of doing good. But the potential gains of systemic change are even greater: if you can find the right area, funding or participating in political campaigns could potentially do even more good. It's not generally necessary to put an exact figure on the expected value of that activity; rough estimates based on reasonable numbers can show you very approximately how great the expected value is. The point is simply that long shots can be worth backing if the payoff is big enough.

When assessing a potential course of action, one should therefore not dismiss it as ineffective by saying 'that'll never happen'. Many ethical ideas that are now regarded as common sense seemed highly radical in the past. The idea that women, or black people, or non-heterosexuals should have the same rights as everyone else was considered ridiculous until very recently, historically speaking. In 1790 Benjamin Franklin, for example, wrote a letter petitioning US Congress to end slavery. Congress debated the petition for two days. The defenders of slavery had no shortage of objections. 'Who is going to compensate the slave-owners?' they asked, and, 'What is the mixing of races going to do to American values and character?' Yet slavery was abolished wholesale, and we now find those objections indefensible. Those activists who campaigned for equal rights for women, black people and the LBGT community were right to do so not because they had a good chance of succeeding in the short term, but because the benefit was so great if they did succeed.

Climate change is another issue where the concept of expected value proves useful, in three different ways. First, it shows that the debate over whether man-made climate change is happening is pretty irrelevant when it comes to what we ought to do. In these debates, one group points to the scientific consensus that man-made climate change is happening while the other argues that the jury is still out. To be clear, there really is near consensus among scientists that man-made climate change is happening. A UN-backed panel of thousands of climate scientists, the Intergovernmental Panel on Climate Change has said, 'It is extremely likely that human influence has been the dominant cause of the observed warming since the mid-twentieth century,' where they define 'extremely likely' to mean at least 95% probability. One article reviewed 4,000 papers that discuss global warming and reported that '97.1% endorsed the consensus position that humans are causing global warming'.

However, this debate is strange for another reason: *even if* scientists had not already shown that man-made climate change is happening, the mere fact that man-made climate change *might* be happening is enough to warrant action. As an analogy, suppose you have a carbon monoxide detector in your home that is a bit sensitive. It gives a false alarm every four times out of five times it goes off, but is otherwise accurate. You're watching TV one evening, and the alarm goes off. What do you do? If you reason to yourself, 'It's probably a false alarm, so I won't bother doing anything,' you'd be making a grave mistake. If it's a false alarm but, to be safe, you turn off the boiler and open the windows, the worst that happens is you've made yourself chilly for an evening and had to pause your favourite TV show unnecessarily. In contrast, if there really is a carbon monoxide leak and you do nothing, you may die. Given this, the sensible thing is to turn off the boiler. The one-in-five chance of death clearly outweighs the four-in-five chance of being a little cold temporarily for no reason.

Our predicament with climate change is no different. If climate change is happening and we don't take action, millions of lives will be lost and the world economy will lose trillions of dollars. If climate change isn't happening and we *do* take action, the costs are much lower. We would have wasted some amount of resources developing low-carbon technology and slowed economic progress a bit, but it wouldn't, literally, be the end of the world.

The second way in which expected value is relevant when figuring out how to respond to the threat of climate change is that it shows why individuals have reason to mitigate climate change just as much as governments do. Over your lifetime, your individual greenhouse gas contribution will only increase the temperature of the planet by about half a billionth of a degree Celsius. That, you might think, is such a small difference as to be negligible, so you shouldn't bother trying to reduce your personal emissions.

This reasoning, however, doesn't consider expected value. It's true that increasing the planet's temperature by half a billionth of a degree probably won't make a difference to anyone, but sometimes it will make a difference, and when it does, the difference will be very large. Occasionally, that increase of half a billionth of a degree will cause a flood or a heatwave that wouldn't have happened otherwise. In which case the *expected* harm of raising global temperatures by half a billionth of a degree would be fairly great. We know that something like this has to be the case because we know that, if millions of people emit greenhouse gases, the bad effects are very large, and millions of people emitting greenhouse gases is just the sum of millions of individual actions.

Finally, and most importantly, expected value is important when assessing just how bad climate change is, and how much of a change we should make. When I first looked into economic assessments of the damages of climate change, I was surprised to find that economists tended to assess climate change as being not all that bad. Most estimate that climate change will cost only around 2% of global GDP. This, of course, is huge when measured in the trillions of dollars lost. But it's not that large when compared to somewhat typical rates of slow economic growth. Economic growth per person over the past decade has been about 2% per year; so a loss of 2% of global GDP due to climate change is therefore equivalent to going one year without economic growth. The thought that climate change would do the equivalent of putting us back one year economically isn't all that scary – 2013 didn't seem that much worse than 2014.

We can see the same thing on an individual level. Carbon dioxide equivalent, or CO_{2eq}, is a way of measuring your carbon footprint that includes greenhouse gases other than carbon dioxide, such as methane and nitrous oxide. For example, one metric ton of methane produces as much warming as twenty-one metric tons of carbon dioxide, so one metric ton of methane is twenty-one metric tons of CO_{2eq}. On typical estimates, the social cost of one metric ton of CO_{2eq} is about $32: incorporating costs both now and in the future, emitting one metric ton of CO_2, or an equivalent amount of greenhouse gases like methane or nitrous oxide, costs all people a total of $32. The average American emits about twenty-one metric tons of CO_{2eq} every year. So the social cost of one American's greenhouse gas emissions is about $670 every year. Again, that's a significant cost, but it's also not the end of the world. For those living in other countries, the cost of greenhouse gas emissions is significantly less again; people in the UK, for example, only emit about nine metric tons of CO_{2eq} every year, so the harm they cause every year is only $275.

However, this standard economic analysis fails to faithfully use expected value reasoning. The standard analysis looks only at the effects from the most likely scenario: a 2–4°C rise in temperature. It doesn't consider what the consequences would be if our best-guess estimates are wrong. This is especially important because the climate is an incredibly complex system that is difficult to predict so we can't be sure that our estimates are correct. When climate scientists make estimates about temperature rise, they have to acknowledge that there is a small but significant risk of a temperature increase that's much greater than 2–4°C. The Intergovernmental Panel on Climate Change gives more than 5% probability to temperature rises greater than 6°C, and even acknowledges a small risk of *catastrophic* climate change, of 10°C or more. To be clear, I'm not saying that this is at all likely, in fact, it's very unlikely. But it is possible, and if it were to happen, the consequences would be disastrous, potentially resulting in civilisational collapse. It's difficult to give a meaningful answer to the question of how bad that would be, but if we think it's potentially catastrophic, then we need to revise our evaluation of the importance of mitigating climate change. In that case, the true expected social cost of carbon could be much higher than $32 per metric ton, justifying much more extensive efforts to reduce emissions than the estimates the economists first suggested.

Just as most of the value from aid programmes comes from the very best of them (see Chapter 3), it's often the case that most of the expected harm from disasters come from the very worst of them. (In other words, the death tolls from disasters form a fat-tailed distribution. Nassim Taleb describes these as 'Black Swans': very rare events that have a very great impact.) For example, most people who've died in war have died in the very worst wars: of the 400 wars in the last 200 years, about 30% of deaths were from World War II alone. This means that if we're concerned by war, we should spend most of our efforts trying to prevent the very largest wars from occurring, or to limit their scope. Similar considerations are true of earthquakes, floods, and epidemics.

In cases where people seem to neglect the risks of worst-case outcomes, helping to prevent these outcomes might be a particularly effective altruistic activity. This is what the Skoll Global Threats Fund focuses on, trying to reduce the chances of global catastrophes arising from climate change, pandemics, and the proliferation of nuclear weapons. The charity evaluator GiveWell is currently investigating these sorts of activities in an attempt to work out how effective donations in these areas can be.

From the previous chapters, you might have gained the impression that effective altruism is limited to those activities with comparatively easy-to-quantify benefits, like deworming schoolchildren or distributing antimalarial bed nets. I hope that this discussion of expected value has helped to show why that's not the case. Even in what seem like 'unquantifiable' areas such as political change and disaster prevention, we can still think rigorously, in an evidence-based manner, about how good those activities are. We just need to assess the chances of success, and how good success would be if it happened. This, of course, is very difficult to do, but we will make better decisions if we at least try to make these assessments rather than simply throwing up our hands and randomly choosing an activity to pursue, or, worse, not choosing any altruistic activity at all.

In this book so far, I've introduced the key questions to help you think like an effective altruist:

How many people benefit, and by how much?

Is this the most effective thing you can do?

Is this area neglected?

What would have happened otherwise?

What are the chances of success, and how good would success be?

Now it's time to examine how we apply those questions to the real world and put effective altruism into action. That is the subject of Part II.

PART II

EFFECTIVE ALTRUISM
IN ACTION

7

OVERHEAD COSTS, CEO PAY AND OTHER CONFUSIONS

Which charities make the most difference?

Suppose I give you $100 and tell you to donate the whole sum to one of three charities, each of which is attempting to address a different problem facing poor countries in Africa. Which would you choose?

First, Books for Africa (BFA). BFA's mission is to improve education by shipping donated books from the USA to the African continent where they are distributed by non-profit partners. Founded in 1988, it has shipped over 28 million books to forty-nine different countries. On its website, the problem and its solution are vividly described:

> Most African children who attend school have never owned a book of their own. In many classrooms, 10–20 students share one textbook . . . Although Books for Africa has made tremendous progress in its mission, the book famine in Africa remains a reality. Where books are available, there are still very few. Empty library

shelves are a constant reminder of Africa's desperate need for printed materials. If we are to see the day when African school children are to have the books they need to learn the skills necessary to provide for themselves and others, Books for Africa must continue to send millions of books.

Former UN secretary general Kofi Annan has personally endorsed BFA, saying, 'Books for Africa is a simple idea, but its impact is transformative. For us, literacy is quite simply the bridge from misery to hope.'

The second organisation is Development Media International (DMI). Its focus is on preventing deaths of African children under five. It aims to do this by designing and broadcasting radio and TV programmes that provide health education, such as encouraging breastfeeding (to improve child health), proper hand washing (to decrease rates of diarrheal disease), and the use of antimalarial bed nets. Sometimes these take the form of minute-long radio ads, broadcast several times a day. Other times they are standalone dramas with educational messages built in. In the charity's words:

6.3 million children worldwide die under the age of five every year. In 2013 one in 11 children in sub-Saharan Africa died before their fifth birthday . . . Many people cannot recognise when their child has a potentially dangerous illness, or do not know what to do about it, so many deaths are due to lack of knowledge rather than lack of healthcare services. If a mother can recognise that her baby has diarrhoea and is able to provide her child with oral rehydration therapy [a piece of advice that DMI promotes], then the child is far more likely to reach the age of five.

DMI currently operates in Burkina Faso, and has plans to run similar programmes in DR Congo, Mozambique and Cameroon.

The third organisation is GiveDirectly. Its programme is simple: it transfers money from donors directly to some of the poorest people in Kenya and Uganda who are then free to use that money however they wish. Using what is called the M-Pesa system, cell phones are used as makeshift bank accounts, thereby enabling an easy transfer of money from foreign bank accounts to the poor. GiveDirectly uses satellite images to find households with thatched roofs (a strong indicator of poverty, compared to iron roofs) and then contacts those households to discuss the programme. If the household is willing, GiveDirectly transfers them a lump sum of $1,000, which is equal to a little more than one year's total income for that household. In their words:

> Recipients use transfers for whatever is most important to them; we never tell them what to do. An independent evaluation of our work in Kenya by Innovations for Poverty Action found that recipients use transfers for a wide variety of purposes that on average generate large income gains. Common uses range from buying food to investing in tangible assets such as housing and live-stock to investing in children's education.

Of these three charities, which do you think can do the most good with your $100 donation? In this chapter I'll provide a framework that will help you determine the answer.

One popular way of evaluating a charity is to look at financial information regarding how the charity spends its money. How much does the charity spend on administration? How much is its CEO paid? What percentage of donations are put directly to the charity's main programmes? This is the approach that Charity Navigator, the oldest and most popular charity evaluator, has taken for the last fifteen years. According to Charity Navigator, 'Savvy donors know that the financial health of a charity is a strong indicator of the charity's programmatic performance. They know that in most cause areas, the most efficient charities spend 75% or more of their budget on their programmes and services and less than 25% on fundraising and administrative fees.'

Using these metrics, let's see how the three charities compare.

Books for Africa's overhead costs are a tiny 0.8% of their total expenditure (which was $24 million in 2013), and their CEO is paid $116,204, which is only 0.47% of that total expenditure. For these reasons, and for their general financial transparency, Charity Navigator has given BFA its highest four-star rating for seven years running. As I write this book, it's rated number 4 on Charity Navigator's list of 'ten top-notch charities', and carries a near-perfect score of 99.93 out of 100.

GiveDirectly isn't rated by Charity Navigator, but would also do well by these metrics. So far, of every $1 that's been donated to GiveDirectly, between 87¢ (in Uganda) and 90¢ (in Kenya) has been transferred to the poor, with the rest spent on enrolment, follow-up and transfer costs. With every $1 they spent on fundraising, they raised $100 in donations, a remarkable number compared to the average of $4 of donations raised for every $1 spent on fundraising. They had an overheads ratio of 6%, spending just $124,000 on administration costs out of an expenditure of $2.2 million. Much of the administration spending was on fixed costs, so as GiveDirectly increases the amount of cash they transfer, the percentage spent on overheads is likely to go down considerably.

In contrast, Development Media International's overheads amount to 44% of its total budget, and there is little financial information on its website. Charity Navigator only evaluates US-based charities, so it does not evaluate DMI, which is based in the UK. However, DMI clearly performs much worse than the two other charities according to Charity Navigator's metrics.

The idea that you should use financial information to compare charities has been highly influential, and Charity Navigator has seen major success as a result. In 2012 its site received a total of 6.2 million visits and it claimed to have influenced approximately $10 billion of charitable donations. Its metrics have become the gold standard for determining whether a charity is efficient, and intuitively this makes sense. If we're donating our hard-earned money to a charity that supports a cause we believe in, we want to feel confident that our donation is actually working to advance that cause rather than being wasted. Based on this metric, you would choose

Books for Africa as the best charity, then GiveDirectly, then Development Media International.

Given the lessons of the previous chapters, however, we should already understand that this approach to evaluating a charity's effectiveness is seriously flawed.

For starters, think about the logic behind this reasoning if you apply it to personal spending. Suppose you're deciding whether to buy a Mac or a PC. What factors would you consider? You'd probably think about the design and usability of the two computers, the hardware, the software, and the price. You certainly wouldn't think about how much Apple and Microsoft each spend on administration, and you wouldn't think about how much their respective CEOs are paid. Why would you? As a consumer you only care about the product you receive for the money you spend; details about the financials of the companies who make the products are almost always irrelevant. If Apple spent a lot of money to attract a more talented management team, you might even consider that a sign that its products were the best on the market!

If we don't care about financial information when we buy products for ourselves, why should we care about financial information when we buy products for other people? Take a silly example: imagine I set up a charity that distributes doughnuts to hungry police officers and I am so enthusiastic about the mission that I manage to spend only 0.1% of the charity's money on overheads, with the rest spent on doughnuts and distribution. Suppose, moreover, that I, as the CEO of this charity, don't take a salary at all.

Would I really have created an amazing charity? Surely, as we discussed in Chapter 2, what we should ultimately care about is the *impact* charities have. When you give $100 to a charity, what does that charity *do* with it? How are people's lives improved as a result?

We can begin to answer this question by comparing the concrete outcomes that donating to each charity achieves. Books for Africa ships one book with every 50¢ donated to them. GiveDirectly gives the poor 90¢ with every $1 donated to them. Development Media International spends $1.5 million to run a mass media campaign promoting health education in a particular country. But those numbers alone don't tell us that much. Is it better to ship 3 million schoolbooks, transfer $1.35 million to poor people, or educate a country's populace about how they can stay healthy (each of which would cost $1.5 million)? To answer that, we have to know how these different expenditures affect people's lives.

The first thing to explore is whether there's high-quality evidence regarding the impact of the programme that the charity implements. Given the dearth of instructional materials in schools in Sub-Saharan Africa, it might seem obvious that distributing textbooks will be beneficial to the students that receive them. But, surprisingly, there's little good evidence in favour of this idea, and some evidence against. Development economists have tested the effect of increasing the number of textbooks in schools in Africa (remember Kremer and Glennerster?) and have found that, in the absence of teacher training, providing textbooks has either no discernible effect on children's school performance, or only a limited effect on the very most able students. Given the evidence that we currently have, there's little ground for thinking that distributing textbooks is a good way to improve educational outcomes in Sub-Saharan Africa.

This might discourage us from choosing Books for Africa as our preferred charity. Certainly, it should make us reject the method of assessing charities by looking at financial information alone. Books for Africa is supposedly 'efficient' for having low administrative costs, but what's really relevant to a charity's effectiveness is how much good is done per dollar spent on the programme that the charity implements, and the evidence we currently have suggests that the benefits of distributing textbooks are small. Books for Africa still seems better to me than most charities, because it's focusing its efforts on the very poorest people in the world, and it's implementing a programme that at least seems like it should work. But we'll see that the evidence in favour of the impact of the other two charities under consideration is much stronger. In my view, therefore, BFA is the least effective of our three candidates for donation.

Given that 'overheads costs' is a poor metric for assessing charities' effectiveness, we need a better set of standards by which to compare them. Below are the five questions I think any donor should ask before deciding where to give. They are based on the criteria used by the charity evaluator GiveWell, which has spent the last eight years investigating which charities improve lives the most with the donations they receive:

1. *What does this charity do?* How many different types of programmes does it run? For each of these programmes, what exactly is it that this charity does? If it runs more than one programme, why is that?

2. *How cost-effective is each programme area?* Is the charity focused on one of the most important causes? How cost-effective does the evidence suggest the programme to be?

3. *How robust is the evidence behind each programme?* What is the evidence behind the programmes that the charity runs? Are there trials showing that the programme is effective? Does the charity rigorously monitor and evaluate the success of its programmes?

4. *How well is each programme implemented?* Do the leaders of the charity have demonstrated success in other areas? Is the charity highly transparent? Does it acknowledge mistakes that it's made in the past? What are the alternative charities you could give to? Are there good reasons for supposing that this charity is better than others?

5. *Does the charity need additional funds?* What would additional funding be used to do? Why haven't other donors already funded the charity to the point it can't use extra money?

This framework enables us to genuinely assess charities in terms of their impact, rather than on flawed metrics like 'administrative overheads'. I'll explain each aspect of the framework in turn, in each case using the framework to compare our two remaining charities – GiveDirectly and Development Media International – against one another.

1. What does this charity do?

This might seem like an obvious question, but often what most people think a charity does is quite different from what it actually does. For example I was surprised to find out that many developed-world medical charities spend only a small fraction of their money on research, with the rest spent on other programmes, even though research is what they emphasise in their marketing and websites. The American Cancer Society spends 43% of its programme expenses on patient support, 21% on prevention, 14% on detection/treatment, and just 22% on research. The ALS Association (of ice bucket challenge fame) spends 41% of its programme expenses on public and professional education, 24% on patient and community services and just 35% on research. That's not a reason in itself against donating to either of these charities, and that's not to say that either of these charities have been misleading in their marketing; but you would assess them differently knowing that donations support numerous programmes rather than just research.

I've already explained what GiveDirectly and DMI do. What we need to know, then, is how good each of these programmes is.

2. How cost-effective is each programme area?

We want to estimate what a charity achieves with a given amount of money, so our focus should always be on *cost-effectiveness* rather than just *effectiveness*. Charity A and Charity B might both be *effective* at distributing deworming drugs (that is to say, they successfully distribute them), but if Charity B can do so at half the cost, then a donation to it will do twice as much good.

The first step in estimating cost-effectiveness is to find out how much the charity spends per person to run its programme. For example it costs about $6 to deliver one antimalarial bed net, which on average protects two children for two years, so it costs $1.50 to protect one child for one year. It costs GiveDirectly $1 to give someone in extreme poverty 90¢; it costs DMI between 40¢ and 80¢ per listener per year to run its education campaigns. Ultimately, however, we should try to discover how this converts into impact on people's wellbeing. These figures don't yet tell us whether GiveDirectly or DMI does more good. To do that we need to assess how these programmes actually affect people's lives.

The obvious first question to ask about GiveDirectly is what the recipients of these cash transfers do with the money. If they spend it on education, that sounds pretty good; if they spend it on drugs and alcohol, that's worrying. It turns out that the most common use of the transfer is to buy assets, typically farm animals, or to convert thatched roofs into iron ones; on average recipients spend 39% of the transfer on assets. These purchases seem to have very high returns, potentially as high as 14% per year for at least a period of several years.

Cash transfers also seem to have several less tangible effects. Recipients of the transfer reported significant increases in subjective wellbeing, reported significant decreases in number of whole days gone without food, and scored significantly higher on an index of female empowerment, though there weren't significant increases in health or education during the time period studied.

The estimated cost-effectiveness of GiveDirectly's programmes is very impressive, but the estimated cost-effectiveness of DMI's programme is even more so.

There's a lot of health knowledge that we have without even realising it. For example we all know that we should wash our hands regularly: it's a lesson that's drilled into us from childhood. Moreover, we know to use soap and that just because our hands *look* clean that doesn't mean they *are* clean. In many poor countries, however, people have never been told this, or they regard soap as a precious commodity and are therefore reluctant to use it for hand washing. This can have severe consequences. Diarrhoea is a major problem in the developing world, killing 760,000 children every year, primarily through dehydration. (For comparison, that's a death toll equivalent to five jumbo jets crashing to the ground every day, killing everyone on board.) A significant number of those deaths could be avoided through simple improvements to sanitation and hygiene, like more regular hand washing with soap.

The ads that DMI run are terribly corny. (In one, a baby has a conversation with a group of diseases who are ultimately defeated by breastfeeding.) Through those ads, however, DMI can teach people crucial pieces of information like the importance of breastfeeding immediately after childbirth or the proper use of bed nets for pennies per person.

When looking at DMI's impact, we can use QALYs as a measurement (where one QALY, remember, represents one year of perfect health). Studies and models of mass-media education have estimated that it costs about $10 to provide one QALY. In Chapter 3 I mentioned that insecticide-treated bed nets provide 1 QALY for just $100 (equivalent to saving a life for $3,400), and I pointed out that this was an astonishing fact. If the estimate of $10/QALY is correct, however, we could do ten times as much good, the equivalent of saving a life for just $360, by donating to DMI.

It's difficult to know how to value the increases in income, psychological wellbeing and empowerment that GiveDirectly provides compared with QALYs and lifesaving, but under any reasonable assumptions about how to make the comparison, on the basis of these estimates DMI looks like the clear winner.

To see this, note that a $1,000 cash transfer represents approximately a doubling of annual household income, where a household consists of about five people. Supposing, very generously, that that doubling of income lasts for ten years thanks to returns on investment. The entire household will therefore be twice as rich as they would otherwise have been for ten years following the transfer. We can then ask which is the larger benefit: saving approximately three lives (as you would by donating $1,000 to DMI), or doubling the income of five people for ten years (as you would by donating to GiveDirectly). It seems clear that saving three lives is providing a larger benefit with the same amount of resources.

Based on estimated cost-effectiveness, therefore, DMI seems like the better bet. In order to fully compare DMI with GiveDirectly, however, we need to complete our framework.

3. How robust is the evidence behind each programme?

Often we should prefer a charity that has very good evidence of being fairly cost-effective to a charity that has only weak evidence of being very cost-effective: if the evidence behind an estimate is weak, it's likely that the estimate is optimistic, and the true cost-effectiveness is much lower.

For example, the evidence behind claims made on charities' websites or marketing materials is often very shaky, and sometimes potentially misleading. On its website, the charity Nothing But Nets says that, 'one $10 bed net can mean the difference between life and death'. In one sense, this is true: bed nets do save lives, so a single bed net *can* save a life. But not every child who is protected by a bed net would otherwise die of malaria, so it's not true that $10 spent distributing bed nets *will* save a life; and if you weren't reading Nothing But Nets' message closely, you might form the impression that that's what is meant. It's cheap to save or improve lives in poor countries, but it's not *that* cheap. (For a sanity check, remember that even the very poorest people in the world live on 60¢ per day: if it cost $10 to save a life, then we'd have to suppose that they or their family members couldn't save up for a few weeks, or take out a loan, in order to pay for the life-saving product.)

Claims of a programme's effectiveness are more reliable when grounded in academic studies. If there's been a 'meta-analysis' – a study of the studies – that's even better. Even then, there can be cause for concern because the programme that a charity implements might be subtly different from the programmes that were studied in the meta-analysis. Knowing that, it's even better if the charity has done its own independently audited or peer-reviewed randomised controlled evaluation of its programmes.

Robustness of evidence is very important for the simple reason that many programmes don't work, and it's hard to distinguish the programmes that don't work from those that do. If we'd assessed Scared Straight by looking just at before-and-after delinquency rates for individuals who went through the programme, we would have concluded it was a great programme. Only after looking at randomised controlled trials could we tell that correlation did not indicate causation in this case and that Scared Straight programmes were actually doing more harm than good.

One of the most damning examples of low-quality evidence concerns microcredit (that is, lending small amounts of money to the very poor, a form of microfinance). Intuitively, microcredit seems like it would be very cost-effective, and there were many anecdotes of people who'd received microloans and used them to start businesses that, in turn, helped them escape poverty. But when high-quality studies were conducted, microcredit programmes were shown to have little or no effect on income, consumption, health, or education. Rather than starting new companies, microloans are typically used to pay for extra consumption like food and healthcare, and the rate of interest on them is often very high. There's even concern that they can cause harm by providing a tempting short-term income boost at the expense of longer-term financial security: people take out a loan in order to pay for food or healthcare costs of family members, but then enter debt that they are unable to repay. The latest evidence suggests that, overall and on average, microlending does have a small positive improvement on people's lives, but it's not the panacea that the anecdotes portray.

With these warnings at the top of our minds, how should we compare GiveDirectly and DMI? Here, GiveDirectly clearly has the edge. Cash transfers are one of the most well-studied development programmes, having been shown to improve lives in many different countries around the world. They also easily pass a sanity check as to whether they will be effective: the recipients of the transfers are very well placed to know their most pressing needs, and they can use additional resources to fill those needs in ways they know will benefit them. Finally, the independent development think-tank Innovations for Poverty Action has run a randomised controlled trial on GiveDirectly, so we can be confident not just about the efficacy of cash transfers in general, but also about cash transfers as implemented by GiveDirectly.

Because transferring cash is such a simple idea, and because the evidence in favour of cash transfers is so robust, we could think of them as the 'index fund' of giving. Money invested in an index fund grows (or shrinks) at the same rate as the stock market; investing in an index fund is the lowest-fee way to invest in stocks and shares. Actively managed mutual funds, in contrast, take higher management fees, and it's only worth investing in one if that fund manages to beat the market by a big enough margin that the additional returns on investment are greater than the additional management costs. In the same way, one might think, it's only worth donating to charitable programmes rather than simply transferring cash directly to the poor if the other programmes provide a benefit great enough to outweigh the additional costs incurred in implementing them. In other words, we should only assume we're in a better position to help the poor than they are to help themselves if we have some particularly compelling reason for thinking so.

In the case of mass-media education, we *do* have a plausible explanation for why it could be more effective than cash transfers: mass-media health education isn't something individuals can buy, and even if they could, they probably wouldn't know just how valuable it is. Markets alone cannot provide mass-media health education, so it needs to be funded and implemented by governments or non-profits.

However, the mere fact we have a plausible explanation for how mass-media education *could be* more cost-effective than cash transfers doesn't show that it *is* more cost-effective. When we look at the evidence for supporting mass-media education, we find it's weaker than the evidence for cash transfers.

There are three main sources of evidence, each of which provides an estimate of approximately $10/QALY for mass-media campaigns. First, there are some published studies of mass-media health education programmes, but these are of far lower quality and relevance than the studies behind GiveDirectly's programme. Second, there is a mathematical model created by DMI prior to rolling out its interventions. But a model is only as good as its assumptions, and the assumptions put into this model may be optimistic. Finally, there are the midline results from the randomised controlled trial that DMI is performing on its own programme. Their programme is based in Burkina Faso, which has many local radio services. This means that they can implement their programme in seven districts, monitor health indicators in an additional seven districts, and then compare mortality and disease prevalence in order to see what effect their programme has had. These midline results are very promising, but they are based on self-reports, which are not as accurate as indisputable indicators such as mortality.

The fact that the evidence for the $10/QALY figure is weaker than the evidence for GiveDirectly's cost-effectiveness estimates provides a reason for preferring GiveDirectly to DMI. Because the evidence behind its programme is better, we can be more confident that GiveDirectly's estimates are approximately accurate, whereas the $10/QALY figure provided by DMI may be optimistic.

4. How well is each programme implemented?

Even if a charity has chosen an extremely cost-effective programme with very robust evidence supporting it, it still might implement that programme badly. For example distribution of antimalarial bed nets is an extremely cost-effective programme if implemented correctly, but if recipients of the bed nets don't believe they're necessary or don't believe they're effective, they may use them for other purposes. A study of bed nets distributed by the Kenyan government found that recipients often used bed nets for catching and drying fish. That's why the Against Malaria Foundation, for example, educates the recipients of its nets about proper use and benefits and later conducts site visits, taking photographs to ensure that the nets are correctly installed after use.

An even more common problem than knowing that a charity implements a programme badly is simply not knowing whether it implements it well. Most charities provide almost no information about the programmes they run, making it difficult to assess their effectiveness.

Both GiveDirectly and DMI seem excellent in terms of the quality of their implementation. GiveDirectly is led by a leading development economist; DMI is led by someone with extensive experience and achievements in radio education, and has an advisory board that includes some of the world's best epidemiologists and development economists. In communication with GiveWell, both charities have openly shared requested information. GiveDirectly even goes so far as to provide information on how many cash transfer recipients reported having to pay bribes to the local agents who transferred them the money (at the time of writing, the figure is 0.4%). This sort of admission is very encouraging: showing that the charity cares about identifying and fixing mistakes, rather than brushing them under the rug.

5. Does the charity need additional funds?

Even after finding a charity that works on an extremely cost-effective programme with robust evidence behind it, we still need to ask whether our contribution will make a difference. Many effective programmes are fully funded precisely because they are so effective. For example developing-world governments usually fund the costs of vaccination programmes for the cheapest vaccines such as those for tuberculosis, polio, diphtheria, tetanus, pertussis, and measles, providing these vaccines through existing health systems. These programmes also receive substantial support from Gavi, the global vaccine alliance, which received $4.3 billion in funding for 2011–15, exceeding its target of $3.7 billion. For these programmes, the main obstacle to universal coverage is logistical rather than a lack of funds.

The same can be true on a smaller scale. Even if there's plenty of room for more funding for a programme in general, it can be difficult for a specific charity to scale up rapidly. If a charity has recently received a windfall, it might not be able to use additional donations effectively. This may have been true of the Against Malaria Foundation in 2013: GiveWell had named it its top-recommended organisation in 2012, and it received a surge in donations totalling $10 million. They struggled to spend that money quickly, which suggested that additional donations to them wouldn't have the same effectiveness as previous donations, so GiveWell didn't recommend them in 2013. (They successfully increased their capacity in 2013, however, so GiveWell recommended them again in 2014.)

Both GiveDirectly and DMI are in a good position to use more funding, but GiveDirectly could do more with additional funds than DMI could. GiveDirectly could productively use an additional $25–$30 million of donations in 2015 and expects to receive about $10 million, whereas DMI could productively use $10 million in 2015 and expects to receive $2–4 million. Moreover, the limit for how much money could be spent on cash transfers is much higher than how much could be spent on mass-media education. Conceivably, hundreds of billions of dollars could be spent on cash transfer programmes; whereas providing mass-media health education in every country in the world would cost much less.

At the moment, this difference doesn't pose a problem, but depending on how each charity's funding situation progresses, it might provide a reason against donating to DMI. If DMI will close their funding gap regardless of whether you donate to them, then your specific donation will do very little.

This brings us to the end of the framework. What should we conclude about which charity will do more good with $100? As you may have guessed, I deliberately chose these two charities because the answer is unclear. Of the considerations we've canvassed, the most important issues are estimated cost-effectiveness versus robustness of evidence. The estimated cost-effectiveness of DMI is higher than that of GiveDirectly, but the evidence behind that estimate is weaker than the evidence behind the estimate of GiveDirectly's cost-effectiveness. Which charity one chooses depends crucially on how sceptical one should be of explicit cost-effectiveness estimates, and that depends on your level of optimism or pessimism about this programme. This is a common difficulty we face when trying to do good: when should you pursue an activity with more robust evidence of more limited impact, versus an activity with much weaker evidence of potentially much greater impact?

If I had to choose between giving to these two charities today, I'd donate the $100 to DMI rather than to GiveDirectly, with my reasoning based on the 'expected value' considerations discussed in Chapter 6. I think that DMI is probably considerably less cost-effective than the $10/QALY figure, but if that figure is even approximately accurate, then DMI is *much* more cost-effective than GiveDirectly. I therefore think the expected value of donating to DMI is higher than that of donating to GiveDirectly. However, I would not fault someone who thought that the robustness of evidence in favour of GiveDirectly was more important than their lower estimated cost-effectiveness, and chose to donate to them instead. Assessing charity effectiveness is difficult, and these are both excellent charities whose programmes provide impressive benefit to the extremely poor.

We've just looked at three specific charities and determined that two of them are indisputably cost-effective. But what about all of the other charities in the world? I don't have the time or the space in this book to apply my framework to every charity, so to end this chapter I'll provide a list of some highly cost-effective charities, based on GiveWell's research, and I'll provide a brief explanation of why each of them passes muster. Before then, I want to clarify a few things.

First, you won't find 'mega-charities' like WorldVision or Oxfam or UNICEF on these lists. These charities run a variety of programmes, and for that reason they are very difficult to evaluate. I also think it's unlikely that, even if we were able to evaluate them in depth, we would conclude that they are as effective as the charities I list here. If a charity implements a variety of programmes, inevitably some of these programmes will be more effective than others. In which case, we should simply focus on funding those very best programmes. For example we argued earlier that disaster relief is generally not the most effective use of funding, but many mega-charities spend a large portion of their energies on just that.

Second, you might be surprised by how few charities are on this list. Aren't there dozens of worthy charities in the world? Yes there are, but that doesn't mean you should give to them all. As we saw in Chapter 3, the best charities are often far better even than very good charities. Given that we've only a limited amount to spend, we should focus on the very best charities rather than merely very good charities.

Finally, you'll notice that most of the charities I discuss implement health-based programmes in poor countries. I've already explained that we should focus on poor countries because it's easier and cheaper to save lives there than it is in developed countries. But what about education, or water provision, or economic empowerment? These are all promising areas, but global health stands out for a couple of reasons. First, it has a proven track record: smallpox eradication is the clearest example, but development aid has made significant contributions towards other areas of health, such as polio, measles, diarrheal disease and guinea worm disease. In contrast, the link between aid and economic growth is less clear. Second, by its nature the evidence behind health interventions is more robust. If we know that the drug albendazole kills the parasitic worm *Ascaris lumbricoides* in the US, we can safely conclude that

OVERHEAD COSTS, CEO PAY AND OTHER CONFUSIONS

it will probably kill that same worm in Kenya or India because human bodies are pretty similar all round the world. In contrast, it's much harder to be confident that an educational programme that works in India will also work in Kenya, where the culture and educational infrastructure are very different.

There can be exceptions to the 'focus on global health' heuristic: GiveDirectly, for example, is an economic empowerment charity. We will also look at a much broader array of causes in Chapter 10, though the arguments for focusing on these causes rather than global health will necessarily be more speculative.

With those caveats out of the way, let's look at some extremely cost-effective charities, as judged by GiveWell (accurate as of January 2015), the leading effective altruism charity evaluator. I'll rate each charity along four dimensions: estimated cost-effectiveness, robustness of evidence, implementation, and room for more funding. These ratings should only be used to compare the charities I list to one another, because, for example, any charity that I assess as 'fairly cost-effective' in the following list would look extremely cost-effective compared to charities not listed here. For completeness and for purposes of comparison, I'll include those we've already read about: GiveDirectly, Development Media International, Deworm the World Initiative and Against Malaria Foundation.

Top charities

GiveDirectly

What does it do? Provides direct unconditional cash transfers to poor households in Kenya and Uganda.

Estimated cost-effectiveness? Fairly cost-effective. $1 in donations results in 90¢ delivered to the poorest households in Kenya and Uganda; this leads to increases in investment, consumption, education spending, and subjective wellbeing.

Robustness of evidence? Extremely robust. There have been a large number of studies of cash transfers proving efficacy, and GiveDirectly has collaborated with independent evaluators to conduct a randomised controlled trial of its own programme.

Implementation? Extremely well implemented. The charity is run in part by a leading development economist. It is very open, transparent and self-sceptical.

Room for more funding? Extremely large. It estimates it could productively use an additional $35 million in 2015, and expects to receive about $15 million in that time. The potential for GiveDirectly to scale up beyond that in future years is very great.

Development Media International

What does it do? Produces and runs radio shows to educate people in Burkina Faso on basic health matters, with plans to cover DR Congo, Mozambique, Cameroon and Côte d'Ivoire.

Estimated cost-effectiveness? Extremely cost-effective. According to Development Media Internationals' interpretation of previous studies, and its own mathematical model, its cost-effectiveness is on the order of $10/QALY.

Robustness of evidence? Fairly robust. It is collaborating with external investigators to conduct a randomised controlled trial on its own programme, but has not yet gathered final mortality data; current data is based on self-reporting.

Implementation? Very well implemented. CEO Roy Head has extensive experience in running radio programmes in developing countries, and DMI works with leading epidemiologists to monitor their effectiveness. The charity has been open, transparent and self-sceptical.

Room for more funding? Very large. In order to scale up to four more countries, it believes it could use about $10 million in 2015, and expects to receive $2–4 million.

Deworm the World Initiative

What does it do? Provides technical assistance to governments in Kenya and India to help those governments run school-based deworming programmes.

Estimated cost-effectiveness? Extremely cost-effective. Because it provides assistance to governments, rather than running deworming programmes itself, the cost to DtWI per child treated per year is extremely low, at about 3¢.

Robustness of evidence? Fairly robust. Two major randomised controlled trials, one of which included long-term follow-up, suggest that deworming has significant education and economic benefits. However, insofar as DtWI provides technical assistance to governments, rather than running the deworming programmes itself, it's more difficult to know for certain that these programmes wouldn't have happened were it not for DtWI's support.

Implementation? Very good. It has been highly transparent about its operations.

Room for more funding? Not very large. It could use an additional $2 million over both 2015 and 2016, and I expect it to receive at least that amount.

Schistosomiasis Control Initiative

What does it do? Provides funding for governments to run school-based and community-based deworming programmes in countries across sub-Saharan Africa, then provides advisory support and conducts monitoring and evaluation. ('Schistosomiasis' is one type of parasitic worm infection; initially SCI focused just on schistosomiasis, hence the name, but now treats other parasitic worm infections, too.)

Estimated cost-effectiveness? Very cost-effective. The cost to SCI of deworming one child is less than $1 per year.

Robustness of evidence? Very robust. Two major randomised controlled trials, one of which included long-term follow-up, suggest that deworming has significant educational and economic benefits.

Implementation? Fairly good. There have been some concerns from GiveWell regarding SCI's transparency and communication about its activities.

Room for more funding? Fairly large. SCI believes it could productively use about $8 million in additional donations in 2015; however, it's not clear how much revenue it will receive in 2015 and it may become fully funded.

Against Malaria Foundation

What does it do? Provides funding to buy and distribute long-lasting insecticide-treated bed nets to poor households across sub-Saharan Africa.

Estimated cost-effectiveness? Very cost-effective. It costs $5 to provide one bed net that covers two children for two years, for an estimated $100/QALY.

Robustness of evidence? Very robust. There have been multiple randomised controlled trials and two meta-analyses supporting the efficacy of bed nets.

Implementation? Extremely good. AMF has been extremely transparent and open in communication.

Room for more funding? Very large. AMF could productively use $20 million in 2015.

Living Goods

What does it do? Runs a network of community health promoters in Uganda who go door-to-door selling affordable health products such as treatments for malaria, diarrhoea and pneumonia, soap, menstrual pads, contraception, solar lanterns and high-efficiency cooking stoves as well as providing healthcare advice.

Estimated cost-effectiveness? Very cost-effective. According to the estimates from the randomised controlled trial it's running on its project, $3,000 spent on its programme would save a life and provide a number of other benefits; GiveWell estimates the cost per life saved at $11,000.

Robustness of evidence? Fairly robust. A high-quality study has been conducted by independent investigators on the very programme that Living Goods is running. However, there is no evidence from multiple studies, as there are for other programmes on this list.

Implementation? Fairly good. Living Goods has been open and fairly transparent in providing information. However, it has only limited ongoing monitoring and evaluation.

Room for more funding? Fairly large. Living Goods' budget will be about $10 million per year for the next three years; it is likely to have a shortfall of about $2–3 million per year.

Iodine Global Network (IGN)

What does it do? Advocates for governments to fortify salt with iodine and thereafter monitors progress of implemented programmes and provides country-specific guidance.

Estimated cost-effectiveness? Extremely cost-effective. Iodine deficiency is a major cause of physical and intellectual stunting in developing countries. Iodine fortification can alleviate these problems at a cost of pennies per person. One estimate put the economic benefits of these programmes at $27 for every $1 spent.

Robustness of evidence? Fairly robust. Fortification of salt with iodine is a well-studied programme and has been shown to lead to significant improvements to people's lives. However, IGN does not implement the iodine fortification programmes itself. It's therefore crucial to determine whether IGN is causing more people to receive iodised salt than they would otherwise have done. This is not yet clear.

Implementation? Very good. IGN is run by leading experts on micronutrient deficiencies, and has been open and transparent.

Room for more funding? Not very large. Though its budget was only $500,000 in 2014, GiveWell believes IGN could productively use $1 million in 2015; it has so far only raised $400,000 towards that goal, giving $600,000 in room for more funding.

My ratings are summarised in Table 1.

	Estimated cost-effectiveness	Robustness of evidence	Quality of implement-ation	Size of room for more funding
GiveDirectly	●●	●●●●	●●●●	●●●●
Development Media International	●●●●	●●	●●●	●●●
Deworm the World Initiative	●●●	●●●	●●●	●
Schistosomiasis Control Initiative	●●●	●●●	●●●	●●
Against Malaria Foundation	●●●	●●●	●●●●	●●●●
Living Goods	●●●	●●	●●	●●
Iodine Global Network	●●●	●●	●●●	●

Table 1: Characteristics of seven top charities

8

THE MORAL CASE FOR SWEATSHOP GOODS

How can consumers make the most difference?

The clothing retailer American Apparel, known for selling 'fashionable basics' like solid-colour T-shirts, proudly claims to be 'sweatshop free'. On its 'about us' webpage, it claims that its garment workers are paid up to fifty times more than the competition:

> A garment worker in Bangladesh earns an average of $600 a year. An experienced American Apparel garment worker can earn $30,000+ and receive benefits such as comprehensive health care. American Apparel garments are created by motivated and fairly-paid employees who don't just have jobs – they have careers. Our culture recognizes outstanding performance and promotes from within. Most importantly, our workers have a voice and influence the direction of the company. At American Apparel we call it Sweatshop-Free, a term we coined in 2002.

The popularity of American Apparel is just one example of a trend towards 'ethical consumerism', where people spend a little more money on goods that are produced by workers who are treated well, thereby using their purchasing power to, hopefully, make the world a better place.

This chapter will look at ethical consumerism through the lens of effective altruism, trying to determine whether it's an effective way of doing good. I'll talk about sweatshops, Fairtrade, low-carbon living and vegetarianism. I'll then tell you why, in my view, ethical consumerism is not all it's cracked up to be – at least, not compared with other ways of making a difference.

Let's start with sweatshops. Sweatshops are factories in poor countries, typically in Asia or South America, that produce goods like textiles, toys, or electronics for rich countries under pretty horrific working conditions. Workers often face sixteen-hour days, six or seven days a week. Sometimes they're prohibited from taking meal or toilet breaks. Air conditioning is rare, so factories can be very hot. Health and safety considerations are commonly neglected and employers sometimes abuse their workers.

Because conditions in sweatshops are so bad, many people have pledged to boycott goods produced in them, and a number of organisations devoted to ending the use of sweatshop labour, such as United Students Against Sweatshops, National Mobilisation Against Sweatshops, SweatFree Communities and the ingeniously named No Sweat Apparel, have proliferated in service to the cause.

For this reason, there's significant public animosity towards big companies such as Nike, Apple and Disney that have been accused of using sweatshop labour to manufacture their products.

This movement has noble intentions: the people who campaign against sweatshops are justifiably horrified that people work in such awful conditions. However, those who attempt to combat sweatshops by refusing to buy goods produced in them are making the mistake of ignoring the key question discussed in Chapter 5: What would have happened otherwise? We assume that if people refuse to buy goods from sweatshops, these factories will succumb to economic pressure and go out of business, in which case their employees will find better employment elsewhere.

But that's not true. In developing countries, sweatshop jobs are the good jobs. The alternatives are typically worse, such as backbreaking, low-paid farm labour, scavenging, or unemployment. The *New York Times* columnist Nicholas D. Kristof illustrated this well when he presented an interview with Pim Srey Rath, a Cambodian woman who scavenges plastic from dumps in order to sell it as recycling. 'I'd love to get a job in a factory,' she said. 'At least that work is in the shade. Here is where it's hot.'

A clear indicator that sweatshops provide comparatively good jobs is the great demand for them among people in developing countries. Almost all workers in sweatshops choose to work there, and some go to great lengths to do so. In the early twenty-first century nearly 4 million people from Laos, Cambodia and Burma immigrated to

Thailand to take sweatshop jobs, and many Bolivians risk deportation by illegally entering Brazil in order to work in sweatshops there. The average earnings of a sweatshop worker in Brazil are $2,000 per year: not very much, but $600 a year more than the average earnings in Bolivia, where people generally work in agriculture or mining. Similarly, the average daily earnings among sweatshop workers are: $2 in Bangladesh, $5.50 in Cambodia, $7 in Haiti and $8 in India. These wages are tiny, of course, but when compared to the $1.25 a day many citizens of those countries live on, the demand for these jobs seems more understandable. Because conditions in sweatshops are so bad, it's difficult for us to imagine that people would risk deportation just to work in them. But that's because, as we discussed in Chapter 1, the extremity of global poverty is almost unimaginable.

In fact, among economists on both the left and the right, there is no question that sweatshops benefit those in poor countries. Nobel Laureate and left-wing economist Paul Krugman has stated, 'The overwhelming mainstream view among economists is that the growth of this kind of employment is tremendous good news for the world's poor.' Jeffrey Sachs, Columbia University economist and one of the foremost proponents of increased efforts to help those in extreme poverty, has said, 'My concern is not that there are too many sweatshops but that there are too few.' The reason there's such widespread support among economists for sweatshops is that low wage, labour-intensive manufacturing is a stepping stone that helps an economy based around cash crops develop into an industrialised, richer society. During the Industrial Revolution, for example, Europe and America spent over a hundred years using sweatshop labour, emerging with much higher living standards as a result. It took many decades to pass through this stage because the technology to industrialise was new, and the twentieth century has seen countries complete this stage of development much more rapidly because the technology is already in place. The four East Asian 'Tiger economies' – Hong Kong, Singapore, South Korea, and Taiwan – exemplify speedy development, having evolved from very poor, agrarian societies in the early twentieth century to manufacturing-oriented 'sweatshop' countries mid-century and finally emerging as industrialised economic powerhouses in recent decades.

Because sweatshops are good for poor countries, if we boycott them we make people in poor countries worse off. This isn't just a hypothetical argument. In 1993 Tom Harkin, a junior Senator from Iowa, brought a child labour bill to Congress. The Child Labor Deterrence Act would have made it illegal for the United States to import goods from countries using child labour. Bangladesh had a large number of children employed in ready-to-wear garment sweatshops at the time. Out of fear that this act would pass, factories quickly laid off 50,000 child workers. According to the US Department of Labor, rather than going to school or even finding better jobs, 'it is widely thought that most of them have found employment in other garment factories, in smaller, unregistered, subcontracting garment workshops, or in other sectors'. Considering that trans-national corporations typically pay much higher wages than domestic sweatshops, the lives of these youths likely became worse. Indeed, an investigation by UNICEF found that many of these laid-off underage garment workers had resorted to even more desperate measures to survive, including street hustling and prostitution.

We should certainly feel outrage and horror at the conditions sweatshop labourers toil under. The correct response, however, is not to give up sweatshop-produced goods in favour of domestically produced goods. The correct response is to try to end the extreme poverty that makes sweatshops desirable places to work in the first place.

What about buying products from companies that employ people in poor countries (unlike American Apparel), but claim to have higher labour standards, like People Tree, Indigenous, and Kuyichi? By doing this, we would avoid the use of sweatshops, while at the same time providing even better job opportunities for the extreme poor.

If we really could effectively pass on benefits to the very poor through consumer pressure, then I would be all in favour of it. In practice, however, I'm not so sure that 'ethical consumption' works as intended. To see this, let's look at the most widespread attempt to give the very poor better working conditions: Fairtrade.

Fairtrade certification is an attempt to give higher pay to workers in poor countries. It's commonly used for consumables grown in developing countries, such as bananas, chocolate, coffee, sugar and tea. The Fairtrade licence is given only to producers who meet certain criteria, such as paying their workers a minimum wage and satisfying specified safety requirements. The Fairtrade licence has two benefits. First, the producers are guaranteed a certain minimum price for the good; for example coffee producers are guaranteed to receive $1.40 per pound of coffee, even if the market rate drops below $1.40. Second, producers are paid a 'social premium' on top of the market rate. For coffee, if the market rate is above $1.40, the producers are paid an additional 20¢ per pound. This social premium is used to pay for democratically chosen community programmes.

Demand for Fairtrade products has grown rapidly. The Fairtrade label was launched only in 1988, and in 2014 $6.9 billion was spent on Fairtrade certified products worldwide. The fact that so many people are willing to pay more to ensure that farmers in other countries are paid a fair wage is heartening. But if we're thinking about buying Fairtrade ourselves, we need to ask how much we're actually benefiting people in poor countries by shelling out a few extra dollars for Fairtrade versus regular coffee. The evidence suggests that the answer is 'disappointingly little'. This is for three reasons.

First, when you buy Fairtrade, you usually aren't giving money to the poorest people in the world. Fairtrade standards are difficult to meet, which means that those in the poorest countries typically can't afford to get Fairtrade certification. For example the majority of Fairtrade coffee production comes from comparatively rich countries like Mexico and Costa Rica, which are ten times richer than the very poorest countries like Ethiopia. In Chapter 1 we saw how fast money diminishes in value and how extreme global inequality is. That means that *even if* buying Fairtrade was a good way of paying farmers more, you might make a bigger difference by buying non-Fairtrade goods that are produced in the poorest countries rather than Fairtrade goods that are produced in richer countries. Because Costa Rica is ten times richer than Ethiopia, $1 is worth more to the average Ethiopian than several dollars is to the average Costa Rican.

Second, of the additional money that is spent on Fairtrade, only a very small portion ends up in the hands of the farmers who earn that money. Middlemen take the rest. The Fairtrade Foundation does not provide figures on how much of the additional price reaches coffee produces, but independent researchers have provided some estimates. Dr Peter Griffiths, an economic consultant for the World Bank, worked out that for one British café chain, less than 1% of the additional price of their Fairtrade coffee reached coffee exporters in poor countries. Finnish Professors Joni Valkila, Pertti Haaparanta and Niina Niemi found out that, of Fairtrade coffee sold in Finland, only 11% of the additional price reached the coffee-producing countries. Professor Bernard Kilian and colleagues from INCAE Business School found that, in the US, while Fairtrade coffee would sell for $5 per pound more than conventional coffee, coffee producers would receive only 40¢ per pound, or 8% of that increased price. In contrast, remember that, if you donate $1 to GiveDirectly, 90¢ ultimately reaches the poor.

Finally, even the small fraction that ultimately reaches the producers does not necessarily translate into higher wages. It guarantees a higher price for goods from Fairtrade-certified *organisations*, but that higher price doesn't guarantee a higher price for the farmers who work for those organisations. Professor Christopher Cramer at the London School of Oriental and African Studies led a team of researchers who conducted a four-year study on earnings of Fairtrade workers in Ethiopia and Uganda. They found that those Fairtrade workers had systematically lower wages and worse working conditions than comparable non-Fairtrade workers, and that the poorest often had no access to the 'community projects' that Fairtrade touted as major successes. Professor Cramer later commented:

> The British public has been led to believe that by paying extra for Fairtrade certified coffee, tea and flowers they will 'make a difference' to the lives of poor Africans. Careful fieldwork and analysis in this four-year project leads to the conclusion that in our research sites Fairtrade has not been an effective mechanism for improving the lives of wage workers, the poorest rural people.

Independent reviews of studies have found much the same thing. Though the evidence is limited (which is itself worrying), the consistent finding among the studies that have been performed is that Fairtrade certification does not improve the lives of agricultural workers. Even a review commissioned by the Fairtrade Foundation itself concluded that 'there is limited evidence of the impact on workers of participation in Fairtrade'.

Given this, there is little altruistic reason to buy Fairtrade products. In buying Fairtrade products, you're at best giving very small amounts of money to people in comparatively well-off countries. You'd do considerably more good by buying cheaper goods and donating the money you save to one of the cost-effective charities mentioned in the previous chapter.

Another major area of ethical consumerism is 'green living'. Per person, UK citizens emit nine metric tons of carbon dioxide equivalent every year. (Recall that carbon dioxide equivalent, or 'CO_{2eq}', is a way of measuring your carbon footprint that includes greenhouse gases other than carbon dioxide, like methane and nitrous oxide. For example one metric ton of methane produces as much warming as twenty-one metric tons of carbon dioxide, so one metric ton of methane is twenty-one metric tons of CO_{2eq}.) As we've seen, climate change is a big deal. It's therefore natural to want to do something about it, and the obvious way is to move to a lower-carbon lifestyle.

Sadly, many popular ways of reducing your greenhouse gas emissions are rather ineffective. One common recommendation is to turn off or shut down electronic devices when you're not using them, rather than keeping them on standby. However, this achieves very little compared to other things you could do: one hot bath adds more to your carbon footprint than leaving your phone charger plugged in for a whole year; even leaving on your TV (one of the worst offenders in terms of standby energy use) for a whole year contributes less to your carbon footprint than driving a car for just two hours. Another common recommendation is to turn lights off when you leave a room, but lighting accounts for only 3% of household energy use, so even if you used no lighting at all in your house you would save only a fraction of a metric ton of carbon emissions. Plastic bags have also been a major focus of concern, but even on very generous estimates, if you stopped using plastic bags entirely you'd cut out 100kg CO_{2eq} per year, which is only 0.4% of your total emissions. Similarly, the focus on buying locally produced goods is overhyped: only 10% of the carbon footprint of food comes from transportation whereas 80% comes from production, so what type of food you buy is much more important than whether that food is produced locally or internationally. Cutting out red meat and dairy for one day a week achieves a greater reduction in your carbon footprint than buying entirely locally produced food. In fact, exactly the same food can sometimes have a higher carbon footprint if it's locally grown than if it's imported: one study found that the carbon footprint from locally grown tomatoes in northern Europe was five times as great as the carbon footprint from tomatoes grown in Spain because the emissions generated by heating and lighting greenhouses dwarfed the emissions generated by transportation.

The most effective ways to cut down your emissions are to reduce your intake of meat (especially beef, which can cut out about a metric ton of CO_{2eq} per year), to reduce the amount you travel (driving half as much would cut out two metric tons of CO_{2eq} per year and forgoing a round-trip flight between London and New York would eliminate a metric ton of CO_{2eq}), and to use less electricity and gas in the home (especially by installing loft insulation, which would save a metric ton of CO_{2eq} for a detached house).

However, there is an even more effective way to reduce your emissions. It's called offsetting: rather than reducing your own greenhouse gas emissions, you pay for projects that reduce or avoid greenhouse gas emissions elsewhere.

Environmentalists often criticise carbon offsetting. Here's the British journalist George Monbiot:

> While the carbon we release by flying or driving is certain and verifiable, the carbon absorbed by offset projects is less attestable. Many will succeed, and continue to function over the necessary period. Others will fail, especially the disastrous forays into tree-planting that some companies have made. To claim a carbon saving, you also need to demonstrate that these projects would not have happened without you – that Mexico would not have decided to capture the methane from its pig farms, or that people in India would not have bought new stoves of their own accord. In other words, you must look into a counterfactual future. I have yet to meet someone from a carbon offset company who possesses supernatural powers.

At the offices of Travelcare and the forecourts owned by BP, you can now buy complacency, political apathy and self-satisfaction. But you cannot buy the survival of the planet.

Monbiot makes his point somewhat melodramatically, but his concern is reasonable. You might feel unsure about how effective many of the offsetting programmes on offer really are. For example many airline companies give you the option when you purchase a flight to pay an extra fee to offset your contribution to the greenhouse gases emitted during that flight. If you do this, you have to trust that the airline will successfully offset those emissions. But you might worry that the airline won't do so effectively: perhaps the project they fund was going to happen anyway; or perhaps they overestimate the greenhouse gas reduction from the projects they finance. If so, then the fee you pay to offset all your emissions will offset only some of them.

However, Monbiot's concern doesn't provide a good argument against carbon offsetting *in general*. It just shows we've got to do some research in order to find a way of offsetting that's genuinely effective. That's what we did at my organisation Giving What We Can. We considered more than one hundred organisations that claim to reduce greenhouse gas emissions with donations and tried to figure out which ones most cost-effectively prevent the release of one metric ton of carbon dioxide equivalent. The charity we ultimately decided was best is called Cool Earth.

Cool Earth was founded in 2007 in the United Kingdom by businessman Johan Eliasch and MP Frank Field, who were concerned with protecting the rainforest and the impact that deforestation might have on the environment. The charity aims to fight global warming by preventing deforestation, primarily in the Amazon. It uses donated money to help develop rainforest communities economically to a point where they do better by not selling their land to loggers. Cool Earth does not buy rainforest directly; instead, it provides economic assistance to local communities, helping the people who inhabit the rainforests establish more profitable ventures than selling trees. This involves, among other things, working to secure property rights, improving community infrastructure and connecting the inhabitants of the forests with markets where they can sell their produce at good prices. The work Cool Earth does therefore incidentally improves the lives of those living in the rainforest while working to prevent climate change.

You might doubt that such an apparently indirect route (via something that looks more like development aid) can really be an effective way of protecting forests. But if a community that wants to preserve the forest can't afford not to sell it, helping that community find an alternative strategy seems like a promising way to make a big difference for comparatively low cost. The evidence suggests that Cool Earth's programme has been effective, with far less deforestation in Cool Earth areas than the surroundings. Moreover, those at Cool Earth think strategically about which regions to provide assistance to. By protecting key areas they can create a 'wall' of rainforest that blocks off a much wider landscape from illegal logging.

Cool Earth claims it costs them about $100 to prevent an acre of rainforest from being cut down, and that each acre locks in 260 metric tons of CO_2. This would mean that it costs just about 38¢ to prevent one metric ton of CO_2 from being emitted.

When we assessed Cool Earth, however, we wanted to try to remain conservative, so we created our own estimates rather than relying on their figures. After looking at their track record, we estimated it cost Cool Earth less than $154 to protect one acre of rainforest, which protected a further four acres by walling off other areas of forest. Thirty per cent of similar areas of rainforest that were not protected by Cool Earth had been logged, suggesting that they were protecting an acre of rainforest for $103. However, we realised that, to some extent, it might be that by protecting a given area of rainforest, Cool Earth simply causes loggers to cut down a different area of rainforest. We took this consideration into account using economic data, and estimated that every acre protected by Cool Earth would prevent 0.5 acres from being felled, giving a cost of $206 per acre protected.

The estimate of 260 metric tons of CO_2 per acre is already low, insofar as it doesn't take into account the carbon dioxide stored in the soil, and doesn't take into account greenhouse gas emissions other than CO_2. But there is a risk that the forest will still be logged in the future, and for this reason we scaled down their estimate to 153 metric tons of CO_2 per acre.

Bringing these numbers together ($206 to prevent 153 metric tons of CO_2) gives our best guess estimate at $1.34 per metric ton. Even after trying to be conservative in our calculations, this number may still be too optimistic. So, to play extra safe, we could assume a 300% margin of error, and use a figure of $5 per metric ton of CO_2 emissions prevented.

Using this figure, the average American adult would have to spend $105 per year in order to offset all their carbon emissions. This is significant, but to most people it's considerably less than it would cost to make large changes in lifestyle, such as not flying. This suggests that the easiest and most effective way to cut down your carbon footprint is simply to donate to Cool Earth.

People sometimes make other objections to carbon offsetting, but they're not very compelling. For example in the article I quoted earlier, George Monbiot claimed that carbon offsetting is a way of 'selling indulgences', in reference to the medieval practice in which Christians would pay the Church in exchange for forgiveness for their sins. On a similar theme, a satirical website, CheatNeutral.com, offers the following service: 'When you cheat on your partner you add to the heartbreak, pain and jealousy in the atmosphere. CheatNeutral offsets your cheating by funding someone else to be faithful and NOT cheat. This neutralises the pain and unhappy emotion and leaves you with a clear conscience.'

However, in both cases the analogies are flawed. In buying indulgences, you don't 'undo' the harm you've caused others or the sins you've done. In contrast, through effective carbon offsetting, you're preventing anyone from being harmed by your emissions in the first place: if you emit carbon dioxide throughout your life but effectively offset it at the same time, overall your life contributes nothing to climate change. Similarly, 'offsetting' your adultery (even if you genuinely could) would still affect *who* is harmed, even if it keeps the total number of adulterous acts constant. In contrast, carbon offsetting prevents anyone from ever being harmed by your emissions; it's the 'equivalent' of never committing adultery in the first place.

Another area where people try to change their purchasing habits in order to make a difference is meat-eating and vegetarianism. As I mentioned earlier, cutting out meat (especially beef) is one effective way to reduce your carbon emissions. However, we've also seen that by donating to Cool Earth you can offset one metric ton of carbon emissions for about $5. If you'd rather pay $5 than go vegetarian, then the environmental argument for vegetarianism is rather weak.

The animal welfare argument for vegetarianism is comparatively stronger. The vast majority of farmed animals are raised in factory farms, which often inflict severe and unnecessary suffering on those animals merely for the sake of slightly cheaper produce. The living conditions of factory farm animals have been extensively documented in books, magazines and documentaries, so I will spare you the grim details here. I personally believe it's important to treat animals humanely, and for that reason I've been a vegetarian for many years.

However, the animal welfare argument is much stronger for some animals than for others, because some sorts of animal produce involve a lot more suffering on the part of the animals than others. In fact, eliminating chicken and eggs removes the large majority of animal suffering from your diet. This is because of the conditions those animals are kept in, and the number of animals needed to provide a given number of calories.

Of all the animals raised for food, broiler chickens, layer hens and pigs are kept in the worst conditions by a considerable margin. The only quantitative estimates of farmed animal welfare I've been able to find come from Bailey Norwood, an economist and agricultural expert. He rated the welfare of different animals on a scale of −10 to 10, where negative numbers indicate that it would be better, from the animal's perspective, to be dead rather than alive. He rates beef cattle at 6 and dairy cows at 4. In contrast his average rating for broiler chickens is −1, and for pigs and caged hens is −5. In other words, cows raised for food live better lives than chicken, hens, or pigs, which suffer terribly. (These numbers are for animals raised in the US; animal welfare in the UK and EU, though less well documented, is generally considered to be better across the board than in the US, but it's still true that chickens and pigs suffer much more than cattle.)

The second consideration is the number of animals it takes to make a meal. In a year, the average American will consume the following: 28.5 broiler chickens, 0.8 layer hens, 0.8 turkeys, 0.37 pigs, 0.1 beef cows, and 0.007 dairy cows; in the UK people eat less meat on average but, like Americans, consume far more chickens and hens than cows. These numbers might suggest that cutting out chicken has a far bigger impact than any other dietary change. However, most broiler chickens live for only six weeks, so insofar as we care about how long the animal spends in unpleasant conditions on factory farms, it's more appropriate to think about animal years rather than animal lives. In a year, the number of animal years that go into the average American's diet are as follows: 3.3 from broiler chickens (28.5 chickens consumed, each of which lives six weeks = 3.3 animal years), 1 from layer hens, 0.3 from turkeys, 0.2 from pigs, 0.1 from beef cows, and 0.03 from dairy cows.

Combining these two considerations, we arrive at the conclusion that the most effective way to cut animal suffering out of your diet is to stop eating chicken, then eggs, then pork: by doing so, you're taking out the worst suffering for the most animals for the longest time.

This may have implications for animal welfare advocates, who often tout vegetarianism's environmental benefits (which we've already discussed) and health benefits, pointing to research that those who don't eat meat are at reduced risk of cardiovascular diseases. These advocates often argue for eliminating beef from your diet, since raising cattle produces a lot of CO_{2eq} emissions and red meat is linked to health problems such as heart disease. However, if people hear the environmental or health arguments and then decrease their beef consumption but compensate even a little bit by eating more chicken, those animal welfare advocates may have caused more animal suffering overall.

Earlier I suggested that offsetting might be an easier and more effective way of reducing your carbon footprint than making large lifestyle changes. Could the same argument apply here? Rather than cutting out meat, couldn't people 'offset' their meat consumption by donating to an animal advocacy charity, thereby causing some other person to become vegetarian who wouldn't otherwise have done so? I don't think so. There's a crucial difference between greenhouse gas emissions and meat consumption: if you offset your greenhouse gas emissions, then you prevent anyone from ever being harmed by your emissions. In contrast, if you offset your meat consumption, you change which animals are harmed through factory farming. That makes eating meat and offsetting it less like offsetting greenhouse gas emissions and more like committing adultery and offsetting it, which we all agree it would be immoral to do.

If you care about animal suffering, you should certainly alter your diet, either by cutting out the most harmful products (at least eggs, chicken and pork), or by becoming vegetarian or vegan. However, there's no reason to stop there. In terms of making a difference to the lives of animals, the impact you can have through your donations seems even greater than the impact you can have by changing your own behaviour. According to Animal Charity Evaluators (a research charity I helped to set up), by donating to charities like Mercy for Animals or The Humane League, which distribute leaflets on vegetarianism, it costs about $100 to convince one person to stop eating meat for one year. If you can donate more than that to animal advocacy charities per year, then your decision about how much to donate to animal advocacy is even more important, in terms of impact, than the decision about whether to become vegetarian yourself.

We've seen that, in general, changing consumption habits is not a very effective way to make a difference compared with the alternatives (though we've also seen how the law of expected value demonstrates that it's still a good idea to change your behaviour in certain cases). Whether our concern is the global poor, climate change, or animal welfare, we've seen that the decision about how much and where to donate is much greater, in terms of impact, than the decision about which products to buy.

On reflection, we should expect it to be this way. By donating, you can ensure that your money is spent only on the most effective activities. Given the difference between the best activities and merely very good activities, this is a big deal. In contrast, spending more in order to buy more 'ethical' produce is not a very targeted way of doing good.

Things may even be worse than that, however. There's some reason to believe that the rise in ethical consumerism could even be harmful for the world, on balance. Psychologists have discovered a phenomenon that they call 'moral licensing' that describes how people who perform one good action often compensate by doing fewer good actions in the future.

For example, in a recent experiment participants were told to choose a product from either a selection of mostly 'green' items (like an energy-efficient light bulb) or from a selection of mostly conventional items (like a regular light bulb). They were then told to perform a supposedly unrelated visual perception task: a square box with a diagonal line across it was displayed on a computer screen, and a pattern of twenty dots would flash up on the screen; the subjects had to press a key to indicate whether there were more dots on the left or right side of the line. It was always obvious which was the correct answer, and the experimenters emphasised the importance of being as accurate as possible, telling the subjects that the results of the test would be used in designing future experiments. However, the subjects were told that, whether or not their answers were correct, they'd be paid 0.5¢ every time they indicated there were more dots on the left-hand side of the line, and 5¢ every time they indicated there were more dots on the right-hand side. They therefore had a financial incentive to lie, and they were alone so they knew they wouldn't be caught if they did so. Moreover, they were invited to pay themselves out of an envelope, so they had an opportunity to steal as well.

What happened? People who had previously purchased a 'green' product were significantly more likely to both lie and steal than those who had purchased the conventional product. Their demonstration of ethical behaviour subconsciously gave them licence to act unethically when the chance arose.

Amazingly, even just *saying* you'd do something good can cause the moral licensing effect. In another study, half the participants were asked to imagine helping a foreign student who had asked for assistance in understanding a lecture. They subsequently gave significantly less to charity when given the chance to do so than the other half of the participants, who had not been asked to imagine helping another student.

Moral licensing shows that people are often more concerned about looking good or feeling good rather than actually doing good. If you 'do your bit' by buying an energy-efficient light bulb, your status as a good human being is less likely to be called into question if you subsequently steal a small amount of money.

Often, the moral licensing effect isn't that decision-relevant. If we're encouraging people to engage in effective actions to make the world a better place, it's not that big a deal if that means they compensate, to some extent, by doing less of other altruistic activities. If we encourage people to do a small action, but frame the request as the first step towards a larger commitment, then the moral licensing effect may not occur. Where it becomes crucial, however, is when people are encouraged to do fairly ineffective acts of altruism and, as a result, are less likely to perform effective ones later. If, for example, encouraging someone to buy Fairtrade causes that person to devote less time or money to other, more effective activities, then promoting Fairtrade might on balance be harmful.

In this chapter we've seen that the benefits of ethical consumerism are often small compared to the good that well-targeted donations can do. In the next chapter we'll look at an area where you really can make an astonishing difference: your career.

9

DON'T 'FOLLOW YOUR PASSION'

Which careers make the most difference?

As Peter Hurford entered his final year at Denison University, he needed to figure out what he was going to do with his life. He was twenty-two, majoring in political science and psychology, and he knew he wanted a career that would both be personally satisfying and would make a big difference. Graduate school was the obvious choice for someone with his interests, but he didn't know what his other options were, or how to choose among them.

How should young people like Peter who want to make a difference in their careers go about making their decisions? What if you're later in your career but are considering changing jobs so you can have a bigger impact? In Chapter 5 we saw that earning to give is one powerful way to make a difference, but it's certainly not the only way. There are a dizzying number of career paths, each with their positives and negatives. At the same time, the decision is a high-stakes one. Your choice of career is a choice about how to spend over 80,000 hours over the course of your life, which means it makes sense to invest a considerable amount of time in the decision. If you were to spend just 1% of your working time thinking about how to spend the other 99%, that would mean you'd spend 800 hours, or twenty working weeks, on your career decision. I doubt many people spend this much time thinking about their careers, but it might be worth it.

Over the last few years at 80,000 Hours we've coached hundreds of people like Peter, as well as people later in their careers, most of whom find the following framework useful in deciding what their next career steps should be. There are many considerations relevant to choosing the right career for you, and this framework ensures that you give due weight to what's most important. You should ask yourself:

- *How do I personally fit with this job?* How satisfied will I be in this job? Am I excited by the job? Do I think I could stick with it for a significant period of time? How good am I, or could I become, at this type of work, compared to other people and compared to other careers I might choose?
- *What's my impact while I'm working at this job?* How many resources can I influence, whether that's the labour I provide, the people or budget I manage, the money I earn, or a public platform I have access to? How effective are the causes to which I can direct those resources?
- *How does this job contribute to my impact later on in life?* How well does this job build my skills, connec-

tions, and credentials? How well does this job keep my options open? How much will I learn in the course of this job about what I might want to do next?

Let's discuss each of these three key factors in turn.

How will I personally fit with this job?

Personal fit is about how good you'll be in a particular job. An important part of this is whether you'll be happy doing the work. People often want job satisfaction as an end in itself, but it's also a crucial factor when thinking about impact: if you're not happy at work, you'll be less productive and more likely to burn out, resulting in less impact in the long term. However, we need to be careful when thinking about how to find a job you'll love. There's a lot of feel-good misinformation out there, and the real route to job satisfaction is somewhat counterintuitive.

On 12 June 2005 Steve Jobs stood in front of the graduating class at Stanford and gave them his advice on what they should do with their lives:

You have to trust in something – your gut, destiny, life, karma, whatever – because believing that the dots will connect down the road will give you the confidence to follow your heart, even when it leads you off the well-worn path, and that will make all the difference.

You've got to find what you love, and that is as true for work as it is for your lovers. Your work is going to fill a large part of your life, and the only way to be truly satisfied is to do what you believe is great work, and the only way to do great work is to love what you do. If you haven't found it yet, keep looking, and don't settle. As with all matters of the heart, you'll know when you find it, and like any great relationship it just gets better and better as the years roll on. So keep looking. Don't settle.

Jobs's message is emotionally resonant and appealing, and career advice is commonly built around slogans like 'follow your heart' or 'follow your passion'. The first paragraph of the advice book *Career Ahead* ends 'You owe it to yourself to do work that you love. This book will show you how.' A popular YouTube video, 'What if money was no object?' narrated by British writer Alan Watts advises similarly. It suggests that, unless you ask yourself 'What makes you itch?' and pursue the answer, you will, 'Spend your life completely wasting your time. You'll be doing things you don't like doing in order to go on living, that is to go on doing things you don't like doing, which is stupid.' At its most extreme, the talk around career choice sounds similar to the talk around romance: when you find your perfect fit, you'll just know.

Taken literally, however, the idea of following your passion is *terrible* advice. Finding a career that's the right 'fit' for you is crucial to finding a career, but believing you must find some preordained 'passion' and then pursue jobs that match it is all wrong. Ask yourself, is following your passion a good way to achieve personal satisfaction in the job you love? Should you pick a career by identifying your greatest interest, finding jobs that 'match' that interest and pursuing them no matter what? On the basis of the evidence, the answer seems to be 'no'.

First, and most simply, most people don't have passions that fit the world of work. In one study of Canadian college students, it was found that 84% of students had passions, and 90% of these involved sport, music and art. But by looking at census data, we can see that only 3% of jobs are in the sport, music and art industries. Even if only half the students followed their passion, the majority would fail to secure a job. In these cases, 'doing what you're passionate about' can be actively harmful.

Indeed, often the fact that you're passionate about something is a good reason why it will be difficult to find a job in that area since you have to compete with all the other people who are passionate about the same thing. This is the situation in sport and music, where only extremely talented (or lucky) people can make a steady living. In the US, fewer than 1 in 1,000 high school athletes will make it into professional sports. For the large majority of people who don't have work-related passions, the advice to 'follow your passion' might merely prompt anxious soul-searching and send them into the wrong careers.

Second, your interests change. Psychologists Jordi Quoidbach, Daniel T. Gilbert and Timothy Wilson have shown that they change much more than we anticipate, so we overrate their importance. Just think about what you were most interested in ten years ago. Chances are, it's completely different from what you're interested in today. If you focus only on what you're currently passionate about, then you risk committing to projects that you soon find you're no longer interested in.

This takes us to our third point against passion, which is that the best predictors of job satisfaction are features of the job itself, rather than facts about personal passion. Instead of trying to figure out which career to pursue based on whatever you happen to be most interested in today, you should start by looking for work with certain important features. If you find that, passion will follow.

Research shows that the most consistent predictor of job satisfaction is engaging work, which can be broken down into five factors (this is known in psychology as the 'job characteristics theory'):

1. **Independence** – To what extent do you have control over how you go about your work?
2. **Sense of Completion** – To what extent does the job involve completing a whole piece of work, so that your contribution to the end product is easily visible, rather than being merely a small part of a much larger product?
3. **Variety** – To what extent does the job require you to perform a range of different activities, using different skills and talents?
4. **Feedback from the job** – How easy is it to know whether you're performing well or badly?

5. **Contribution** – To what extent does your work 'make a difference', as defined by positive contributions to the wellbeing of other people?

As well as job satisfaction, each of these factors also correlates with motivation, productivity and commitment to your employer. Moreover, these factors are similar to those required to develop flow, the pleasurable state of being so immersed in an activity that you're completely free of distractions and lose track of time, which some psychologists have argued is the key to having genuinely satisfying experiences.

There are other factors that also matter to your job satisfaction, such as whether you get a sense of achievement from the work, how much support you get from your colleagues, and 'hygiene' factors, such as not having unfair pay or a very long commute. But again, these factors have little to do with whether the work involves one of your 'passions' – you find them in many different jobs.

The evidence therefore suggests that following your passion is a poor way to determine whether a given career path will make you happy. Rather, passion grows out of work that has the right features. This was true even of Steve Jobs. When he was young, he was passionate about Zen Buddhism. He travelled in India, took plenty of LSD, shaved his head, wore robes and seriously considered moving to Japan to become a monk. He first got into electronics only reluctantly, as a way to earn cash on the side, helping his tech-savvy friend Steve Wozniak handle business deals while also spending time at the All-One commune. Even Apple Computers' very existence was fortuitous: while Jobs and Wozniak were trying to sell circuit boards to hobbyists, the owner of one local computer store said he would only buy fully assembled computers, and they jumped at the chance to make more money. It was only once they started to gain traction and success that Jobs's passion for Apple and computing really bloomed.

What about following your 'heart', your 'gut', or your 'itch' to find work you love? The evidence suggests that won't work either, since we're bad at predicting what will make us happy.

The way we predict how some event will affect us emotionally is by running a simulation in our heads: when I imagine feeling anxious while taking an exam, I'm imagining taking an exam, which makes me feel anxious. This anxiety is an indicator of the feeling I expect to have when I actually take the exam. From a psychological perspective, this ability to simulate the effects of an as-yet unexperienced event is a remarkably powerful skill, one which humans possess to a degree far beyond other animals. But the simulations we run bias us in a number of predictable ways. For example our tastes and preferences change considerably over time, in ways we don't accurately predict. You might plan your life believing you'll never want to have kids, but then find when you're thirty that your preferences change dramatically.

Our simulation-based predictions of the future are also often incomplete. Simulating future events is hard to do, and we can't possibly focus on every minute aspect of the event, so our brain just includes the most important details. However, this means we may miss out on some non-essential features that would make a big difference to our emotional responses. For example it's been found that professors on average end up much less happy after getting tenure than they predicted they would be prior to getting tenure. One possible explanation for this is that they focused too much on the positive features of getting tenure – the sense of achievement and recognition – to the neglect of others, such as an increased number of dull departmental meetings. When deciding which career to pursue, therefore, we are likely to focus our attention on factors that come to mind easily such as salary and working hours. This might lead us to ignore other factors that are actually crucial to predicting happiness. Simply 'following your heart' without paying attention to what really predicts job satisfaction can easily lead you astray.

For all these reasons, 80,000 Hours prefers to talk about 'personal fit' rather than 'following your heart' or 'following your passion'. How can you work out where you have the best personal fit? As we've just seen, it's difficult to predict where you'll be most satisfied and where you'll perform the best just by thinking about it. Indeed, it's hard for anyone to know which job you'll be best at. Even corporate recruiters regularly make mistakes, and they have huge amounts of resources at their disposal to find the people who fit best.

This means it's best to take an empirical approach, trying out different types of work, and using your track record to predict how well you'll perform in the future. At the start of your career, be open minded about where you'll eventually be able to perform best.

Beyond track record, if you want to predict how well you'll perform, the first step is to learn as much about the work as you can. Go and speak to people in the job. Ask what traits they think are most important to success and see how you measure up. Ask about the main reasons people end up leaving the job. Find out how people who are similar to you have performed in the past. Look at whether you think you'd find the work satisfying based on the factors mentioned earlier. The 'follow your passion' slogan assumes it's as easy as looking inward to figure out what you ought to be doing. In contrast, identifying a job with what we call good 'personal fit' involves finding out as much about a job as you can, because it's features of the job itself that are much more important in determining how well you succeed and enjoy your work than whether that job corresponds with your pre-existing passions.

These considerations affected Peter Hurford's decision. While at university, he was most interested in political science and had enjoyed completing several research projects with a professor there. He had always presumed he'd go to grad school to study political science. However, after reading our research on personal fit, he widened his search considerably. Instead of trying to figure out what career path fitted his current passions best, he drew up a list of fifteen possible options across a range of areas, and thought about each of them in turn, spoke to people who knew about them and thought about which he might perform best in based on his skills and experience to date. He was able to rule out some of his options after just a little investigation: consulting would involve a lot of travel, which he'd hate; medicine would require a lot of retraining, which didn't seem worth it. In the end, he was able to narrow his options down to five plausible candidates. Graduate school stayed on the list, but was joined by options he hadn't thought as much about previously: law school, non-profit work, computer programming and market research.

He thought he would fit well within any of these five categories, so he tried to decide between these primarily on the basis of his long-run potential for impact. This takes us to the next two aspects of the career effectiveness framework.

What will be my impact while I'm working at this job?

The second issue in our framework is how much impact you'll have within the job. Typical advice on making a difference through your career emphasises this factor heavily. The most obvious way to do this is to work in the social sector: social-impact-focused careers websites list job opportunities at charities or in corporate social responsibility. However, like 'following your passion', this advice can be misleading.

First, to make a difference in the social sector, the organisation you work for must be effective. If your charity job had been at PlayPumps International, then, no matter how enthusiastically or efficiently you worked, you'd have made very little positive impact. It's difficult to assess how effective an organisation is, but the frameworks given in the chapters on effective charities and effective causes can help you, as can the key questions described in the first part of this book.

Second, you need to provide substantial value over the person the charity would have hired instead. If you offer unusual skills or are particularly good at that job compared to others who could have worked there, then you can offer significant additional value. If these conditions don't hold and you don't add more value than whomever would have been in your place, your impact might be small. In the most extreme case, if you are simply very good at interviewing and not that great an employee, you could even cause harm by displacing someone better who would have been in your shoes.

Third, there are many other ways of making a difference. Earlier, we saw the arguments in favour of earning to give, and helping others through your donations rather than through your direct labour. As we'll discuss later in this chapter, there are also very compelling ways of making a difference that aren't in the social sector, such as entrepreneurship, research, journalism, or politics.

In general, we recommend people think of three primary routes by which they can have impact on the job. The first is through the labour you provide. This can be the work you do if you are employed by an effective organisation, or the research you do if you are a researcher. The second is the money you can give. The third is the influence you can have on other people. In order to work out the total impact you can have, you should look at all three of these; whereas advice that is focused solely on the charity sector looks only at the first.

Next, you need to assess how effective are the causes or organisations to which you can direct these resources. The more effective the cause or organisation, the more good those resources will do. For your labour, that's the effectiveness of the organisation you work for. For your donations, that's the effectiveness of the organisation you donate to. What you're able to influence depends heavily on your situation: you might be able to influence the expenditure of the charity you work for; you might be able to influence the donations of your co-workers; or you might be able to influence the general public through a public platform. In each case, the more effective the causes you're able to support, the more impact you'll have.

The fourth and most important reason why 'work in the social sector' might be bad advice is that if you're just starting out, it's much more important to build skills and credentials than it is to have an impact on the job. There are a few reasons for this. First, there are many ways of boosting your potential for influence later that have high return on investment, such as getting an advanced degree or an MBA, learning to programme, or building your network. Whereas your first position might last a few years, your subsequent career will last decades. Spending a few years building your abilities now, therefore, can pay off with increased impact over a much longer period. In addition, the most senior people within a field generally have a disproportionate amount of influence and impact within that field. Maximising your chances of getting into more senior and influential positions is therefore a key part of maximising your impact.

For these reasons, especially when starting out, you should focus on building your skills, network and credentials, rather than trying to make an impact right away. This is how many of the most effective charities we've discussed have been founded. GiveDirectly, Schistosomiasis Control Initiative, Deworm the World Initiative and Development Media International were all founded by academics who discovered innovative ways to help the poor. Rob Mather, who founded Against Malaria Foundation, had spent many years building skills in strategy consulting before moving into the charity sector. This meant he had a good grasp of how to run an organisation well, and that, once he came to set up AMF, he didn't need to take a salary.

Building career capital can be important later in your career as well if you're not sure which causes to support. Instead of trying to make an immediate impact, you can instead invest in yourself while continuing to learn about which causes are most important, preparing yourself to make a bigger difference in the future.

With these considerations in mind Peter Hurford didn't place too much weight on the immediate impact he could have in the job he did. If he looked at immediate impact only, earning to give and non-profit work were his best options, with graduate school and law school following. However, these options differed significantly in terms of the impact they'd enable him to have later on in his life, and that was more important to him. This takes us to the final section of the framework.

How would this job contribute to my impact later on in life?

There are a number of ways in which a given job can help you have a larger impact later on in life. Through your initial work, you develop 'career capital' – skills, a network, and credentials – which will help you take a higher-impact job later on. If you develop organisational skills then, all other things being equal, you will be more effective in your next job. If you get to know a large number of people through your work, you are more likely to be connected with job opportunities. If you work at a high-prestige firm like Google or McKinsey, that line on your CV will make you more attractive to future potential employers.

In addition to career capital, there are two other ways in which your initial job will affect the impact you have later on in your career. First is how well it keeps your options open. It's easier, for example, to move from the for-profit sector to the non-profit sector than vice versa. Similarly, it's easier to move from academia into industry than it is the other way around; for people who are highly uncertain about whether they want to leave academia after their PhD, this asymmetry provides a reason for staying in academia until they have better information. Keeping your options open also provides a reason for building transferable skills – such as sales and marketing, leadership, project management, business knowledge, social skills, personal initiative and work ethic – rather than highly specific skills such as piano tuning or maritime law.

Second, there is 'exploration value': how much do you learn about what careers you might choose in the future in the course of doing the job? Especially when you're just starting out, you won't know much about what opportunities are out there and which will fit you best. Your first few jobs will give you valuable information that will inform your later decisions. This can provide a reason in favour of trying things that are less well known to you at first. Perhaps, after university, you have a good understanding of what pursuing a Master's and a PhD would involve, but you have very little understanding of the for-profit world, in terms of either how much you'd enjoy it or how well you'd fit there. Exploration value provides a reason in favour of working in the for-profit sector for a year or two: you might discover that the opportunities there suit you well.

People embarking on their careers often neglect these considerations, tending to think of choosing a career as an all-or-nothing proposition: a one-off life decision that you make aged twenty-one that you can't change later. A way to combat this mistake is to think of career decisions like an entrepreneur would think about starting a company. In both career choice and entrepreneurship, you start out with a tiny amount of relevant information, but you have to use that information to cope with a huge number of variables. Moreover, as things progress, these variables shift: you're constantly gaining new information and new, often entirely unexpected, opportunities and problems arise. For these reasons, armchair speculation about what will and won't happen isn't very useful.

In the case of entrepreneurship, Eric Ries has argued forcefully for this idea and created the popular Lean Startup movement. The idea behind the Lean Startup is that many entrepreneurs make the mistake of getting excited about some product or idea and then doing everything they can to push it onto the world even before they've tested it to see if there's a market for it. When companies do this, products often fail because they were reasoning from the armchair when they should have been experimenting. Ries argues that entrepreneurs should think of their ideas or products as hypotheses, and continually test, ultimately letting the potential customers determine what the product should be.

In the case of career choice, many people make an analogous mistake. They try to decide, early on, what their career should be and then they doggedly try to pursue that career, ignoring other possibilities that might arise and failing to consider that the job might not be right for them. (Sometimes this is caused by the idea of having a 'calling' that you try to force onto the world, without testing to find out if it's something that the world actually needs.) Instead of trying to work out what your calling is and then forming a rigid plan on the basis of that calling, you should think like a scientist, testing hypotheses. This has three implications.

First, it means you should think of your career as a work in progress. Rather than having a fixed career plan, try to have a career 'model' – a set of provisional goals and hypotheses that you're constantly revising as you acquire new evidence or opportunities. It's better to have a bad plan than no plan, but only if you're open to changing it.

Second, find out where you're uncertain, then reduce that uncertainty. Before making a decision, don't merely try to weigh up all the pros and cons as you currently see them (though that is a good thing to do). Ask yourself: 'What is the single most important piece of information that would be most useful for my career decision? Now, what can I do in order to gain that information?'

Third, test yourself in different paths. In science you try to test hypotheses. Similarly, if you can, you should try to run 'tests' of different career plans; this is important because it's often very difficult to predict which careers will work out and which won't. For example one person we coached started an internship at an asset-management firm. Having no experience in the field, she didn't know whether she'd like it, but she guessed she wouldn't. It turned out she hated the job. In a sense, she 'failed'. But that failure meant she could be much more confident in pursuing a different (academic) path, instead. Her bad experience was very valuable.

Peter's decision

For all these reasons, Peter regarded his potential impact later in life as the most important factor to consider when deciding which career to pursue. This made law school look considerably worse than he had previously thought: he'd be committed to one path, learning a very specific set of skills, ending up after three years with considerable debt.

Similar reasoning made software engineering or market research look more promising than non-profit work. Both options would allow him to have a big immediate impact (via his donations if he was working as a software engineering or market researcher; via his labour if he was working at a non-profit), and he also felt he would gain better long-term skills, and learn more, if he pursued options in software engineering or market research than he would if he worked for non-profits straight out of university.

As a result, in his final year at university he invested heavily in developing his computer programming skills, which enabled him to get a job as a software engineer at a start-up in Chicago that offers online loans to people with near-prime credit ratings. The organisation he's working for is certainly improving the world, but it isn't the most effective organisation he could work for. However, it is allowing him to build his skills in programming and statistics, and will also allow him to gain business and financial experience, which will potentially open doors later on. Finally, the job gives him enough free time to focus on his non-profit projects, which will further allow him to work out whether he should ultimately transition into full-time non-profit work, or whether he should stick to his current path and focus on earning to give.

By using this framework, you can assess the different career options available to you, but what are some of the best options? There are a huge number of possible paths, so I've used this framework to carve out some 'career strategies' that I and the others at 80,000 Hours think are particularly promising. (As our research progresses, these are likely to change somewhat, so it's worth also monitoring the 80,000 Hours website for updated information.) I'll divide top career options into 'solid bets', where one is very likely to make a positive impact, and 'high-potential long shots' where one has a smaller chance of making a very large impact.

Solid bets

Direct work for a highly effective organisation

We don't often recommend that people go into non-profit work straight out of university, because you will typically build fewer skills and credentials than you would in for-profit companies, which typically have greater resources to invest in training. However, there are still many situations where starting off working in a non-profit can be a good bet. If you're considering working for a non-profit, ask yourself the following questions:

- Is the organisation particularly effective?
- Will I learn a lot working here?
- Is the organisation money-rich but talent-poor?
- Am I sure I want to work within non-profits long-term?

Given these conditions, GiveWell is an example of a non-profit that could represent an excellent place to work. It's highly effective, it's very well-run and gives excellent training to those who work there. It also needs talent much more than it needs money. One way in which you can assess whether an organisation is money-constrained or talent-constrained is simply to ask the organisation if it would prefer you donate to it or work for it. For example in 2011 Alexander Berger had just graduated from Stanford with an MA in policy, organisation, and leadership studies. He was unsure whether to earn to give or to take up a position at GiveWell. When he asked how much GiveWell would be willing to pay to have him as an employee, he found it was considerably beyond the amount he could donate if he earned to give.

There are also personal reasons why working for non-profits might be a good option. For example if you are fired up by a specific cause, it might feel important to you to be in the midst of the action. Alternatively, you might worry that your values will wane if you were to pursue something with either indirect benefits, like earning to give, or later benefits, like building skills. Perhaps you find it helpful and inspiring to surround yourself with like-minded people, and working for a place that shares these values will keep you committed to your ultimate goals. Personal considerations like these should be taken very seriously.

Finally, it's worth bearing in mind that non-profits are not the only effective organisations you can work for. Most of the incredible progress that humanity has made over the last few hundred years has been due not to the activities of non-profits but to technology and innovation generally spurred by for-profit companies and governments. If you can find a company that is benefiting many people, or is correcting market failure in some way (such as by developing renewable alternatives to fossil fuels), this might be an effective means to have an impact. I'll discuss the potential of for-profits more under the 'entrepreneurship' section later in this chapter.

Earning to give

Earning to give enables you to start having a significant positive impact via the most cost-effective organisations right from the beginning of your career. Often, it also allows you to build valuable skills and a network that will prove very useful later on in life.

If you're aiming to pursue earning to give over the long term, it's important to work out the long-run earning potential of different careers. On the internet, you can often find the pay at a given level of experience within a field, but it's harder to find out how difficult it is to get to that level of experience, and how high paying the alternatives are for those who move out of that career type. Moreover, within a given career path the earnings within specific sub-fields and from company to company can also vary dramatically.

We've researched this to help make the decision easier. Unsurprisingly, the very highest paying careers are extremely competitive, such as finance in 'front-office' positions, followed by consulting with somewhat lower earnings. Both of these careers also come with a high chance of dropping out, since at each stage, if you fail to be promoted, you'll probably have to switch into a different job with lower pay. Even taking this into account, however, they're still among the career paths with the highest expected earnings. Tech entrepreneurship and quantitative trading in hedge funds offer even higher expected earnings, though tech entrepreneurship comes with even higher risks (entrepreneurs have less than a 10% chance of ever selling their shares in the company at profit) and quantitative trading requires exceptionally strong mathematical skills.

Among less risky careers, medicine is probably the highest-earning option, especially in the US, though earnings are probably less than in finance. Law is less appealing than one might think because you probably won't earn as much as you would in consulting or finance.

Outside the hyper-competitive fields mentioned, there are still some very good options. Software engineering is a lucrative career with an unusually low barrier for entry, and many of the people we've coached chose to pursue that career. Chris Hallquist, for example, completed a philosophy degree at the University of Wisconsin, Madison. His degree didn't naturally lead to other career paths, so he looked at a wide range of options. He considered law, but decided that the market for lawyers was too poor. Programming, in contrast, was highly promising. He was able to apply to App Academy, a three-month intensive programming school, and from there he got a job at a start-up in San Francisco with a six-figure salary.

Sales and marketing can also be good options. As well as being fairly high paying for a given level of competitiveness, they provide particularly useful skills if you want to move into the social sector later in your career. Accountancy and actuarial work are also high paying for their level of competitiveness.

For those without a university degree, the highest-paying careers are usually in skilled trades or in public services such as the police force. Other options are aviation and the energy sector. For those with an associate degree, the highest-paying careers are air traffic control, or within the medical profession: radiation therapists, nuclear medicine technologists or dental hygienists, for example.

One important issue to consider for all careers, but especially when earning to give through trade professions, is whether a job will be around in the future. A job might be outsourced (as IT support has been to some extent), or automated as a result of new technology. For example before the advent of alarm clocks, people called 'knocker uppers' were employed to knock on the windows of sleeping people in the morning, so that they could get to work on time. Similarly, computers have decreased the need for jobs that involve basic number-crunching, refrigerators have decreased the need for milkmen, robotic assemblers have decreased the need for assembly line workers. The technology for self-driving cars is already here, so it may be unwise to become a taxi or truck driver because there is a good chance that this industry will become automated over the next couple of decades. Improvements in technology are reducing demand for clerks and secretaries. In general, jobs that require social skills (like public relations), creativity (like fashion design), or precise perception and manipulation (like boiler making) are the least likely to become automated. Jobs that require physical proximity or high levels of training are also unlikely to be outsourced.

Another important consideration regarding earning to give is the risk of losing your values by working in an environment with people who aren't as altruistically inclined as you are. For example David Brooks, writing in the *New York Times*, makes this objection in response to a story of Jason Trigg, who is earning to give by working in finance:

> You might start down this course seeing finance as a convenient means to realize your deepest commitment: fighting malaria. But the brain is a malleable organ. Every time you do an activity, or have a thought, you are changing a piece of yourself into something slightly different than it was before. Every hour you spend with others, you become more like the people around you.
>
> Gradually, you become a different person. If there is a large gap between your daily conduct and your core commitment, you will become more like your daily activities and less attached to your original commitment.

This is an important concern, and if you think that a particular career will destroy your altruistic motivation, then you certainly shouldn't pursue it. But there are reasons for thinking that this often isn't too great a problem. First, if you pursue earning to give, but find your altruistic motivation is waning, you always have the option of leaving and working for an organisation that does good directly. At worst, you've built up good work experience. Second, if you involve yourself in the effective altruism community, then you can mitigate this concern: if you have many friends who are pursuing a similar path to you, and you've publicly stated your intentions to donate, then you'll have strong support to ensure that you live up to your aims. Finally, there are many examples of people who have successfully pursued earning to give without losing their values. Bill Gates and the other members of the Giving Pledge (a group of billionaires who have pledged at least 50% of their earnings to charity) are the most obvious examples, but there are many more. When Jim Greenbaum graduated from the University of Virginia in the early 1980s, his primary aim was to make as much money as he could in order to use that money to make the world a better place. He founded a telecommunications company, Access Long Distance, in 1985, selling it fourteen years later. Now aged fifty-six, he's as committed to philanthropy as he ever was, donating over 50% of his assets. There is certainly a risk of losing one's values by earning to give, which you should bear in mind when you're thinking about your career options; but there are risks of becoming disillusioned whatever you choose to do, and the experience of seeing what effective donations can achieve can be immensely rewarding.

Skill-building

'Skill-building' is a short-term strategy, which can be a very good option if you aren't sure about what you ultimately want to do. The idea behind this path is that you build up general-purpose career capital in order to keep your options open as much as possible, giving you time to figure out your long-run plans for having an impact and giving you skills that will be useful in what you choose to do.

Given this strategy, consultancy is a great first step. For example Habiba Islam graduated from Oxford University in PPE in 2011. She considered going into politics, and still thinks of that as a potential long-term aim, but she decided to work in consulting first. This makes sense: by working in consulting for a few years, you get a good all-round business education, you get to meet a wide variety of people, and you get clear evidence on your CV that you're capable of working hard and meeting deadlines. You're also able to earn to give, having an impact through your donations, in the meantime.

Other areas that are good for skill-building are sales and marketing, because this training seems useful if you want to move into the social sector, where the ability to advertise particular messages persuasively is important. Another alternative is to get a PhD in a useful area. This is what Jess Whittlestone did: having studied maths and philosophy previously, she pursued a PhD in the behavioural sciences at Warwick Business School. This gives her the option of going into research, but if not she has still gained an important credential as well as knowledge of statistics and organisational decision-making that will become useful later on. In addition, during a PhD your time is often more flexible than when employed full-time, which means you have more opportunity to start or pursue other projects on the side. Jess, for example, has used the opportunity to write popular science articles in her spare time, giving her the option to become a full-time writer after her PhD if she chooses.

High-potential long-shots

Working for an effective organisation, earning to give and skill-building are all safe bets because if you pursue them, you can be confident that you will either have an impact immediately or that you're putting yourself in a good position to have an impact later on. However, as we saw in the chapter on expected value, we should also be interested in lower-probability higher-payoff activities, and there are some promising careers where your impact takes this form. Let's look at them.

Entrepreneurship

Entrepreneurship is an extremely promising option, giving you both the potential to effect massive change, build valuable career capital, and, if pursuing for-profit entrepreneurship, make large profits that can be donated to effective causes. Entrepreneurship is also an area with lower barriers to entry than other careers, and many people without university degrees have become successful entrepreneurs. However, most start-up enterprises fail, and one has to be prepared to accept that fact. In addition, entrepreneurship usually comes with very long working hours and high levels of stress. Not everyone is cut out to start their own business.

To illustrate how valuable non-profit entrepreneurship can be, consider GiveDirectly, which we discussed in the chapter on effective charities. With an economics PhD from Harvard, the founder, Paul Niehaus, had very good earning-to-give options. However, he clearly made the right choice to set up GiveDirectly. Since its official launch in 2011, GiveDirectly has raised more than $20 million in donations – an amount that is currently growing rapidly. Even after taking into account the fact that most of those donations would have been donated anyway (albeit probably to less effective charities), Niehaus has done far more good by founding GiveDirectly than he would have if he'd earned to give.

If you're starting a non-profit, one good strategy is to focus on a particularly important cause (which we'll discuss in the next chapter). Another important question is to ask why the problem your new organisation is addressing has not been solved already, or won't be solved in the future. Ask yourself:

- Why hasn't this problem been solved by markets?
- Why hasn't this problem been solved by the state?
- Why hasn't this problem already been solved by philanthropy?

In many cases, the answers to these questions will suggest that the problem is very difficult to solve, in which case it may not be the most effective problem to focus on. In other cases, the answers might suggest that you really can make good progress on the problem. If the beneficiaries of your action don't participate fully in markets and aren't governed by a well-functioning state, then there is a clear need for philanthropy. For example we should expect the interests of future people to be systematically underrepresented because they don't participate in present-day markets or elections.

For-profit entrepreneurship can be even more compelling as an option than non-profit entrepreneurship. Though it generally will be more difficult to focus your activities on the most important social problem within for-profit entrepreneurship, there is a much greater potential to grow quickly, and there is the additional benefit of larger earnings that can be used for good purposes later on in life. Economists also suggest that innovative entrepreneurship is undersupplied by the market. Professor William Nordhaus at Yale University has estimated that innovators only collect 2% of the value they generate; that is, for every $1 an innovative company makes in profit, society has benefited by $50. By becoming an innovative entrepreneur, you are on average producing benefits to society that far exceed your paycheck.

The delightfully named Lincoln Quirk pursued this option, quitting graduate school in order to found a company called Wave, which makes it easier and cheaper for immigrants in the US to send remittances to their home country. Currently, if immigrants wish to send remittances, they have to use Western Union or MoneyGram. They have to go to a physical outlet to make the transfer, and pay 10% in transfer costs. Lincoln Quirk and his co-founder Drew Durbin have built software that allows transfers from a mobile phone in the US to a mobile phone in Kenya, and they only take 3% of the transfer costs. For now, they are just focused on Kenya, because that has particularly good infrastructure for this project, but they plan to expand significantly.

The potential positive impact of this idea is huge. Annual global remittances are over $400 billion, several times the total global foreign aid budget. The potential impact Lincoln's start-up could have, by making the costs of remittances a few per cent cheaper, therefore amounts to tens of billions of dollars in increased financial flow from rich countries to poorer countries every year. Even just from Maryland to Kenya, annual remittances are over $350 million; within one state Wave could therefore increase the amount going to Kenya every year by $24 million. After only a few months of operation, they already have thousands of users who have collectively transferred millions of dollars to Kenya.

Research

When Norman Borlaug was awarded the Nobel Peace Prize in 1970, the committee suggested that he'd saved one *billion* lives. Was he a politician? Or a military leader? Or a superhero? No, he was a fairly regular guy from Iowa who worked in agricultural research. He wasn't a typical academic: his credentials were limited and he used techniques that had been available to the Victorians. Moreover, the innovation that made his name was rather boring – a new type of short-stem disease-resistant wheat. That wheat, however, was able to radically increase crop yield across poor countries. It helped to cause the 'green revolution'. Even after taking into account the fact that similar innovations may have happened even if he hadn't done his research, Borlaug's impact should be measured in the prevention of tens of millions of deaths.

In terms of researchers with impact, Borlaug isn't a lone example: in any list of the most influential people of all time, scientists and researchers make up a large percentage. Scientists who have clearly had a huge positive effect on the world include Fritz Haber and Carl Bosch, who invented synthetic fertiliser; Karl Landsteiner, who discovered blood groups, thus allowing blood transfusions to be possible; Grace Eldering and Pearl Kendrick, who developed the first whooping cough vaccine; and Françoise Barré-Sinoussi and Luc Montagnier, who discovered HIV.

In each of these cases, even after taking into account that these developments would have eventually happened anyway, the good each of these researchers did should be measured in the millions of lives saved. And clearly many other researchers, from Isaac Newton to Daniel Kahneman, have made a huge contribution to human progress even if it's not easy to quantify their impact in terms of lives saved.

Like innovative entrepreneurship, research is an area that is drastically undersupplied by the market because the benefits are open to everyone, and because much of the benefit of research occurs decades into the future. Governments try to fix this problem to some extent through state-funded research, but academic research is very often not as high-impact as it could be – the incentive facing many academics is work on the most theoretically interesting questions rather than the most socially important questions. This means that, by deliberately pursuing research that has a large impact, one could make a significant difference that wouldn't have happened otherwise.

However, the distribution of achievements in research (as suggested by number of publications, awards and citations) is heavily fat-tailed: a large proportion of scientific achievement comes from a very small number of scientists. This suggests that research might only be the best option if it's an area you really excel in. But if you might be able to become such a person, it's an option you should take seriously.

If you're thinking about going into research, it's important to bear in mind the job prospects: fields vary dramatically in both the difficulty of getting an academic job post-PhD, and in the difficulty of finding jobs outside of academia. Within philosophy, for example, there are about four times as many doctoral candidates as there are tenure-track positions; as a result, many aspiring academic philosophers end up unable to find a job in academia. In contrast, within economics the number of people who seek academic employment more closely matches the number of academic jobs. Another important consideration is the extent to which one can have an impact outside of academia. Again, an economics PhD is a good bet, being generally well respected in policy and business.

With these considerations in mind, 80,000 Hours currently suggests that the areas with the greatest potential to do high-impact research while simultaneously gaining career capital that keeps your options open are economics, statistics, computer science and some areas of psychology. This, however, shouldn't deter you if you have some particular interest or expertise within an area of research that is relevant to a particularly high-priority cause-area.

One good way to have impact within research is to combine fields. There are far more combinations of fields than there are individual fields and research tends to be influenced by traditional disciplinary distinctions, so research at the intersection of two disciplines is often particularly neglected and can for that reason be very high-impact. For example Daniel Kahneman and Amos Tversky were psychologists who caused a revolution within economics: they applied methods developed in psychology to test assumptions about rational choice that were prevalent within economics, thereby leading to the new field of 'behavioural economics'. By giving us a better understanding of human behaviour, this field has improved our ability to cause desirable behaviour change, including in development. Similarly, effective altruism has made the progress it has by combining concepts from moral philosophy and economics.

Combining fields can be especially useful when one moves from a more theoretical area to an area with real-world applications. Within academia, the most prestigious research fields – which often therefore attract the best researchers – are often those that have the fewest practical applications. (A friend of mine has jokingly commented that a Fields Medal – the equivalent of a Nobel Prize in mathematics – indicates two things about the recipient: that they were capable of accomplishing something truly important, and that they didn't.) If you are a top researcher and are willing to sacrifice some amount of status within academia, you can have considerable impact by moving into more applied areas of research.

Politics and advocacy

Politics is another area where one has a small chance of extremely large influence. For someone entering party politics in the UK, most of their expected impact comes from the chance of ending up in the Cabinet or as prime minister. Even though the chances of being that successful are small, your potential influence, if you do succeed, is very great indeed. As discussed in Chapter 6, this was the reason Laura Brown pursued a career in party politics.

Though we only discussed British politics in that chapter, similar considerations apply everywhere.

Advocacy also has potentially high payoffs, as one could influence the behaviour of many thousands of people and help to influence debates around particular policies, though this is particularly difficult to quantify. One could become an effective advocate through journalism, or by pursuing an early career in academia and then moving to become a 'public intellectual'. Someone from the effective altruism community who's pursued this path is Dylan Matthews. He studied moral and political philosophy at Harvard. He considered continuing his studies at graduate school, but instead pursued journalism, in part because doing so gave him a platform from which to champion particularly important causes. He worked for the *Washington Post* and now works for Vox.com. In this position, he's been able to promote and discuss ideas he thinks are important, such as more liberal immigration policies, a universal basic income, and the idea of earning to give.

In advocacy, we would expect the distribution of impact to be highly fat-tailed: it's a 'winner takes all' environment, where a small number of thought leaders command most of the attention. We don't have data on impact through advocacy in general, though the distribution of book sales, which one could use as a proxy, is highly fat-tailed, as is the distribution of Twitter follower counts. Again, therefore, this is an area you might only want to go into if you think you have an unusually good chance of being successful.

Volunteering

So far I've discussed how you can choose a career in order to make a difference. Similar considerations apply to volunteering, though there's an additional challenge. As a volunteer, you're often not trained in the area in which you're helping, which means the benefit you provide might be limited. At the same time you're often using up valuable management capacity. For that reason, volunteering can in fact be harmful to the charity you're volunteering for. Anecdotally, we have heard from some non-profits that the main reason they use volunteers is because those volunteers subsequently donate back to the charity.

This means you should try to volunteer only in ways that cost an organisation relatively little. For example by contributing high-quality work to Wikipedia, you can provide a significant benefit to many people at almost no cost to others. Some organisations also have opportunities that are designed to take on board volunteers with little cost. Mercy for Animals, for example, is a vegetarian advocacy organisation. It has volunteers contact people who have commented on videos on factory farming on Facebook. These volunteers then discuss the option of going vegetarian with them. This provides a significant benefit while costing the charity very little in management time. An alternative route to having an impact without imposing a burden on charities is to work additional hours instead of volunteering and donate the money you make.

However, you don't need to limit yourself to this.

Instead, I'd encourage you to think about volunteering primarily in terms of the skills and experiences you'll gain, which will enable you to have a greater impact later in your life. Because the total time you'll spend volunteering will be only a tiny fraction of the total time you'll spend on your career, the impact volunteering has on other areas of your life will generally be much greater than the impact you have via the volunteering itself.

For example, as an undergraduate I went to Ethiopia to teach at a school. The impact I had there was limited (as far as I can tell, I mainly just allowed the real teacher to take some time off – which is a benefit, but a small one compared to other things I could have done with my time and money, especially given the costly flights). However, the impact that seeing extreme poverty up close had on me was significant: it shaped the choices I have made in the years since then and it helps motivate me when I'm doing activities that are more abstract than teaching at that school. The main impact of that trip to Ethiopia was its effect on me.

It might feel odd to volunteer simply to benefit yourself, but I think that, as long as one is thinking of volunteering as the first step towards generally moving your life in the direction of making a difference, there's nothing problematic about this. Like anything, benefiting others requires some training, and volunteering can be a good way to get experience.

Later career moves

What if you're later on in your career and want to make a difference?

Later in life, the same framework we introduced at the start applies, but career capital becomes a lot less important, and facts about your specific situation (the skills and experience that you've developed) become a lot more important. For people who didn't set out to build skills that are useful for making a difference, earning to give can be a particularly good option. Often, people move from high-paying jobs to something that directly makes a difference even though they have limited expertise in the area they move into, when they could have done much more good by keeping their high salary and earning to give.

For example, after graduating with a PhD in philosophy from Brown University in the seventies, Frederick Mulder left academia in order to become an art dealer. He became very successful, but progressively wanted to use his career to make a difference. He thought being an art dealer was of neutral moral value – or perhaps slightly negative, he told me, because of the amount of flying he has to do – but realised that moving out of art and into the non-profit world wasn't the best way for him to use his talents. 'There are many things that I'd like to see done in the world,' he said, 'but I can't do them myself because I don't have those skills. So what better than to use the resources I can generate by doing something I love in order to help someone else do something really important that needs to be done?' He continued in his career, donating every year between 10% and 80% of his earnings.

If you've built up useful skills, on the other hand, then it can be a good option to contribute those skills directly to an effective area. This is what Rob Mather of the Against Malaria Foundation did. He had extensive experience in business and sales, which meant he understood how to run an organisation and pitch ideas, and he had developed an incredible capacity to make things happen. (His first foray into altruism was organising a swimming-based fundraiser and he managed to get 100,000 swimmers to participate.) His background also meant that he didn't need to take a salary, something that impressed donors in the early stages. His sales skills allowed him to get a huge amount of pro bono support from a variety of companies. As a result, he's built a charity that is among the top-recommended at GiveWell, has raised over $30 million, and has distributed more than 10 million long-lasting insecticide-treated bed nets, saving thousands of lives.

Choosing a career is one of the most important decisions you'll ever make, and I hope that the framework I've presented in this chapter will help you to think through this decision.

In order to use your career to make a difference, one rule of thumb that I mentioned is to work on a particularly important cause. However, so far I've primarily discussed only the cause of fighting global poverty. What about all the other problems in the world? How can we decide which are most important to focus on? In the next chapter, I tackle this question.

POVERTY VS CLIMATE CHANGE VS . . .

Which cause should you focus on?

In the summer of 2013 President Barack Obama referred to climate change as 'the global threat of our time'. He's not alone in this opinion. The US Secretary of State John Kerry called climate change 'the greatest challenge of our generation'; Former Senate Majority Leader Harry Reid has said that, 'Climate change is the worst problem facing the world today,' and the co-chair of the Intergovernmental Panel on Climate Change, Thomas F. Stocker, called climate change 'the greatest challenge of our time'.

Are Obama and these other commentators correct? Is climate change the most important cause in the world today – a greater global priority than extreme poverty? How could we decide?

A lot of people have asked these questions. Though foundations and social entrepreneurs often talk about trying to maximise their impact, they usually just focus on maximising their impact within the cause or causes that

they're personally passionate about (like poverty, or education, or climate change), rather than thinking strategically
about which causes they should focus on. If we're really
trying to do the most good we can, however, then we need
to think carefully about cause selection. We'll be able to
help more people to a greater degree within some cause
areas than we will in others, which means that, in order to
have the biggest impact we can, we have to think carefully
about what causes we choose to focus on.

So far the organisations I've recommended as extremely
cost-effective have all been focused on global poverty. We
can have a high degree of confidence that these charities
do a substantial amount of good. However, you might
reasonably think that the very best way of helping others
isn't to fight global poverty, or that the best way of fighting
global poverty is through activities the benefits of which
are more difficult to quantify than those of the charities
I've mentioned. Moreover, you might want to do good
with your time (whether through volunteering or your
work) rather than your money. In which case, your own
particular skills, experiences and opportunities become a
lot more important, and these might not fit as well with
global poverty as they do with other areas. This means we
need to think about cause selection.

In this chapter I'm not going to attempt to definitively
answer the question of what cause is most important to
focus on, which would be impossible to do in a whole
book, let alone a single chapter. Instead I'm going to
introduce a framework for thinking about the question,

and then use that framework to suggest some causes that, on the basis of research at GiveWell and the Centre for Effective Altruism, I think should be given high priority. Again, bear in mind that decisions about cause selection involve value judgements to an even greater degree than some of the other issues I've canvassed in this book so the conclusions you reach might be quite different from the ones I reach. Though effective altruism aims to take a scientific approach to doing good, it's not exactly physics: there is plenty of room for differences of opinion. This doesn't, however, make thinking rigorously about which cause one chooses to focus on any less important.

On the framework I propose, you can compare causes by assessing them on how well they do on each of the following three dimensions:

First, *Scale*. What's the magnitude of this problem? How much does it affect lives in the short run and long run?

Second, *Neglectedness*. How many resources are already being dedicated to tackling this problem? How well allocated are the resources that are currently being dedicated to the problem? Is there reason to expect this problem can't be solved by markets or governments?

Third, *Tractability*. How easy is it to make progress on this problem, and how easy is it to tell if you're making progress? Do interventions within this cause exist, and how strong is the evidence behind those interventions?

Do you expect to be able to discover new promising interventions within this cause?

If we're thinking about contributions of time rather than just money, then there is a fourth important dimension:

Personal fit. Given your skills, resources, knowledge, connections and passions, how likely are you to make a large difference in this area?

We discussed 'personal fit' in the previous chapter on career choice, and most of that discussion applies equally well to the choice of causes. This chapter will therefore focus on the first three criteria, but you should keep in mind that, if you're thinking about working or volunteering in an area, the considerations I give need to be mediated by your personal fit with the cause.

Scale refers to the size of the problem, which should usually be measured in terms of total actual or potential impact on others' wellbeing. For example cancer, as I noted earlier, is a bigger problem than malaria because it is responsible for 7.6% of all ill health (measured in QALYs lost) worldwide, whereas malaria is responsible for 3.3% of ill health worldwide.

All other things being equal, the larger the problem, the higher-priority the cause should be. This is for a couple of reasons. First, many activities make a proportional impact on a problem. If you can develop a new cheap treatment for either cancer or malaria, you should probably develop the cheap treatment for cancer. Cancer causes more ill health and death than malaria so, when that treatment is rolled out, it will have a larger total benefit. Political change is another area where you can have a proportional effect on a problem: if you can improve the healthcare policy of either a single region or the whole country, the fact that national policy would affect a far larger number of people is clearly relevant.

Second, the scale of a problem also determines how long we should expect the problem to persist. There's no point in investing significant time and resources into learning about a cause if that problem will be resolved a few years later. Similarly, if the problem is very big, then it will take a large amount of resources before the most effective opportunities are used up.

The second aspect of the framework is *Neglectedness*, which refers to how many resources are being invested into this cause, relative to its scale. Because of diminishing returns, all other things being equal, the more resources that have been invested in a specific cause, the more difficult it will be to make progress within that cause with a given amount of resources, because typically many of the most cost-effective opportunities will have already been taken.

This is an easy consideration to forget. If something seems like a huge problem – perhaps the biggest problem in the world – it is natural to think one should focus on it. But if that problem already has a large amount of resources invested in it, then additional resources might be better spent elsewhere. For example HIV/AIDS, tuberculosis and malaria traditionally received much more attention than conditions like intestinal worms. One reason for this, I think, is that these other conditions cause a much greater amount of ill health (measured in number of deaths, or QALYs lost) than intestinal worms do, and thereby attracted a disproportionate share of attention. However, precisely because intestinal worms had much less attention, the cheapest and most effective ways of treating them were still available. In fact, it wasn't until Alan Fenwick, executive director of the Schistosomiasis Control Initiative, coined the term 'Neglected Tropical Diseases' that these conditions became more prominent in the discussion of global health. The term had two benefits. First, it classified a wide range of conditions under one heading. This meant that, even though the burden of disease from schistosomiasis, for example, was small compared to the global burden from HIV/AIDS, the global burden of disease from *all* neglected tropical diseases was comparable to the global burden from HIV/AIDS. Second, the name highlighted the fact that these diseases were neglected.

When you read the rest of this chapter, you might be surprised that you haven't heard much about many of the causes I suggest are high-priority. That just shows the importance of considering neglectedness when choosing a cause. The causes we hear the most about are precisely those where it will be harder to make a big difference; the causes that get less attention are those where we may be able to have a massive impact.

The third aspect of the framework is *Tractability*, which means the long-run average of people's ability to turn resources into progress toward solving the problem. Even if a problem is hugely important and highly neglected, that doesn't mean it's an important cause to focus on. There might simply be very little we can do about it. For example aging is a problem that is huge in scale: almost two-thirds of global ill health is a result of aging. It's a problem that's highly neglected: there are only a tiny number of research institutes focused on trying to prevent the causes of aging (rather than to treat its symptoms, like cancer, stroke, Alzheimer's, and so on). However, the reason it's neglected is because many scientists believe it to be highly intractable. Preventing the aging process is just a very difficult problem to solve.

In previous chapters I discussed explicit cost-effectiveness estimates (e.g. a QALY costs $100). This is useful when thinking in the short term. If we have good evidence on specific interventions, we can compare cost-effectiveness directly. But these estimates only apply to specific interventions, and the estimated cost-effectiveness of specific programmes within a cause area will change over time. This means that, when thinking about investing time and effort into a cause, it's important not just to look at our current best-guess estimates, but to make estimates about the long-run tractability of the cause as well.

To illustrate the framework of Scale, Neglectedness and Tractability, let's see how it provides a strong case for focusing on global poverty rather than domestic poverty. The scale of global poverty is much larger, in both numbers and extremity, than domestic poverty within first-world

countries. There are 46.5 million Americans living in relative poverty, defined as living on less than $11,000 per year,
but there are 1.22 billion people worldwide living in extreme
poverty, defined as living on less than $550 per year. Second,
global poverty is much more neglected than domestic
poverty. In 2014, $500 billion was spent on welfare in the
United States, whereas total aid and philanthropy to poor
countries was only $250 billion in that year. Most impor-
tantly, as we've seen, extreme poverty is far more tractable
than domestic poverty, with current cost-effectiveness estimates suggesting that you can do one hundred times as
much to provide the same size of benefit to someone in
extreme poverty as you can to someone domestically.

It is relatively easy to compare global and domestic
poverty, because the former seems more promising on all
three dimensions. In other cases, it's not so easy: one cause
might be better on one dimension but worse on another. In
what follows I'll give a number of examples of what seem
like highly promising causes. As in Chapter 7, in which I
discussed charities, I'll score each cause from 'not very' to
'extremely', on each dimension. We'll see that it's difficult
to find causes that score very highly on every dimension.
Criminal justice reform seems unusually tractable, but
comparatively low on scale. Increasing international labour
mobility scores highly on scale, but does very poorly on
tractability. Which cause to focus on is therefore something that involves difficult judgement calls: it's not clear
how to weigh these different criteria against one another,
and people may reasonably disagree on how to do so.

A couple of caveats before we begin. First, in each case, I'm only going to be able to describe the cause and why, in short, I think it's promising (I provide references to further reading in the endnotes for those who are interested). This chapter should therefore be taken as an invitation to explore causes other than extreme poverty, with recommendations rather than a definitive argument for why these are the most important causes. Second, for some of these causes, it's not as easy for casual donors to make a big difference in the same way they can if they donate to the charities listed in Chapter 7; some of these causes are more in need of good people than more money.

With those caveats in mind, let's look at some high-priority causes.

US criminal justice reform

What's the problem? At any one time, 2.2 million people are incarcerated in the US. That's 0.7% of its population, giving it one of the highest incarceration rates in the world. As a comparison, the UK has an incarceration rate of 0.14%; Canada's is 0.1%; Japan's is 0.05%. At the same time, the US has the highest level of intentional homicide (which is a good proxy for rates of criminality in general) in the developed world, at 4.7 per 100,000 people per year (in comparison, the UK's homicide rate is 1 per 100,000 people per year; Canada's is 1.6; Japan's is 0.3). This suggests that the high incarceration rate is not deterring crime, and may even be increasing it. Since the 1990s, incarceration rates in the US have increased dramatically despite a fall in violent crime in that period. According to expert criminologists, incarceration rates could be reduced (especially for low-risk offenders) by 10% or more while keeping levels of criminality the same, or even reducing them.

In this book I've argued that the highest-impact ways of doing good typically won't be aimed at providing benefits to people in rich countries, so it might seem surprising to see US criminal justice reform on this list. But though opportunities to make a truly massive difference in the West are rarer than opportunities to make a massive difference elsewhere, that doesn't mean they're nonexistent. What distinguishes criminal justice reform from other sorts of domestic issues is that, while being fairly great in scale, it is an issue that is both neglected and unusually tractable at this point in time.

Scale: Fairly large. A reduction of the prison population by 10% would have a variety of benefits. It would of course greatly benefit all the people (over 200,000 each year) who would not have to spend time in prison (often for crimes such as drug possession, which does not pose as great a threat to society as violent crime). As well as the misery of life in prison itself, costs of a prison sentence include: forgone earnings, the reduction of future income and the costs borne by families, especially children, of having a family member in prison.

Incarceration also costs the government about $25,000 per person per year, whereas parole costs only about $2,000 per year, meaning the government could save billions annually. If even larger reductions in incarceration rates were feasible (remembering that even a 50% reduction would still mean that the US incarceration rate is three and a half times as high as Canada's), then the scale would be considerably greater again.

Neglectedness: Fairly neglected. GiveWell estimates that only about $20 million is spent per year by organisations other than governments on prison reform to substantially reduce incarceration rates. (A further $40 million per year is spent on other sorts of prison reform, such as campaigning to abolish the death penalty.)

Tractability: Extremely tractable. Owing to a combination of declining rates of criminality and a particularly poor economy following the recession, there appears to be an unusual level of bipartisan support for prison reform. The Pew Charitable Trust provides an example of progress in this area: as of summer 2014, it had assisted with twenty-nine reform packages in twenty-seven states since 2007, at a cost of just $25 million, with a forecasted reduction in prison population in those states of 11%. On the assumption that these forecasts are accurate and that these reforms would not have happened without Pew's intervention, the cost per year of life in prison averted would be as low as $29.

What promising organisations are working on it?

The Pew Charitable Trusts Public Safety Performance Project aims to make criminal justice policy more effective and evidence-based by providing technical assistance to states, doing policy evaluations, providing information on what works, and fostering broad political support for specific policies.

BetaGov (accepts donations via *GiveWell*), led by Professor Angela Hawken of Pepperdine University, is a start-up centre that provides tools to help practitioners conduct experimental trials of policies.

The University of Chicago Crime Lab (accepts donations) runs randomised controlled trials to provide evidence-based criminal justice policy advice to governments.

International labour mobility

What's the problem? Increased levels of migration from poor to rich countries would provide substantial benefits for the poorest people in the world, as well as substantial increases in global economic output. However, almost all developed countries pose heavy restrictions on who can enter the country to work.

Scale: Very large. Location rather than other factors accounts for 85% of the global variation in earnings: the extremely poor are poor simply because they don't live in an environment that enables them to be productive. Economists Michael Clemens, Claudio Montenegro and Lant Pritchett have estimated what they call the 'place premium' – the wage gain for foreign workers who move to the United States. For an average person in Haiti, relocation to the US would increase income by about 680%; for a Nigerian, it would increase income by 1,000%. Some other developing countries have comparatively lower place premiums, but they are still high enough to benefit migrants dramatically. Most migrants would also earn enough to send remittances to family members, thus helping many of those who do not migrate. An estimated 600 million people worldwide would migrate if they were able to.

Several economists have estimated that the total economic gains from free mobility of labour across borders would be greater than a 50% increase in world GDP. Even if these estimates were extremely optimistic, the economic gains from substantially increased immigration would be measured in trillions of dollars per year. (I discuss some objections to increased levels of immigration in the endnotes.)

Neglectedness: Very neglected. Though a number of organisations work on immigration issues, very few focus on the benefits to future migrants of relaxing migration policy, instead focusing on migrants that are currently living in the US.

Tractability: Not very tractable. Increased levels of immigration are incredibly unpopular in developed countries, with the majority of people in Germany, Italy, the Netherlands, Norway, Sweden and the United Kingdom favouring reduced immigration. Among developed countries, Canada is most sympathetic to increased levels of immigration; but even there only 20% of people favour increasing immigration, while 42% favour reducing it. This makes political change on this issue in the near term seem unlikely.

What promising organisations are working on it?

ImmigrationWorks USA (accepts donations) organises, represents, and advocates on behalf of small business owners who would benefit from being able to hire lower-skill migrant workers more easily, with the aim of 'bringing America's annual legal intake of foreign workers more realistically into line with the country's labour needs'.

The Center for Global Development (accepts donations) conducts policy-relevant research and policy analysis on topics relevant to improving the lives of the global poor, including on immigration reform, then makes recommendations to policymakers.

Factory farming

What's the problem? Fifty billion animals are raised and slaughtered in factory farms every year. Relatively small changes to farming practices could substantially improve these animals' welfare. Raising animals for consumption also produces substantial greenhouse gas emissions.

Scale: Up to very large, depending on value judgements. The scale of the problem depends on how much weight you put on the interests of non-human animals. Many people regard the suffering of non-human animals as morally important. Given these values, the scale of the problem of factory farming would seem very great. The meat industry is also one of the largest contributors to climate change, amounting to 14.5% of global greenhouse gas emissions.

Neglectedness: Extremely neglected. Total expenditure from non-profits on factory farming practices is less than $20 million per year.

Tractability: Fairly tractable. Rates of meat consumption are decreasing, and there appear to be reliable ways to persuade people towards a vegetarian diet. In the EU there have been moves to improve conditions in factory farms, such as a ban on battery hen cages. In the US, however, there is a strong farming lobby that opposes political change on the issue.

What promising organisations are working on it?

Mercy for Animals (accepts donations) conducts investigations to expose animal cruelty in farming and engages in education and outreach such as online videos and advertisements related to animal welfare.

The Humane League (accepts donations) engages in education and outreach, primarily through online videos and advertisements, on-the-ground leafleting, and Meatless Mondays campaigns.

The Humane Society of the United States (accepts donations), whose Farm Animal Protection Campaign aims to end the most extreme confinement practices in factory farming by working with farmers to improve the treatment of animals in food production, and lobbying for better laws and against anti-whistleblower legislation.

Mercy for Animals and The Humane League are top-recommended by the independent evaluator Animal Charity Evaluators; The Humane Society of the United States Farm Animal Protection Campaign is rated as a 'standout' organisation.

2–4°C climate change

What's the problem? Greenhouse gas emissions will probably lead to a 2–4°C rise in average global temperatures. This will cause trillions of dollars of economic damage, the loss of hundreds of thousands or millions of lives, and significant reductions in biodiversity.

Scale: Fairly large. Economists typically estimate that a 2–4°C rise in temperature would cause a reduction in GDP by about 2%. However, most of the damage from climate change will occur in the future when people even in poor countries are considerably richer than they are now. For example according to the second most pessimistic model in the Stern Review (a particularly grave assessment of climate change published in 2006), by 2100 the economic costs from climate change will amount to $400 per person, reducing the average GDP per person in developing countries from $11,000 to $10,600.

Economic assessments of the costs of climate change typically look at human costs only. If you also value preservation of the natural environment, you should regard climate change as considerably worse than the economists' models suggest. For example climate change may potentially lead to the extinction of 20–30% of species.

Neglectedness: Not very neglected. Climate change is well known as a major social issue. The US government spends about $8 billion per year on climate change efforts, the UK spends about £1 billion per year on climate change projects in developing countries and several hundred million dollars are spent each year by foundations.

Tractability: Fairly tractable. There are reliable ways in which individuals can reduce the amount of global greenhouse gas emissions. The opportunity to effect political change is unclear, however, as political progress has been slow. For example the 2009 United Nations Climate Change Conference in Copenhagen was the largest meeting of the heads of state in history, but it achieved very little.

What promising organisations are working on it?

Cool Earth (accepts donations) helps indigenous peoples in Peru and DR Congo protect the rainforest in which they live from illegal logging.

ClimateWorks (accepts donations) campaigns for public policies that will decrease the output of greenhouse gas emissions.

Catastrophic climate change

What's the problem? Given current climate models, we are unable to rule out the possibility that greenhouse gas emissions will lead to what I call catastrophic climate change, with temperature rises of 10°C or more. Though the chance of this occurring is very small, the outcome would be very grave, which means the expected value of preventing this possibility may be very high.

Scale: From fairly large to extremely large, depending on value judgements. How one evaluates risks of global catastrophe depends crucially on how much value one places on maintaining a flourishing civilisation long into the future. The chances of such bad outcomes are very small, but if you regard civilisational collapse as *extremely* bad, then it could be very important to prevent these worst-case scenarios.

Neglectedness: Fairly neglected. Most focus on climate change is on reducing emissions. This is a good thing whether or not the best-guess climate change predictions are correct. However, there has been comparatively little research done into the likelihood of catastrophic climate change, or into mitigation and adaption strategies in extreme warming scenarios. About $11 million per year is spent on research into geoengineering (see below).

Tractability: Fairly tractable. The most pressing need is to fund further research into both assessing the likelihood of worst-case scenarios and to developing strategies to reduce their likelihood. One potential opportunity is research into geoengineering, which could be used as a measure of last resort. Geoengineering is the attempt to deliberately cool the planet, for example by pumping sulphates (which are gases that reflect sunlight and in turn cool the planet) into the stratosphere. Geoengineering itself may pose significant risks such as depletion of the ozone layer, but if it turns out we're facing very large temperature increases then the risks may be justified. Moreover, geoengineering is cheap enough that in the future individual countries could unilaterally undertake risky geoengineering projects. It would therefore be desirable to have a good understanding of the impacts and risks of geoengineering ahead of time. However, it may be that increased research into this area could detract from other mitigation and adaption strategies.

What promising organisations are working on it?

The Oxford University Geoengineering Programme advocates to conduct transparent and socially informed research into the social, ethical and technical aspects of geoengineering.

The Solar Radiation Management Governance Initiative provides advice on the regulation of geoengineering, seeking to ensure that research into solar radiation management (one form of geoengineering) is conducted in a responsible manner.

General mitigation of climate change is also a way to reduce catastrophic risk, so Cool Earth and ClimateWorks, previously mentioned, are also promising charities in this area.

Other global catastrophic risks

What's the problem? There are a number of low-probability risks that could have disastrous outcomes. These include risks of nuclear war, pandemics, and bioterrorism.

Scale: From fairly large to extremely large, depending on value judgements. As with catastrophic risk from climate change, how one evaluates risks of global catastrophe depends crucially on how much value one places on maintaining a flourishing civilisation long into the future.

Neglectedness: Fairly neglected. Because global catastrophes are unprecedented and unlikely, they may not receive the attention they deserve. The amount of philanthropic funding on these issues is comparatively small: about $30 million per year on nuclear security, and only a few million per year on biosecurity. However, there is considerable funding and involvement from governments. Only a very small amount of funding (on the order to $1–2 million) is spent on global catastrophic risks in general, such as research to identify currently overlooked risks of global catastrophe.

Tractability: Fairly tractable. There are opportunities for funding academic research into catastrophic risks in general, and there are some opportunities for increasing policy influence. However, none of these activities have as clear a path to impact as, for example, donating to fight extreme poverty.

What promising organisations are working on it?

The Nuclear Threat Initiative (accepts donations) works on a variety of projects to reduce the spread of nuclear, biological and chemical weapons.

The Future of Humanity Institute and *The Centre for the Study of Existential Risk* (both accept donations) are interdisciplinary research institutes at the Universities of Oxford and Cambridge, respectively, that assess the magnitudes of global catastrophic risks and try to develop risk-mitigation strategies.

The foregoing is summarised in Table 2.

	Scale	Neglected-ness	Tractability
Extreme poverty	● ● ●	● ●	● ● ● ●
US criminal justice reform	●	● ●	● ● ● ●
International labour mobility	● ● ●	● ● ●	●
Factory farming	Up to ● ● ● depending on value judgements	● ● ● ●	● ● ●
2–4°C climate change	● ●	●	● ●
Catastrophic climate change	● ● to ● ● ● ● depending on value judgements	● ●	● ●
Other global catastrophic risks	● ● to ● ● ● ● depending on value judgements	● ● ●	● ●

Table 2: A cause-assessment framework

CONCLUSION:
BECOMING AN EFFECTIVE ALTRUIST

What should you do right now?

This book has presented effective altruism's approach to making a difference. By outlining the five key questions of effective altruism, and the frameworks for choosing a charity, a career, and a cause (all restated in the appendix), I hope that I have provided the tools to help you increase your impact in all areas of your life. I hope you will bear this perspective in mind the next time you reach for your wallet after seeing a charity fundraiser, think about signing up to volunteer, or go shopping and wonder whether to buy ethically produced goods.

We've seen that, by employing effective altruism's way of thinking, we each have the power to do a tremendous amount of good. A donation of $3,400 (£2,200) can provide bed nets that will save someone's life, deworm seven thousand children, or double the income of fifteen people for a year. Those charities with less concretely measurable benefits, such as those working on criminal justice reform, or more relaxed immigration policy, or catastrophic climate change, may, in terms of expected value, do even more good again.

The film *Schindler's List* tells the story of the war hero Oskar Schindler, a Polish entrepreneur who ran munitions factories for the Nazis. Initially he was an opportunist, happy to take advantage of the war for his own gain, but as he saw the horrors that the Nazis inflicted on the Jews, he realised he couldn't simply stand by and watch. So he bribed officials to spare his Jewish workers, ultimately saving more than a thousand of them.

Though Schindler's story is inspiring, you might think that war is a particularly unusual time, and therefore altruism like Schindler's isn't really that relevant to our lives. What we've seen in this book is that this isn't true. Every one of us has the power to save dozens or hundreds of lives, or to significantly improve the welfare of thousands of people. We might not get books or films written about us, but we can each do an astonishing amount of good, just as Schindler did.

If you feel empowered by what you have read, by far the most important thing for you to do is ensure that this feeling doesn't dissipate over the coming weeks or months. Here are four ideas about how best to do that.

1: Establish a habit of regular giving

Go onto the website of a highly effective charity and sign up to make a regular donation, even if it's just a small amount each month. This is the easiest and most tangible way of having a great and immediate positive impact. Even if you think that the main way you'll help others in life won't be through your donations, starting to give is a good way of solidifying your intentions, and of proving to yourself that you mean business.

Some of the top charities I've mentioned in this book are Against Malaria Foundation, Cool Earth, Development Media International, Deworm the World Initiative, GiveDirectly and the Schistosomiasis Control Initiative. Pick whichever you believe to be best and begin a habit of effective donations. Even a modest monthly donation to any of these charities will have a big impact.

2: Write down how you're going to incorporate effective altruism into your life

Get a pen and paper, or open up an electronic document, and make some notes about the changes you plan to make. Make the plan specific and concrete. If you're going to start giving, write down what proportion of your income you'll donate and when you intend to start. If you're going to change what you buy, write down what changes you plan to make and by when. If you're going to pursue a career that makes a difference, specify which dates you're going to set aside in order to find out more information relevant to your next steps.

3: Join the Effective Altruism community

Go to www.effectivealtruism.org and sign up to the Effective Altruism mailing list. That way you can learn more about effective altruism and about how to get involved in the community, and read stories of people putting effective altruism into practice. You can also talk with others in the Effective Altruism forum, and there you can find out more about issues that I haven't been able to cover in this book, including whether to give now or invest and give later, or the impact of giving on your personal happiness.

4: Tell others about effective altruism

Tell people on Facebook, Twitter, Instagram or your blog some of your thoughts about what you've read. If you find the arguments in this book convincing, then your friends, family and colleagues might do so too. If you can get one person to make the same changes you make, you've doubled your impact.

It can be awkward to raise the idea of effective altruism – you don't want to come across as holier-than-thou, or critical of projects that are less effective – but there are ways to do so naturally. For your birthday, instead of presents you could ask for donations to a highly effective charity, creating a webpage on Causevox.com; Charity Science, a fundraising website set up by two people in the effective altruism community, helps you to do this on their Take Action page. If it's the holiday giving season, you could offer to match any donations made by your colleagues up to a certain amount. You could organise discussion groups on career choice, or cause selection, or ethical consumerism.

If you want to go further than these actions, you might wish to take Giving What We Can's pledge to donate 10% of your income. You could read the career advice on 80,000 Hours, or apply for one-on-one career coaching there. Or you might wish to set up a local group, starting discussions about effective altruism in your area, with your friends or through your church or university. Further information on all this is available at effectivealtruism.org.

Whatever you choose to do, think of today as a pivotal step on your journey to making the world a better place. Each of us has the potential to have an enormous positive impact. I hope this book has both inspired you to do so and given you the tools you need to get there.

APPENDIX: SUMMARY

Thinking like an effective altruist

The five key questions of effective altruism

How many people benefit, and by how much?

Like James Orbinski, the doctor who engaged in triage during the Rwandan genocide, we need to make hard decisions about who we help and who we don't; that means thinking about how much benefit is provided by different activities. The quality-adjusted life year, or QALY, allows us to compare the impact of different sorts of health programmes.

Is this the most effective thing you can do?

The very best health and education programmes are hundreds of times better than 'merely' very good programmes. Smallpox eradication did so much good that it alone shows development aid to be highly cost-effective on average.

Is this area neglected?

Natural disasters get far more funding than ongoing causes of death and suffering such as disease; for that reason, disaster relief usually isn't the most effective use of funds. Diseases such as malaria that affect people in the developing world get far less funding than conditions like cancer; for that reason you have a much bigger impact treating people with malaria than with cancer.

What would have happened otherwise?

After going through the Scared Straight programme, juveniles were more likely to commit crimes than they would have done otherwise, so the programme did harm overall. In careers like medicine, you're sometimes simply doing good work that would have happened anyway; if you earn to give, however, you make a difference that wouldn't otherwise have occurred.

What are the chances of success, and how good would success be?

Some activities – such as voting, entering politics, campaigning for systemic change or mitigating risks of global catastrophe – are effective not because they're likely to make a difference but because their impact is so great if they do make a difference.

Which charity should you donate to?

What does this charity do?

How many different types of programmes does it run? For each of these programmes, what exactly is it that this charity does? If it runs more than one programme, why is that?

How cost-effective is each programme area?

Is the charity focused on one of the most important causes? How cost-effective does the evidence suggest the programme to be?

How robust is the evidence behind each programme?

What is the evidence behind the programmes that the charity runs? Are there trials showing that the programme is effective? Does the charity rigorously monitor and evaluate the success of its programmes?

How well is each programme implemented?

Do the leaders of the charity have demonstrable success in other areas? Is the charity highly transparent? Does it acknowledge mistakes that it's made in the past? What are the alternative charities you could give to? Are there good reasons for supposing that this charity is better than those alternatives?

Does the charity need additional funds?

What would additional funding be used to do? Why haven't other donors already funded the charity to the point it can't use extra money?

Which career should you pursue?

How will I personally fit with this job?

How satisfied will I be in this job? Am I excited by the prospect of doing this job? Do I think I could stick with it for a significant period of time? How good am I, or could I become, at this type of work, compared with other people and compared with other careers I might choose?

What will be my impact while I'm working at this job?

How many resources will I be able to influence, whether via the labour I provide, the people or budget I manage, the money I earn, or a public platform I have access to? How effective are the causes to which I could direct those resources?

How would this job contribute to my impact later on in life?

How well will this job build my skills, connections, and credentials? Will it enable me to keep my options open? How much will I learn while doing this job about what I might want to do next?

Which cause should you focus on?

Scale

How big is the problem? How much does it affect lives in the short run and long run?

Neglectedness

How many resources are already being dedicated to tackling this problem? How well allocated are the resources that are currently being dedicated to the problem? Is there reason to expect that markets or governments won't solve this problem unaided?

Tractability

How easy is it to make progress on this problem, and how easy is it to monitor progress? Do interventions exist to make progress within this cause, and how strong is the evidence behind those interventions? Do you expect to be able to discover promising new avenues for progress?

Personal fit

Given your skills, resources, knowledge, connections and passions, how likely are you to make a large difference in this area?

ACKNOWLEDGEMENTS

This book has benefited from the input of very many people, sufficiently so that I'm not sure I can really call it 'my' book. For helping make effective altruism actually happen, and for providing volumes of online discussion of the key ideas that I present in this book, I thank everyone in the effective altruism community, and especially everyone at the Centre for Effective Altruism. I also thank the staff at GiveWell, whose research underpins substantial parts of this book.

For very helpful feedback on the manuscript, I thank Alexander Berger, Jason Boult, Niel Bowerman, Uri Bram, Ryan Carey, Nick Cooney, Roman Duda, Sam Dumitriu, Sebastian Farquhar, Austen Forrester, Iason Gabriel, Evan Gaensbauer, Daniel Gastfriend, Eric Gastfriend, Aaron Gertler, Josh Goldenberg, Alex Gordon-Brown, Katja Grace, Topher Hallquist, Elie Hassenfeld, Roxanne Heston, Hauke Hillebrandt, Ben Hoskin, Chris Jenkins, Holden Karnofsky, Greg Lewis, Amanda MacAskill, Larissa MacFarquhar, Georgie Mallett, Michael Marcode de Freitas, Sören Mindermann, David Moss, Luke Muehlhauser, Sally Murray, Vipul Naik, Anthony Obeyesekere, Rossa O'Keeffe-O'Donovan, Toby Ord, Michael Peyton Jones,

Duncan Pike, Alex Richard, Jess Riedel, Josh Rosenberg, Matt Sharp, Carl Shulman, Peter Singer, Imma Six, Pablo Stafforini, Shayna Strom, Tim Telleen-Lawton, Derek Thompson, Ben Todd, Helen Toner, Robert Wiblin, Boris Yakubchik, Vincent Yu, Pascal Zimmer and the many others with whom I've discussed these ideas.

I owe an enormous debt to my research assistant Pablo Stafforini, who is rapidly becoming part of my extended mind. I thank Roxanne Heston, Mihnea Maftei and Robin Raven for providing interview transcriptions. For financial support towards Effective Altruism Outreach, of which this book is a project, I'm grateful to Markus Anderljung, Ryan Carey, Austen Forrester, Tom Greenway, Sam Hilton, George McGowan, William Saunders, Chris Smith, Pablo Stafforini and Matt Wage. For the final-year DPhil stipend and postdoctoral research fellowship that paid my bills while I wrote this, I thank, respectively, the Society for Applied Philosophy and Emmanuel College, Cambridge.

For all his encouragement and advice, I thank my agent, William Callahan of Inkwell Management, without whom the literary world would have utterly confounded me. For their extraordinarily in-depth comments and suggestions on multiple drafts of the manuscript, which improved the book in every way, I thank my editors, Brooke Carey and Laura Hassan.

For their ongoing love and support I thank my parents, Mair and Robin Crouch, my brothers, Iain and Thomas Crouch, and my partner, Amanda MacAskill.

NOTES

Introduction: Worms and Water Pumps

page 2 *'African girls have almost nothing'*: Private conversation with author, September 2014.

page 3 *'innovative, early stage development projects'*: World Bank Development Marketplace: http://wbi.worldbank.org/wbi/content/development-marketplace-1.

page 3 *'They thought the PlayPump was incredible'*: Private conversation with author, September 2014.

page 3 *launched a bottled-water brand called One Water*: One Difference, http://onedifference.org/.

page 3 *became the official bottled water of the Live8 concert and the Make Poverty History campaign*: Ralph Borland, 'Radical plumbers and PlayPumps: objects in development', PhD thesis, Trinity College Dublin, 2011, p. 37.

page 3 *'pumping water is child's play'*: 'Why pumping water is child's play', BBC News, 25 April 2005.

page 3 *'The magic roundabout'*: Kevin Bloom, 'Playing for real', *Mail & Guardian* (Johannesburg), 26 March 2004.

page 3 *'wonderful innovation'*: Bill Clinton, Laura Bus and Jean Case, 'How the new philanthropy works', *Time*, 25 September 2006.

page 4 *Rapper Jay-Z raised tens of thousands of dollars*: 'Jay-Z helps U.N. focus on water crisis', *USA Today*, 9 August 2006.

page 4 *a $16.4 million grant*: Amy Costello, 'PlayPump project receives major U.S. funding', *FRONTLINE/World*, 20 September 2006.

page 4 *'When I first looked at this water pump'*: Mark Melman, 'The making of a "philanthropreneur"', *Journal of Values Based*

Leadership, 15 March 2008, www.valuesbasedleadershipjournal. com/issues/vol1issue2/field_melman.php

page 4 *'it really rocks me'*: John Eastman, 'Trevor Field of PlayPumps International', *Black and White*, 14 April 2008, www.blackandwhite-program.com/interview/trevor-field-playpumps-international.

page 4 *one by UNICEF*: UNICEF, 'An evaluation of the PlayPump water system as an appropriate technology for water, sanitation and hygiene programmes', October 2007, www-tc.pbs.org/frontline-world/stories/southernafrica904/flash/pdf/unicef_pp_report.pdf.

page 4 *one by the Swiss Resource Centre and Consultancies for Development (SKAT)*: Ana Lucía Obiols and Karl Erpf, *Mission report on the evaluation of the PlayPumps installed in Mozambique*, The Swiss Resource Centre and Consultancies for Development, April 2008, www-tc.pbs.org/frontlineworld/stories/southernafrica904/flash/pdf/mozambique_report.pdf.

page 5 *women of the village ended up pushing the roundabout them-selves*: 'When children are not available, adults (especially women) have no choice but to operate the PlayPump. While some women in South Africa and Mozambique reported that they did not mind rotating the "merry-go-round", in Mozambique they also reported that they got embarrassed where the people watching them did not know the linkage between the "merry-go-round" and the water pumping (e.g. where the pump is near a public road). All women interviewed in Zambia reported that they did not like operating the pump.' UNICEF, 'An evaluation of the PlayPump water system', p. 10.

page 5 *'From 5 a.m.'*: Amy Costello, *Southern Africa: Troubled Water*, PBS video 23:41, 29 June 2010, www.pbs.org/frontlineworld/stories/southernafrica904/video_index.html.

page 5 *One reporter estimated*: Andrew Chambers, 'Africa's not-so-magic roundabout', *Guardian*, 24 November 2009.

page 5 *The pumps often broke down within months*: Borland, 'Radical plumbers and PlayPumps: objects in development', ch. 3.

page 6 *at $14,000 per unit*: UNICEF, 'An evaluation of the PlayPump water system', p. 13.

page 6 *PBS ran a documentary*: Costello, 'South Africa: troubled water'.

page 6 *'money down the drain'*: Chambers, 'Africa's not-so-magic roundabout'.

page 7 *'I got sent down to big projects that had failed'*: Private conversation with author, May 2014.

page 9 *it's illegal to market a drug*: Federal Food, Drug, and Cosmetic

Act, Regulatory information & legislation, U.S. Food and Drug Administration, section 505.

page 9 *Kremer tested the different ICS programs*: For a general overview, see Michael Kremer, 'Randomised evaluations of educational programs in developing countries: some lessons', *American Economic Review*, vol. 93, no. 2 (May 2003), pp. 102–6.

page 9 *he looked at the efficacy of providing schools with additional textbooks*: Paul Glewwe, Michael Kremer and Sylvie Moulin, 'Many children left behind? Textbooks and test scores in Kenya', *American Economic Journal: Applied Economics*, vol. 1, no. 1 (January 2009), pp. 112–35.

page 9 *Kremer looked at providing flipcharts*: Paul Glewwe, Michael Kremer, Sylvie Moulin and Eric Zitzewitz, 'Retrospective vs. prospective analyses of school inputs: the case of flip charts in Kenya', *Journal of Development Economics*, vol. 74, no. 1 (June 2004), pp. 251–68.

page 10 *he found no discernible improvement from decreasing class sizes*: Abhijit Banerjee and Michael Kremer, 'Teacher–student ratios and school performance in Udaipur, India: a prospective evaluation', mimeo, Brookings Institution, Washington, D.C., 2002.

page 10 *parasitic infections that affect more than a billion people worldwide*: 'More than 1.5 billion people, or 24% of the world's population are infected with soil-transmitted helminth infections worldwide' ('Soil-transmitted helminth infections', World Health Organization fact sheet no. 366, April 2014, www.who.int/mediacentre/factsheets/fs366/en/).

page 10 *'We didn't expect deworming'*: Private conversation with author, November 2014.

page 10 *deworming reduced it by 25%*: Edward Miguel and Michael Kremer, 'Worms: identifying impacts on education and health in the presence of treatment externalities', *Econometrica*, vol. 72, no. 1 (January 2004), pp. 159–217.

page 11 *Enabling a child to spend an extra day in school*: Ibid.

page 11 *Deworming decreases all these risks*: The extent of the health gains, however, is a matter of some controversy. For discussion, see GiveWell, 'Combination deworming (mass drug administration targeting both schistosomiasis and soil-transmitted helminths)', December 2014, www.givewell.org/international/technical/programs/deworming.

page 11 *compared to those who had been dewormed*: Sarah Baird, Joan Hamory Hicks and Edward Miguel, 'Worms at work: long-run impacts of child health gains', working paper, Harvard

University, 2012, http://scholar.harvard.edu/files/kremer/files/klps-labor_2012-03-23_clean.pdf.

page 11 *deworming was such a powerful program*: Michael Kremer, 'The origin and evolution of randomised evaluations in development', talk at J-PAL's tenth anniversary event, 7 December 2013, http://youtu.be/YGL6hPgpmDE.

page 12 *over 40 million deworming treatments*: 'Where we work', Evidence Action, Deworm the World Initiative, www.evidenceaction.org/dewormtheworld.

page 12 *an extreme example of a much more general trend*: David Anderson of the Coalition for Evidence-Based Policy comments that '1) the vast majority of social programs and services have not yet been rigorously evaluated, and 2) of those that have been rigorously evaluated, most (perhaps 75% or more), including those backed by expert opinion and less-rigorous studies, turn out to produce small or no effects, and, in some cases negative effects.' 'Guest Post: Proven programs are the exception, not the rule', GiveWell Blog, 18 December 2008, http://blog.givewell.org/2008/12/18/guest-post-proven-programs-are-the-exception-not-the-rule/.

page 14 *If it weren't for the independent investigations*: In fact, the feedback that the still-operating Roundabout Water Solutions gets from the schools they work with is very positive. The headmaster of one school says: 'I hereby use the opportunity to heartily thank you for the round-about which you donate to our school. You have enable us to get access to water for our learners as well as our community . . . Allow me to also say may the Good Lord bless you for services rendered by you. WATER IS LIFE!!!!!!!!!!'. Why is the feedback that they receive so positive, even though the PlayPump itself is of dubious value? A second letter provides a clue: 'We are so grateful for the clean running water. We used to drink with beasts in the river. We are children of a struggling school/government having abandoned her work of providing schools with basic services. We the learners of the aforesaid school can be very glad for any other project like painting our buildings and/or our grade R to grade 6 are still learning in mud structures, if we could get another sponsor, even if you could refer or recommend us to other sponsors in this regard.' That is, it would be in the interest of schools to provide extensive gratitude to Roundabout Water Solutions even if the PlayPump did no good at all. There's little cost to writing a thank-you letter, and if the recipient of PlayPumps do so, they might later receive other gifts that are more useful.

This just shows the sheer difficulty of ensuring that you're having an impact. Another example comes from Canadian Engineer Owen Scott, who wrote: 'Each time I've visited a PlayPump, I've always found the same scene: a group of women and children struggling to spin it by hand so they can draw water. I've never found anyone playing on it. But, as soon as the foreigner with a camera comes out (aka me), kids get excited. And when they get excited, they start playing. Within 5 minutes, the thing looks like a crazy success' ('The Playpump III – "The challenge of good inquiry"', Owen in Malawi blog, 3 November 2009, http://thoughtsfrommalawi.blogspot.co.uk/2009/11/play-pump-iii-challenge-of-taking-photos.html). That is, you'll get positive feedback from installing PlayPumps almost no matter how (in)effective it is.

page 14 *'deworming is probably the least sexy development program there is'*: Private conversation with author, June 2014.

page 16 *Along with Toby Ord*: Toby and I were both heavily influenced by the arguments for the moral importance of giving to fight poverty made by Peter Singer in 'Famine, affluence and morality', *Philosophy and Pubic Affairs*, vol. 1, no. 1 (Spring 1972), pp. 229–43 and *The Life You Can Save*, New York: Random House, 2009. On the basis of his arguments, we both made commitments to donate everything we earn above £20,000 per year – about £1 million each over our careers, or 50% of our lifetime earnings. Because we were putting so much of our own money on the line, the importance of spending that money as effectively as possible seemed imperative. Peter Singer has since become a powerful advocate for effective altruism: see *The Most Good You Can Do*, New Haven: Yale University Press, 2015.

page 16 *the number of hours you typically work in your life*: If you work forty hours per week, fifty weeks a year for forty years that's exactly 80,000 hours. For many careers, the real number of hours worked will be quite a bit more than that.

Chapter 1: You Are the 1%

page 19 *The term came from a popular statistic*: Dawn Turner Trice, 'How the 1 percent live, and give', *Chicago Tribune*, 29 December 2011; Social Security Administration, 'Measures of central tendency for wage data', www.ssa.gov/oact/cola/central.html. In an effort to avoid technical vocabulary whenever possible, throughout this book I use 'typical' to refer to 'median' and 'average' to refer to 'mean'.

page 19 *while typical household income:* Congressional Budget Office, 'Trends in the distribution of household income between 1979 and 2007', October 2011, www.cbo.gov/sites/default/files/10-25-HouseholdIncome_0.pdf.

page 19 *'probably higher than in any other society':* Thomas Piketty, *Capital in the Twenty-First Century,* Cambridge, Mass.: Harvard University Press, 2014, p. 265.

page 20 *Consider the graph of global income distribution:* The data on world income distribution is drawn from several sources. The figures for between the richest 1% and the richest 21% are based on micro data from national household surveys carried out in 2008, kindly provided by Branko Milanovic. The figures for the poorest 73% are based on the 2008 data from PovcalNet (http://iresearch. worldbank.org/PovcalNet/index.htm?1), adjusted based on the approximation that the surveys covered unbiased samples of the poorest 80% of the world's population. The figure of $70,000 for the top 0.1% is from Milanovic's *The Haves and the Have-Nots: A Brief and Idiosyncratic History of Global Inequality,* New York: Basic Books, 2011. All figures have been adjusted for the Consumer Price Index measure of inflation. To find out how rich you are, you can use the Giving What We Can Calculator at: www.givingwhatwecan.org/get-involved/how-rich-am-i.

page 20 *That spike goes off the chart:* According to Equilar, the data provider for the *New York Times,* the highest paid CEO in 2014 was Charif Souki, president of Cheniere Energy, who took home $141,949,280 ('2014 Equilar top 200 highest paid CEO rankings', www.equilar.com/nytimes/the-new-york-times-200-highest-paid-ceos). Assuming that the distance on the page between $0 and $100,000 is 2 inches (the next graph has the *y*-axis labelled), the spike would be 2,839 inches, or 237 feet. At ten feet per storey, that's over twenty-three storeys high. That's only looking at income, however. If we included changes in net wealth on this graph, the spike would be considerably longer again. In 2014, the person with the greatest gain in net wealth was Zhang Changhong, whose wealth increased by $982.5 million (*Forbes,* 'The world's billionaires', www.forbes.com/billionaires/list/#tab:overall; '#864 Zhang Changhong', Forbes, www.forbes.com/profile/zhang-changhong/; true as of 9 December 2014). If we put him on this graph, the spike would be 1,638 feet, a full 400 feet taller than the Empire State Building.

page 21 *the typical income for working individuals:* Social Security Administration, 'Measures of central tendency for wage data'.

page 23 *that's 1.22 billion people who earn less than $1.50 per day:* World Bank, 'Poverty overview', www.worldbank.org/en/topic/poverty/ overview. This figure is true as of 2010. The extreme poverty line is usually expressed as $1.25/day. However, that's $1.25/day in 2005 prices. In order to make the figure more easily understandable, I've updated the figure in line with inflation: $1.50 in 2014 prices is approximately the same as $1.25 in 2005 prices.

page 23 *they live on an amount of money equivalent to what $1.50 could buy in the US*: Martin Ravallion, Shaohua Chen and Prem Sangraula, 'Dollar a day revisited', policy research working paper 4620, World Bank, May 2008. Extreme poverty is generally understood as referring to earnings below $1.25 per day in 2005 prices, or equivalently, as earnings below $1 per day in 1996 prices.

page 23 *According to the way these figures are calculated*: United Nations, 'Millennium Development Goal Indicators', http://mdgs.un.org/ unsd/mdg/Metadata.aspx?IndicatorId=0&SeriesId=580.

page 23 *in poor countries in sub-Saharan Africa it is only fifty-six years*: 'Life expectancy at birth, total (years)', World Bank, http://data. worldbank.org/indicator/SP.DYN.LE00.IN/countries/LS-ZF-XN?display=graph&hootPostID=cc8d300b9308f8acab94418eff21 32ac.

page 24 *Professors Abhijit Banerjee and Esther Duflo*: Abhijit Banerjee and Esther Duflo 'The economic lives of the poor', *Journal of Economic Perspectives*, vol. 21, no. 1 (Winter 2007), pp. 141–67.

page 25 *we make ourselves $1 poorer*: I have used US dollars throughout the book for the sake of consistency: most of the figures I rely on are presented by the original authors in dollars; converting them to pounds using the exchange rate at the time of writing risks being misleading if the exchange rate subsequently changes.

page 25 *I'll just discuss one*: The reliability of this method is discussed in Alan B. Krueger and David A. Schkade, 'The reliability of subjective well-being measures', *Journal of Public Economics*, vol. 92, nos. 8–9 (August 2008), pp. 1833–45.

page 25 *Estimates via other methods*: For an overview of these methods, see Ben Groom and David Maddison, 'Non-identical quadruplets: four new estimates of the elasticity of marginal utility for the UK', working paper no. 141, Centre for Climate Change Economics and Policy, August 2013.

page 25 *Their results are given in Figure 3*: Betsey Stevenson and Justin Wolfers, 'Subjective well-being and income: is there any evidence of satiation?' *American Economic Review*, vol. 103, no. 3 (May 2013), pp. 598–604. In this graph, each line represents how levels of subjective wellbeing within a country change as income changes. For example a Brazilian earning $3,000 per year will on average report a score of 6.5 in life satisfaction, whereas a Brazilian earning $8,000 will on average report a score of 7. Note that the same income level is associated to different levels of reported life-satisfaction in different countries. Nonetheless, it remains true for all countries that, as incomes rise, so does life satisfaction. The graph is plotted on a logarithmic scale: each increment in the horizontal axis represents a doubling of income. The graph thus shows that it takes increasingly more income to attain a given increase in subjective wellbeing.

Subjective wellbeing is measured by asking subjects to rate how satisfied they are with their lives as a whole. Although this is one accepted measure of happiness, it is not the only one. An alternative way of measuring how happy people are, known as the experience sampling method, involves asking subjects to rate how well they are feeling at the present moment. See Reed Larson and Mihaly Csikszentmihalyi, 'The experience sampling method', *New Directions for Methodology of Social & Behavioral Science*, vol. 15 (March 1983), pp. 41–56. An advantage of the experience sampling method over reports of subjective wellbeing is that it does not ask subjects to recollect and aggregate past experience – tasks which humans are not very good at, see B. L. Fredrickson and Daniel Kahneman, 'Duration neglect in retrospective evaluations of affective episodes', *Journal of Personality and Social Psychology*, vol. 65, no. 1 (July 1993), pp. 45–55. Using this method, it's been found that, once household income passes $75,000 – which equals a personal income of $30,000 – additional income makes people no happier. This method would therefore considerably strengthen my conclusion: for many people, giving up additional money incurs no loss of happiness at all.

page 28 *The 100x Multiplier*: One point to clarify: The 100x Multiplier refers to the discrepancy in the benefit of $1 to you as a member of an affluent country versus the benefit of $1 to someone in extreme poverty. That doesn't yet entail, however, that we should prefer to give $1 to someone in extreme poverty rather than $99 to the typical US citizen. This is because increases in income have effects on the wider economy. If I give $99 to Jo Bloggs in the US, doing so benefits her, but it also benefits others, too, such as the people that Jo Bloggs buys goods from using that $99 (and these others may live in other, much poorer, countries). The same is true of the $1 given to the person in extreme poverty. But, importantly, nothing I've said so far shows that the ratio of the benefits from those wider effects are also 100:1. That's why we can't yet conclude that it does 100x as much good in general to give $1 to the extreme poor than to give $1 to someone in an affluent country. We can just conclude that, when thinking about me versus the person in extreme poverty (considered in isolation from the rest of the world), giving the extremely poor person $1 provides 100x as large a benefit as giving me $1.

page 28 *For those of us living in rich countries*: Note that the figure of one hundred is a baseline. I believe that if we try hard, we should be able to do even more good for even less personal cost. This is for two reasons. First, we've only looked at one problem: global poverty. As discussed in Chapter 10, there may be even better opportunities for helping others, in which case The 100x Multiplier is an underestimate. Second, while I just described giving in terms of choosing between a benefit to yourself or others, that's not a good way of thinking about it because giving benefits the giver as well as the receiver. If anything, my life has become happier since I've started donating some of my income. That's the upside of the 'warm glow' effect. Indeed, academic studies suggest I'm not alone. In one case, experimental subjects ended up more satisfied when they were given money and told to use that money to benefit others than when they were told to use that money to benefit themselves. (See Elizabeth Dunn, Lara Aknin and Michael Norton, 'Spending money on others promotes happiness', *Science*, vol. 319, no. 5870 (21 March 2008), pp. 1687–8.) So in fact we should expect that, if we focus on the most effective activities, the benefits to others will be greater and the costs to ourselves will be less than The 100x Multiplier would suggest. (For an overview, see Andreas Mogensen, 'Giving without sacrifice? The relationship between income, happiness, and giving', www. givingwhatwecan.org/sites/givingwhatwecan.org/files/attachments/giving-without-sacrifice.pdf)

page 29 *In a mere 200 years*: Louis Johnston and Samuel H. Williamson, 'What was the U.S. GDP then?' MeasuringWorth, 2014, www. measuringworth.com/.

page 29 *the graph of gross domestic product per person*: Angus Maddison, 'Statistics on world population, GDP and per capita GDP, 1–2008 AD', University of Groningen. www.ggdc.net/maddison/content. shtml.

page 29 *For almost all of human history*: See also Angus Maddison's *Contours of the World Economy 1–2030 AD*, Oxford University Press, 2007.

page 30 *transform the lives of thousands of people*: For further discussion of global inequality and economic progress over time, see Milanovic, *The Haves and the Have-Nots*, and Gregory Clark, *A Farewell to Alms: A Brief Economic History of the World*, Princeton: Princeton University Press, 2007.

Chapter 2: Hard Trade-offs

page 33 *The problems in Rwanda had begun to build up decades earlier*: For a summary of the main events of the Rwandan genocide, see Jonathan Glover, *Humanity: A Moral History of the Twentieth Century*, New Haven: Yale University Press, 1995, ch. 14. A comprehensive discussion may be found in Gérard Prunier, *The Rwanda Crisis: History of a Genocide*, New York: Columbia University Press, 1995.

page 34 *'There were so many, and they kept coming'*: James Orbinski, *An Imperfect Offering: Humanitarian Action for the Twenty-First Century*, New York: Walker, 2008, p. 226.

page 37 *how many people benefit . . .* : Is this just utilitarianism? No. Utilitarianism is the view, roughly speaking, that one is always required to do whatever will maximise the sum total of wellbeing, no matter what. The similarity between effective altruism and utilitarianism is that they both focus on improving people's lives: but this is a part of any reasonable moral view. In other respects, effective altruism can depart significantly from utilitarianism. Effective altruism doesn't claim that you are morally required to do as much good as you can, only that you should use at least a significant proportion of your time or money to help others. Effective altruism doesn't say that you may violate people's rights for the greater good. Effective altruism can recognise sources of value other than happiness, like freedom and equality. In general, effective altruism is a much broader and ecumenical philosophy than utilitarianism.

page 38 *the '$50 for five books' figure is accurate:* Charities' claims about what your donation will buy are often highly misleading, representing a 'best case' figure, or a figure that doesn't take into account 'hidden' costs. I talk about this more in Chapter 7. Moreover, even if it does cost $50 to buy and provide five books, it's not really true that if you donate $50 you will cause five additional books to be bought. United Way of New York City spends its money on a wide variety of programmes, spending $55 million in total in 2013. Your $50 will be added to its total income and in effect will be distributed across all its programme areas. For the purpose of this discussion, however, I assume that an additional $50 donated to United Way of New York City will provide an extra five books.

page 39 *he should opt to perform the simpler surgeries*: Some philosophers have argued that, in cases of this sort, we should decide by tossing a coin, or by using a lottery that gives more weight to the greater number. See, for example, John Taurek, 'Should the numbers count?', *Philosophy and Public Affairs*, vol. 6, no. 4 (Summer 1977), pp. 293–316, and F. M. Kamm, *Morality, Mortality*, volume I: *Death and Whom to Save from It*, Oxford University Press, 1993. I am not persuaded by these arguments. If we think that all people matter equally, we should save more people rather than few. As the Oxford philosopher Derek Parfit writes: 'Why do we save the larger number? Because we *do* give equal weight to saving each. Each counts for one. That is why more count for more' ('Innumerate Ethics', *Philosophy and Public Affairs*, vol. 7, no. 4 (Summer 1978), p. 301.)

page 39 *For health benefits*: In this discussion I've left out the most common metric used by economists to measure harms and benefits, which is called *willingness to pay*. According to this metric, the size of a benefit of something to a person is measured by how much that person is willing to pay for it. If Jones is willing to pay $1 for an apple, but Smith is willing to pay $10 for an apple, then, if we used this metric, we would conclude that giving Smith an apple provides ten times as great a benefit as providing Jones with an apple. The reason I don't rely on this metric is that it treats an additional dollar as being of equal worth no matter who has it. But this is clearly wrong. If Smith is a multimillionaire, whereas Jones is poor, then $1 will be much less valuable to Smith than $1 is to Jones. This problem becomes particularly severe if we try to compare activities that benefit people in rich countries with activities that benefit people in poor countries. For example, Americans are on average willing to pay fifteen times as much as Bangladeshis to reduce their risk of dying by 1% (John Broome, *Weighing Lives*, Oxford University Press, 2004, p. 263). If we used the willingness-to-pay metric, we'd have to conclude that American lives are worth fifteen times as much as Bangladeshi lives. But that's clearly wrong. The real reason Americans are willing to pay much more to avoid risks of death than Bangladeshis is simply that they have much more money that they can spend.

page 40 *on average people rate a life with untreated AIDS*: 'Global burden of disease 2004 update: disability weights for diseases and conditions', World Health Organization, www.who.int/healthinfo/global_burden_disease/GBD2004_DisabilityWeights.pdf.

page 42 *official lists of quality-of-life estimates:* Estimates are provided in Joshua A. Salomon et al., 'Common values in assessing health outcomes from disease and injury: disability weights measurement study for the Global Burden of Disease Study 2010', *Lancet*, vol. 380 (2012), table 2; available at www.jefftk.com/gbdweights2010.pdf; the 2004 estimates (created using a slightly different methodology) are available at www.who.int/healthinfo/global_burden_disease/GBD2004_DisabilityWeights.pdf.

In both articles, the authors talk about disability-adjusted life-years, or 'DALYs': very approximately, one DALY is just the negative of one QALY. (So it's good to gain QALYs and bad to gain DALYs.) QALYs tend to be used in domestic settings, whereas DALYs are used in global health.

Note that the disability weight estimates should be taken as exactly that: estimates, which may be too high or too low in a given context. For that reason, we shouldn't slavishly follow explicit estimates of cost per QALY that rely on these numbers; instead we should think of them as one important tool in our attempt to do the most good.

page 43 *quality of life with AIDS*: In this example I use the disability weights from the 2004 WHO Global Burden of Disease, available at www.who.int/healthinfo/global_burden_disease/GBD2004_DisabilityWeights.pdf

page 44 *academics continue to debate*: An overview of the QALY, and issues in defining it and measuring how bad different conditions are, is given in Milton C. Weinstein, George Torrance and Alistair McGuire, 'QALYs: the basics', *Value in Health*, vol. 12, sup. s1 (March–April 2009), pp. S5–S9. Note that these problems should not cause us to reject entirely the attempt to think in terms of quantitative harms and benefits. David Spiegelhalter, Winton Professor of The Public Understanding of Risk at the University of Cambridge, puts the point nicely: 'Of course the QALY approach is not perfect, but some mechanism is needed to provide consistent comparisons across different medical interventions, based on aggregate benefit and cost. Otherwise the money could go to those with the most appealing emotional argument' ('Experts dismiss claims NHS drug decisions are "flawed"', National Institute for Health and Care Excellence, 25 January 2013, https://www.nice.org.uk/news/article/experts-dismiss-claims-nhs-drug-decisions-are-flawed).

page 45 *We could use these methods*: This has been suggested by both philosophers and economists: see, for example, Broome, *Weighing Lives*, p. 261.

page 45 *$50,000 to train and provide*: See www.guidedogsofamerica.
org/1/mission/#cost.

page 46 *a critical piece on effective altruism*: Ken Berger and Robert
M. Penna, 'The elitist philanthropy of so-called effective altruism',
Stanford Social Innovation Review blog, 2013, www.ssireview.org/blog/
entry/the_elitist_philanthropy_of_so_called_effective_altruism.

page 46 *As they clarified in correspondence*: Personal communication,
November 2013.

page 47 *came across the Fistula Foundation*: More information about
the Fistula Foundation and about obstetric fistula can be found at
www.fistulafoundation.org.

Chapter 3: How You Can Save Hundreds of Lives

page 51 *'aid is malignant'*: Dambisa Moyo, *Dead Aid: Why Aid Is Not
Working and How There Is a Better Way for Africa*, New York: Farrar,
Straus and Giroux, 2009, p. 47.

page 51 *The White Man's Burden*: William Easterly, *The White Man's
Burden: Why the West's Efforts to Aid the Rest Have Done so Much
Ill and so Little Good*, New York: Penguin, 2006; quote from p. 4.

page 52 *The total annual economic output of the world is $87 trillion*:
World GDP for 2013 was $87.25 trillion in terms of purchasing
power parity, and $74.31 trillion in nominal terms. Central
Intelligence Agency, *The CIA World Factbook 2014*, https://www.
cia.gov/library/publications/the-world-factbook/geos/xx.html

page 53 *the US spends about $800 billion on social security*: Congressional
Budget Office, 'Monthly budget review – summary for fiscal
year 2013', 7 November 2013, https://www.cbo.gov/sites/default/
files/44716-%20MBR_FY2013_0.pdf

page 53 *a decade of sales of cosmetics amounts to $1.7 trillion*: Perry
Romanowsky, 'A cosmetic industry overview for cosmetic chem-
ists', *Cosmetics Corner*, 14 April 2014, http://chemistscorner.
com/a-cosmetic-market-overview-for-cosmetic-chemists/.

page 53 *the US military had simply lost track of $2.3 trillion*: Aleen
Sirgany, *The War on Waste*, CBS, 29 January 2002.

page 53 *the average population of sub-Saharan Africa in that time*:
The total population of Sub-Saharan Africa was 177 million in
1950, and 815 million in 2010. (Dominique Tabutin and Bruno
Schoumaker, 'The demography of Sub-Saharan Africa from the
1950s to the 2000s [A survey of changes and a statistical assess-
ment]', *Population*, vol. 59, nos. 3–4 (2004), p. 525.) Assuming a
constant growth rate during that period, we sum the estimated
population for every year in this period and take the mean.

page 53 *Now it's 56 years*: Ibid., p. 538; The World Bank, 'Sub-Saharan Africa', http://data.worldbank.org/region/sub-saharan-africa.

page 54 *the eradication of smallpox*: For details, see David Koplow, *Smallpox: The Fight to Eradicate a Global Scourge*, Berkeley: University of California Press, 2003, and D. A. Henderson, *Smallpox: The Death of a Disease – the Inside Story of Eradicating a Worldwide Killer*, New York: Prometheus Books, 2009.

page 54 *smallpox killed 1.5 to 3 million people every year*: Koplow, *Smallpox*, p. 1; Henderson, *Smallpox*, p. 13.

page 55 *The eradication of smallpox is one success story from aid*: I owe this argument for the cost-effectiveness of aid on average to Toby Ord.

page 55 *The total aid spending of all countries*: Easterly, *The White Man's Burden*, p. 4.

page 55 *if doing so costs less than about $7 million per life saved*: Binyamin Appelbaum, 'As U.S. agencies put more value on a life, businesses fret', *New York Times*, 17 February 2011, p. A1.

page 55 *it still would have prevented a death*: The diehard aid critic might suggest that non-health aid hasn't just been *ineffective*, but that it's been downright *harmful*. However, if so we need to ask just how harmful it's been. Even just given the example of smallpox, in order for foreign aid to have been net harmful, the costs must have exceeded 122 million lives lost – which, as we noted, is greater than that of all war. No respectable development economist would suggest that foreign aid has been this harmful. For example, Professor Adrian Wood at Oxford University's Department for International Development comments that: 'The one thing we can be clear about is the evidence that almost certainly aid does not reduce growth' (Select Committee of Economic Affairs, House of Lords, *The Economic Impact and Effectiveness of Development Aid: 6th Report of Session 2010–12*, London: Stationery Office, 2012, p. 23, n. 45).

Moreover, studies published since Moyo and Easterly's books indicate a positive relationship between aid and economic growth; see Arndt Channing, Sam Jones and Finn Tarp, 'Aid, growth, and development: have we come full circle?', *Journal of Globalization and Development*, vol. 1, no. 2 (December 2010), pp. 1–29, and Camelia Minoiu and Sanjay G. Reddy, 'Development aid and economic growth: a positive long-run relation', *Quarterly Review of Economics and Finance*, vol. 50, no. 1 (2010), pp. 27–39. This is so even though, given the small size of aid flows to poor countries, one would not expect a detectable impact on economic growth. As Owen Barder of the Centre for Global Development comments: 'Given the modest volumes of aid, we should not expect an impact on growth which is bright enough to shine through the statistical fog' (Select Committee of Economic Affairs, *The Economic Impact and Effectiveness of Development Aid*, p. 23, n. 42).

page 55 *This calculation not only shows*: Critics may question whether the smallpox campaign was a form of overseas development aid, understood as the flow of funds from donor to recipient nations. But note that smallpox is usually included as a success story in studies about the effectiveness of aid, even those written by aid sceptics. See, e.g., Roger Riddell, *Does Foreign Aid Really Work?*, Oxford University Press, 2007, p. 184. More to the point, the WHO Smallpox Eradication Unit was partially funded by official aid funds: international donors supplied one-third of the funding for the programme. And it appears that these contributions played a key role in its success, which would probably not have occurred without international funding (Ruth Levine, *Case Studies in Global Health: Millions Saved*, Sudbury, Mass.: Jones and Bartlett, 2007, pp. 1–8). But even if we credit foreign aid with only one-third of the benefits that resulted from the smallpox eradication programme, that would still leave us with at least a life saved per $225,000 spent in aid, which is still very good value for money.

page 56 *'There are well known and striking donor success stories'*: William Easterly, 'Can the West save Africa?', *Journal of Economic Literature*, vol. 47, no. 2 (June 2009), pp. 406–7.

page 56 *'even those of us labeled as "aid critics"'*: William Easterly, 'Some cite good news on aid', Aid Watch, 18 February 2009, http://aidwatchers.com/2009/02/some-cite-good-news-on-aid/.

page 59 *most people live in a small number of cities*: For this and the other examples mentioned, see Mark Newman, 'Power laws, Pareto distributions and Zipf's law', *Contemporary Physics*, vol. 46, no. 5 (2005), pp. 323–51.

page 59 *The effectiveness of different aid activities forms a fat-tailed distribution*: Ramanan Laxminarayan, Jeffrey Chow and Sonbol A. Shahid-Salles, 'Intervention cost-effectiveness: overview of main messages', in Dean Jamison et al. (eds.), *Disease Control Priorities in Developing Countries*, 2nd edn, Oxford University Press, 2006, pp. 41–2.

page 59 *First, developing-world education*: Abdul Latif Jameel Poverty Action Lab, 'Student participation', www.povertyactionlab.org/policy-lessons/education/student-participation.

page 61 *the estimated cost-effectiveness of different health programs*: Jamison et al. (eds.), *Disease Control Priorities in Developing*

Countries., p. 62 (for Kaposi's sarcoma); Omar Galárraga, M. Arantxa Colchero, Richard G. Wamai and Stefano M. Bertozzi, 'HIV prevention cost-effectiveness', *BMC Public Health*, vol. 9, sup. 1 (2009), pp. S1–S5 (for condom promotion and antiretroviral therapy); GiveWell, 'GiveWell estimate of AMF cost per net', November 2014, www.givewell.org/files/DWDA%20 2009/Interventions/Nets/GiveWell%20cost-effectiveness%20 analysis%20of%20LLIN%20distribution%202014.xls (for distribution of bed nets). To be conservative, I've rounded down GiveWell's estimate of QALYs per $1,000 provided by bed net distribution through donations to the Against Malaria Foundation (they give six estimates of the cost per QALY, the harmonic mean of which is $68.90). Their estimate is also only an estimate of the QALYs/$ as a result of prevention of death of under-fives. It doesn't take into account prevention of death of children over five, or prevention of illness. GiveWell are keen to emphasise, however, that these are only estimates. The real number may be higher or lower than their model suggests.

page 62 *costing less than the governments of the US or the UK are willing to spend to provide one QALY*: Laxminarayan, Chow and Shahid-Salles, 'Intervention cost-effectiveness', p. 62.

page 63 *According to the most rigorous estimates*: 'Against Malaria Foundation', GiveWell.

Chapter 4: Why You Shouldn't Donate to Disaster Relief

page 65 *'I want to study medicine'*: Private conversation with author, April 2014.

page 65 *According to one study*: Oliver Robinson, 'Planning for a fairer future', *Guardian*, 14 July 2006.

page 66 *jobs that make a difference*: '5 more do-good jobs you've never considered', *Oprah*, 19 April 19 2012, www.oprah.com/money/ Jobs-That-Make-a-Difference-in-the-World.

page 67 *Which is more valuable: water or diamonds?*: The apparent difficulty in answering this question is known as the 'paradox of value'. It was discussed by Nicolaus Copernicus and John Locke, among others, but the most influential presentation appears in a passage of Adam Smith's *Wealth of Nations*:

> The things which have the greatest value in use have frequently little or no value in exchange; and, on the contrary, those which have the greatest value in exchange have frequently little or no value in use. Nothing is more useful than water: but it will purchase scarce anything; scarce anything can be had in

exchange for it. A diamond, on the contrary, has scarce any value in use; but a very great quantity of other goods may frequently be had in exchange for it. (book I, ch. 4)

page 67 *why the cost of a gallon of water from the tap in New York City*: 'Residential water use', New York City Department of Environmental Protection, www.nyc.gov/html/dep/html/residents/wateruse.shtml.

page 67 *they are therefore scarce in the way that water isn't*: Diamonds aren't, in fact, as rare you might think. They are so expensive because for most of the twentieth century the supply of them has been artificially restricted by the De Beers monopoly, in order to keep prices high. For more information, see Eric Goldschein, 'The incredible story of how De Beers created and lost the most powerful monopoly ever', *Business Insider*, 19 December 2011, www.businessinsider.com/history-of-de-beers-2011-12?op=1&IR=T.

page 69 *the Tōhoku region of Japan was hit*: R. A. Hindmarsh, *Nuclear Disaster at Fukushima Daiichi: Social, Political and Environmental Issues*, New York: Routledge, 2013; Kevin Voigt, 'Quake moved Japan coast 8 feet, shifted Earth's axis', CNN, 20 April 2011.

page 69 *an earthquake hit Haiti*: Clarens Renois, 'Haitians angry over slow aid', *The Age*, 5 February 2010; 'Haiti quake death toll rises to 230,000', BBC News, 11 February 2010.

page 70 *the total international aid raised*: Report of the United Nations in Haiti 2011, Chapter 7, www.onu-haiti.org/Report2011/Chapter7.html; 'Disaster donations top ¥520 billion', *Japan Times*, 8 March 2012, p. 1. In the ensuing years Haiti received continued aid support, such that the total pledged to Haiti increased to $13.3 billion (Office of the Special Envoy to Haiti, 'International assistance to Haiti key facts as of December 2012', www.lessonsfromhaiti.org/download/International_Assistance/1-overall-key-facts.pdf).

page 70 *'The Japanese Red Cross Society'*: 'Japan and Pacific: earthquake and tsunami', International Federation of Red Cross and Red Crescent Societies, information bulletin no. 2, 12 March 2011, p. 1.

page 71 *it raised only $500 million in international aid*: The various sources of international aid are listed in Wikipedia at 'Reactions to the 2008 Sichuan earthquake', https://en.wikipedia.org/wiki/Reactions_to_the_2008_Sichuan_earthquake.

page 71 *For every death the Japanese earthquake caused*: As mentioned in the text, $5 billion was raised for the Japanese earthquake, which caused 15,000 deaths. $5 billion ÷ 15,000 ≈ $330,000.

page 71 *for every person that dies from poverty-related causes worldwide*:

According to the OECD, globally $135 billion was spent on foreign aid in 2013 (Claire Provost, 'Foreign aid reaches record high', *Guardian*, 8 April 2014). US private philanthropy is $37.3 billion (Carol Adelman, Jeremiah Norris, and Kacie Marano, *The Index of Global Philanthropy and Remittances: 2010*, Washington, D.C.: Hudson Institute, 2010, p. 12), Non-US private philanthropy is $15.3 billion (ibid., p. 41). This brings total overseas aid and philanthropy to approximately $188 billion per year. A rough conservative estimate of 12.7 million poverty-related deaths can readily be determined, giving $15,000 of overseas aid and philanthropy per poverty-related death. The statistics used in this calculation (with corresponding number of deaths in parentheses) are deaths from: malnutrition (3.1 million); lower respiratory infections (3.1 million); tuberculosis (1.5 million); HIV/AIDS (1.5 million); diarrheal diseases (1.5 million); preterm birth complications (1.1 million); malaria (600,000); maternal conditions (280,000). See World Health Organization, fact sheets nos. 94, 104, 310, 330, 348 360, 2014 and World Food Program, 'Hunger statistics', 2014, www.wfp.org/hunger/stats.

page 71 *'Emergency health interventions'*: Claude de Ville de Goyet, Ricardo Zapata Marti and Claudio Osorio, 'Natural disaster mitigation and relief', in Dean T. Jamison et al., *Disease Control Priorities in Developing Countries*, 2nd edn, Washington, D.C., World Bank, 2006, ch. 61, p. 1153.

page 72 *Not only is $50,000 enough*: Matthew J. Burton and David C. W. Mabey, 'The global burden of trachoma: a review', *PLoS Neglected Tropical Diseases*, vol. 3, no. 10 (27 October 2009), e460. The authors give estimates of cost per surgery ranging from $6.13 to $41; to be conservative, I've rounded this up to $100. Even still, we should bear in mind that both the cost for a guide dog and the cost for a trachoma surgery are only estimates, and that the estimates for cost-effectiveness of a given programme in published articles or on charity websites may be more optimistic than the real cost-effectiveness of programmes when actually implemented. Correcting for this won't, however, change the central point.

page 73 *$217 billion per year is spent on cancer treatment*: 'Breakaway: the global burden of cancer – challenges and opportunities', Economist Intelligence Unit, 2009, p. 25, http://graphics.eiu.com/upload/eb/EIU_LIVESTRONG_Global_Cancer_Burden.pdf. This figure does not include costs due to loss of productivity, which amount to $69 billion per year.

page 73 *Malaria is responsible for 3.3% of QALYs lost worldwide*: These figures come from the Global Burden of Disease website, http://

vizhub.healthdata.org/gbd-compare/. The Global Burden of Disease measures the health cost of different illnesses in 'DALYs': very approximately, these are the same as QALYs, but where 1 QALY = –1 DALY. So it's a good thing to gain QALYS; it's a bad thing to gain DALYs.

page 73 *It was eliminated from the US in 1951*: Margaret Humphreys, *Malaria: Poverty, Race, and Public Health in the United States*, Baltimore: Johns Hopkins University Press, 2001, ch. 7.

page 74 *any program that provides one QALY for less than $50,000*: Milton C. Weinstein, 'How much are Americans willing to pay for a quality-adjusted life year?', *Medical Care*, vol. 46, no. 4, (April 2008), pp. 343–5; Scott D. Grosse, 'Assessing cost-effectiveness in healthcare: history of the $50,000 per QALY threshold', *Pharmacoeconomics & Outcomes Research*, vol. 8, no. 2 (April 2008), pp. 165–78; Chris P. Lee, Glenn M. Chertow and Stefanos A. Zenios, 'An empiric estimate of the value of life: updating the renal dialysis cost-effectiveness standard', *Value in Health*, vol. 12, no. 1 (2009), pp. 80–7.

page 74 *providing the same benefit in poor countries*: 'Combination deworming (mass drug administration targeting both schistosomiasis and soil-transmitted helminths)', GiveWell, December 2013.

page 75 *This is what Greg did initially*: Gregory Lewis, 'How much good does a doctor do?', unpublished paper.

page 75 *878,194 doctors in the US*: Aaron Young, Humayun J. Chaudhry, Jon V. Thomas and Michael Dugan, 'A census of actively licensed physicians in the United States, 2012', *Journal of Medical Regulation*, vol. 99, no. 2 (2013), pp. 11–24.

page 75 *work by an epidemiologist named John Bunker*: John Bunker, 'The role of medical care in contributing to health improvements within societies', *International Journal of Epidemiology*, vol. 30, no. 6 (December 2001), pp. 1260–3.

Chapter 5: The Best Person Who Ever Lived is an Unknown Ukrainian Man

page 80 *'The 75 Best People in the World'*: 'The 75 best people in the world', *Esquire*, January 2012.

page 80 *Ohio-born doctor D. A. Henderson*: For background, see D. A. Henderson and Petra Klepac, 'Lessons from the eradication of smallpox: an interview with D. A. Henderson', *Philosophical Transactions of the Royal Society B*, vol. 368, no. 1623 (5 August 2013).

page 82 *Viktor Zhdanov, a Ukrainian virologist*: For biographical details about Zhdanov, see Alice Bukrinskaya, 'In memory of

Victor Zhdanov', *Archives of Virology*, vol. 121, no. 1/4 (1991), pp 237–40.

page 82 *'I avail myself of this occasion'*: Cited in Frank Fenner, 'Development of the global smallpox eradication programme', in *Smallpox and Its Eradication*, Geneva: World Health Organization, 1988, pp. 366–418.

page 84 *the paramedic would have been able to do the same thing*: Unlike in TV shows, in the real world paramedics are almost never able to restart someone's heart using defibrillation. However, for the purposes of the thought experiment let's assume that the defibrillation was certain to work.

Page 85 *an episode of* Beyond Scared Straight: 'Oakland County, Michigan', *Beyond Scared Straight*, Season 2, Episode 2, A&E, 2011.

page 87 *Nine high-quality studies*: Anthony Petrosino, Carolyn Turpin-Petrosino, Meghan E. Hollis-Peel and Julia G. Lavenberg, 'Scared Straight and other juvenile awareness programs for preventing juvenile delinquency: a systematic review', *Campbell Systematic Reviews*, vol. 9, no. 5 (2013).

page 87 *'The analyses show'*: Ibid., p. 7.

page 87 *In a separate study*: Steve Aos, Roxanne Lieb, Jim Mayfield, Marna Miller and Annie Pennucci, 'Benefits and costs of prevention and early intervention programs for youth', Washington State Institute for Public Policy, 17 September 2004, www.wsipp.wa.gov/ReportFile/881/Wsipp_Benefits-and-Costs-of-Prevention-and-Early-Intervention-Programs-for-Youth_Summary-Report.pdf.

page 88 *only one third of kids*: Petrosino, Turpin-Petrosino, Hollis-Peel and Lavenberg, 'Scared Straight and other juvenile awareness programs for preventing juvenile delinquency', p. 31.

page 88 *I suspect the apparent effectiveness of Scared Straight*: Another part of the explanation may be that juveniles are simply less likely to offend as they get older; this effect is well documented. See Thomas P. Locke, Glenn M. Johnson, Kathryn Kirigin-Ramp, Jay D. Atwater and Meg Gerrard, 'An evaluation of a juvenile education program in a state penitentiary', *Evaluation Review*, vol. 10 no. 3 (June 1986), p. 282.

page 89 *one hypothesis is that the inmates*: Thomas Dishion, Joan McCord and François Poulin, 'When interventions harm. Peer groups and problem behavior', *American Psychologist*, vol. 54, no. 9 (September 1999), pp. 755–64.

page 92 *The average salary of a doctor in the UK*: 'Annual survey of hours and earnings, 2013: provisional results', Office of National Statistics, www.ons.gov.uk/ons/publications/re-reference-tables.html?edition=

tcm%3A77-328216. Average salaries are considerable higher in the US, at about $250,000 per year. See 'Occupational outlook handbook: physicians and surgeons', Bureau of Labor Statistics, www.bls.gov/ooh/healthcare/physicians-and-surgeons.htm#tab-5.

page 93 *By pursuing a particularly lucrative speciality*: For discussion, see Ryan Carey, 'Increasing your earnings as a doctor', 80,000 Hours blog, 17 July 2014, https://80000hours.org/2014/06/increasing-your-earnings-as-a-doctor/#fn:3.

page 94 *the average is about 2%*: 'Charitable giving in America: some facts and figures', National Center for Charitable Statistics, http://nccs.urban.org/nccs/statistics/Charitable-Giving-in-America-Some-Facts-and-Figures.cfm.

Chapter 6: Why Voting Is Like Donating Thousands of Dollars to Charity

page 96 *'The possibility of a severe accident occurring'*: Phred Dvorak and Peter Landers, 'Japanese plant had barebones risk plan', *Wall Street Journal*, 31 March 2011.

page 97 *'the root cause of the Fukushima crisis'*: Mari Yamaguchi, 'Gov't panel: nuke plant operator still stumbling', Associated Press, 23 July 2012.

page 100 *one ecstasy session*: Advisory Council on the Misuse of Drugs, *MDMA ('Ecstasy'): A Review of Its Harms and Classification Under the Misuse of Drugs Act 1971*, London: Home Office, 2009.

page 100 *going scuba diving*: Richard D. Vann and Michael A. Lang (eds.), *Recreational Diving Fatalities Workshops Proceedings, 8–10 April 2010*, Durham, N.C.: Divers Alert Network, 2011, www.diversalertnetwork.org/files/Fatalities_Proceedings.pdf.

page 100 *going skydiving*: 'Skydiving safety', United States Parachute Association, www.uspa.org/AboutSkydiving/SkydivingSafety/tabid/526/Default.aspx.

page 100 *Flying in a space shuttle*: Out of 833 crewmembers on space shuttle flights (with some flying multiple times), fourteen people have died (Tariq Malik, 'NASA's space shuttle by the numbers: 30 years of a spaceflight icon', Space.com, 21 July 2011, www.space.com/12376-nasa-space-shuttle-program-facts-statistics.html)

page 100 *climb Mount Everest beyond base camp*: P. G. Firth et al., 'Mortality on Mount Everest, 1921–2006: descriptive study', *British Medical Journal*, vol. 337 (December 2008), p. 1430.

page 100 *The same concept*: Richard Wilson, 'Analyzing the daily risks of life', *Technology Review*, vol. 81, no. 4 (February 1979), p. 45.

page 101 *Whereas an hour on a train*: Many of these facts also appear in the excellent book *The Norm Chronicles*, by David Spiegelhalter and Michael Blastland, New York: Basic Books, 2014.

page 102 *Psychologists have found*: See George F. Loewenstein, Eike U. Weber, Christopher K. Hsee and Ned Welch, 'Risk as feelings', *Psychological Bulletin*, vol. 127, no. 2 (March 2001), pp. 267–86.

page 103 *'Nobody in their right mind'*: 'Your FREAK-quently asked questions, answered', Freakonomics blog, 20 January 2011, http://freakonomics.com/2011/01/20/freakonomics-radio-your-freak-quently-asked-questions-answered/.

page 104 *the odds of an individual vote swaying the outcome of the 2008 Presidential election*: Andrew Gelman, Nate Silver and Aaron Edlin, 'What is the probability your vote will make a difference?', *Economic Inquiry*, vol. 50, no. 2 (April 2012), pp. 321–6. The authors reached this estimate by using election forecasts to calculate the probability that (1) a given state is necessary for an electoral college to win and that (2) the election for that state is exactly tied – the two quantities that jointly determine whether a single vote is decisive in a US presidential election.

page 104 *Although this $1,000 per citizen figure is hypothetical*: This is also the hypothetical figure used in Aaron S. Edlin, Andrew Gelman and Noah Kaplan, 'Vote for charity's sake', *Economists' Voice*, vol. 5, no. 6 (October 2008), pp. 1–4.

page 108 *economists estimate*: F. Bailey Norwood and Jayson Lusk, *Compassion, by the Pound: The Economics of Farm Animal Welfare*, New York: Oxford University Press, 2011, p. 223.

page 108 *Professors of political science at Harvard and Stockholm University*: Andreas Madestam, Daniel Shoag, Stan Veuger and David Yanagizawa-Drott, 'Do political protests matter? Evidence from the Tea Party Movement', *Quarterly Journal of Economics*, vol. 128, no. 4 (2013), pp. 1633–85.

page 109 *'I expect to fail'*: Private conversation with Laura Brown, July 2014.

page 109 *work by my organisation 80,000 Hours*: Carl Shulman, 'How hard is it to become prime minister of the United Kingdom?', 80,000 Hours blog, 17 February 2012, https://80000hours.org/2012/02/how-hard-is-it-to-become-prime-minister-of-the-united-kingdom/.

page 110 *At 80,000 Hours we did*: Paul Christiano, 'An estimate of the expected influence of becoming a politician', 80,000 Hours blog, 12 February 2014, https://80000hours.org/2014/02/an-estimate-of-the-expected-influence-of-becoming-a-politician/.

page 112 *£732 billion*: 'Total Managed Expenditure is expected to be around £732 billion in 2014–15', Budget 2014, page 5, https://www.gov.uk/government/uploads/system/uploads/attachment_data/file/293759/37630_Budget_2014_Web_Accessible.pdf

page 112 *influence by a half*: Our belief that these assumptions are conservative is based on surveys of the British politics literature and discussions with Westminster sources. Qualitative discussions of the roles of different aspects of the political system (such as Parliament, civil service, and international bodies) determining policy, on which these estimates are partially based, can be found in: Dennis Kavanagh, David Richards, Andrew Geddes and Martin Smith, *British Politics: Continuities and Change*, 5th edn, Oxford University Press, 2006; Martin Smith, *The Core Executive in Britain*, Basingstoke: Palgrave Macmillan, 1999; Gillian Peele, *Governing the UK: British Politics in the Twenty-First Century*, 4th edn, Malden, Mass./Oxford: Wiley/Blackwell, 2004.

page 114 *in part on the basis*: As will be seen in Chapter 9, considerations such as 'personal fit' are also very important when considering choice of a career.

page 116 *'It is extremely likely that human influence'*: IPCC, 'Summary for policymakers', in *Climate Change 2014: Impacts, Adaptation, and Vulnerability*, Cambridge University Press, 2014, p. 3.

page 116 *'97.1% endorsed the consensus position that humans are causing global warming'*: John Cook et al., 'Quantifying the consensus on anthropogenic global warming in the scientific literature', *Environmental Research Letters*, vol. 8, no. 2 (April–June 2013). Even people whom the media label as 'climate sceptics' agree. 'It is quite odd that so much of the argument on global warming had been on whether or not a human influence can be seen,' wrote Bjørn Lomborg, perhaps the most famous 'climate sceptic', in the chapter on global warming of his controversial book *The Skeptical Environmentalist*: 'Even with lots of countervailing (negative feedback) climate effects, it would seem unlikely that there would not be some form of warming coming from increased CO_2.' (*The Skeptical Environmentalist: Measuring the Real State of the World*, Cambridge University Press, 2001, pp. 265–6.) Later, he made his position even clearer, stating that climate change is, 'undoubtedly one of the chief concerns facing the world today' (quoted in Matthew Moore, 'Climate "sceptic" Bjørn Lomborg now believes global warming is one of world's greatest threats', *Daily Telegraph*, 31 August 2010). What I'm saying here in this secant is not that the jury is out on climate change, but that *even if it were we should still be taking action*.

page 117 *millions of lives will be lost*: The World Health Organization estimates that without significant action to reduce carbon emissions, climate change will be causing approximately 250,000 additional deaths *per year* between 2030 and 2050. These deaths are primarily caused through climate change's impacts on heat exposure in elderly people, diarrhoea, malaria, and childhood under-nutrition. See Simon Hales, Sari Kovats, Simon Lloyd and Diarmid Campbell-Lendrum (eds.), *Quantitative Risk Assessment of the Effects of Climate Change on Selected Causes of Death, 2030s and 2050s, 2014*, World Health Organization, 2014, http://apps.who.int/iris/bitstream/10665/134014/1/9789241507691_eng.pdf?ua=1.

page 117 *the world economy will lose trillions of dollars*: Estimates of the economic costs of climate change range from a benefit to the global economy of 2% or so of GDP, to a decrease of 20% of global GDP or more. Most estimates suggest climate change will damage the global economy by a few per cent of global GDP (Richard Tol and Gary Yohe, 'A review of the Stern Review', *World Economics*, vol. 7, no. 4 (December 2006)). As global GDP is currently approximately $80 trillion and growing (*CIA World Factbook*, 2014, https://www.cia.gov/library/publications/the-world-factbook/geos/xx.html), the damage from climate change to the global economy is expected to be trillions of dollars.

page 117 *the costs are much lower*: Nicolas Stern et al., *The Economics of Climate Change: The Stern Review*, Cambridge University Press, 2007.

page 117 *low-carbon technology*: Some of the money invested in low-carbon technology would have been beneficial, such as the investments into solar photovoltaics which are a useful technology for producing electricity in remote regions, and in the future potentially for generating electricity at low cost. Other investments, such as funding for carbon capture and storage technologies to bury carbon dioxide emissions under the ground, would probably have been less beneficial in the absence of climate change (though these investments would probably still have had some positive impact in improving our ability to do activities such as enhanced oil recovery).

page 117 *slowed economic progress a bit*: The *Stern Review* estimates that mitigating climate change would cost approximately 1% of GDP every year, which is money that we would otherwise be spending on other things, which currently would be approximately $1 trillion per year. See Stern et al., *The Economics of Climate Change*.

page 118 *half a billionth of a degree Celsius*: Current estimates of the warming caused per trillion metric tons of carbon emitted are between 0.8 and 2.5 degrees Celsius (IPCC, *Climate Change 2013: The Physical Science Basis*, Cambridge University Press, 2013, ch. 12). The average emissions per capita for someone living in the US are approximately five metric tons of carbon (Carbon Dioxide Information and Analysis Centre, http://cdiac.ornl.gov/trends/emis/top2009.cap). US current life expectancy is about eighty years (World Health Organization, *World Health Statistics 2013*, Geneva: World Health Organization, 2013). If we assume lifetime emissions at this average rate, then an average US citizen would contribute approximately half a billionth of degree of warming. The average emissions per capita for someone living in the UK are about half that of someone living in the US, so an average British citizen would contribute approximately one quarter of a billionth of a degree of warming (Department of Energy and Climate Change, '2013 UK greenhouse gas emissions, final figures', 2015, https://www.gov.uk/government/statistics/final-uk-emissions-estimates).

page 118 *that increase of half a billionth of a degree*: Scientists are unable to say whether or not a given extreme weather event was *caused* by climate change, but they can say whether a given event was *made more likely* by climate change. So we should expect a small increase in carbon emissions will slightly increase the chances of certain types of extreme weather events occurring. See IPCC, *Climate Change 2013*, ch. 10.

page 118 *the* expected *harm of raising global temperatures*: The amount by which your individual emissions would increase the chance of a given extreme event occurring are very small. However there are many possible extreme events that could occur as a result of increased climate change, and so the chances of your individual emissions causing an extreme event at some point are non-negligible.

page 118 *Economic growth per person over the past decade*: Gross World Product has grown at a rate of 3.5% over the past nine years ('World economic outlook databases', International Monetary Fund, 2014, www.imf.org/external/ns/cs.aspx?id=28), while the global population growth rate over this period has been 1.2% (United Nations Department of Economic and Social Affairs Population Division, 'World population prospects: the 2012 revision', 2012, http://esa.un.org/unpd/wpp/Excel-Data/EXCEL_FILES/1_Population/WPP2012_POP_F01_1_TOTAL_POPULATION_BOTH_SEXES.XLS). Dividing gross world product growth by global population growth yields an average economic growth rate per person of 2.2%.

page 119 *the social cost of one metric ton of CO_{2eq} is about $32*: The median of 311 published estimates of the social cost of carbon is $116/metric ton of carbon (Richard Tol, 'An updated analysis of carbon dioxide emission abatement as a response to climate change', 2012, www.copenhagenconsensus.com/sites/default/files/climateemissionsabatement.pdf). Note that this is measured in metric tons of carbon, and so to convert to metric tons of carbon dioxide we need to multiply this figure by the ratio of their relative molecular masses, 12/44, giving a social cost of carbon of $32 per metric ton of carbon dioxide. If we were to use the mean rather than the median estimate, we would get a social cost of carbon of $48 per metric ton of CO_2.

page 119 *The average American emits about twenty-one metric tons of CO_{2eq} every year*: This figure does not include emissions from land-use change or forestry. (World Resources Institute, 2014, http://cait2.wri.org/wri/Country%20GHG%20Emissions?indicator[]=Total%20GHG%20Emissions%20Excluding%20Land-Use%20Change%20and%20Forestry%20Per%20Capita&year[]=2011&sortDir=desc&chartType=geo)

page 119 *people in the UK*: Department of Energy and Climate Change, '2013 UK greenhouse gas emissions, final figures'.

page 120 *even acknowledges a small risk of* catastrophic *climate change*: I'm using the term 'catastrophic climate change' to refer to warming significantly beyond the usual 2–4°C range. Most scenarios in which this occurs involve one or more tipping points in the climate system that may increase global warming more than otherwise anticipated. We should distinguish this from 'runaway climate change', which astronomers refer to as a situation where a planet such as Earth heats so much that the water on the planet boils off. That's considerably more extreme (and very considerably less likely) than what I'm referring to by catastrophic climate change.

page 120 *the consequences would be disastrous*: The chances of climate change bringing an end to the human race are extremely small, but the consequences of such an extinction event would be so severe as to warrant further thinking. In order for runaway climate change to happen, a number of feedbacks in the climate system would need to push temperatures considerably higher than we expect. The sorts of feedbacks that could contribute include: frozen methane trapped in melting arctic ground ice; extensive forest fires in rainforests; frozen methane on deep sea beds; and ice melting and revealing darker ground which absorbs more sunlight. To cause human extinction this extreme climate change would probably need to give rise to societal collapse, perhaps triggered by water or crop shortages. The situation could be exacerbated if geoengineering, previously used to cool the planet, was discontinued during the societal collapse, which could cause even more warming. Even in a situation of this sort it is unlikely that the human race would end, however.

page 120 *the death tolls from disasters form a fat-tailed distribution*: A comprehensive overview is in Anders Sandberg, 'Power laws in global catastrophic and existential risks', unpublished paper.

page 120 *'Black Swans'*: Nassim Nicholas Taleb, *The Black Swan: The Impact of the Highly Improbable*, New York: Random House, 2007.

page 120 *most people who've died in war have died in the very worst wars*: Steven Pinker, *The Better Angels of Our Nature: Why Violence Has Declined*, New York: Viking, 2011.

page 121 *This is what the Skoll Global Threats Fund focuses on*: 'Mission and strategy', Skoll Global Threats Fund, www.skollglobalthreats.org/about-us/mission-and-approach/.

page 121 *GiveWell is currently investigating these sorts of activities*: Alexander Berger, 'Potential global catastrophic risk focus areas', The GiveWell Blog, 26 June 2014, http://blog.givewell.org/2014/06/26/potential-global-catastrophic-risk-focus-areas/.

Chapter 7: Overhead Costs, CEO Pay and Other Confusions

page 125 *'Most African children who attend school'*: Books for Africa, 'Why books?', https://www.booksforafrica.org/why-books.html. A similar organisation, Books to Africa, exists in the UK.

page 126 *'Books for Africa is a simple idea'*: Books for Africa, 'Home', www.booksforafrica.org/.

page 126 *'6.3 million children worldwide die under the age of five every year'*: Development Media International, 'Priority issues', www.developmentmedia.net/priority-issues and 'Demand creation', www.developmentmedia.net/demand-creation.

page 127 *'Recipients use transfers for whatever is most important to them'*: GiveDirectly, 'Operating model', https://www.givedirectly.org/howitworks.php.

page 128 *'Savvy donors know'*: Charity Navigator, 'Top 10 Best Practices of Savvy Donors', www.charitynavigator.org/index.cfm?bay=content.view&cpid=419&print=1.

page 129 *Development Media International's overheads amount to 44% of its total budget*: Conversation with Will Snell, of Development Media International, July 2014. As came up in conversation, what counts as 'overhead' is fairly arbitrary. He comments:

NOTES

The overheads calculation all depends on definitions:

Defined at the minimum level (London office rent and associated expenditure, non-project staff, non-project related travel, IT/comms), our overheads are around 16% of total expenditure.

Defined at the mid-level (all HQ expenses, including staff who work directly on project delivery from London such as our research manager), our overheads are around 44% of total expenditure.

Defined at the maximum level (the [randomised controlled trial]), our overheads are 100% of total expenditure because we do not currently have any other live projects!

page 129 *In 2012 its site received a total of 6.2 million visits*: 'Where we are headed (2013 and beyond)', Charity Navigator, www.charitynavigator.org/index.cfm?bay=content.view&cpid=1193#.VJddHsAA.

page 130 *this approach to evaluating a charity's effectiveness is seriously flawed*: There are many other problems with focusing on overheads; some of these are described in Holden Karnofsky, 'The worst way to pick a charity', GiveWell blog, 1 December 2009, http://blog.givewell.org/2009/12/01/the-worst-way-to-pick-a-charity/; Dean Karlan, 'Why ranking charities by administrative expenses is a bad idea', Freakonomics blog, 9 June 2011, http://freakonomics.com/2011/06/09/why-ranking-charities-by-administrative-expenses-is-a-bad-idea/; and Dan Pallotta, *Uncharitable: How Restraints on Nonprofits Undermine Their Potential*, Medford, Mass.: Tufts University Press, 2008, ch. 3. One crucial problem is that it's often highly indeterminate what counts as overheads and what doesn't. There is one aspect of the 'overheads' metric that it's potentially important to maintain, however, which is the focus on keeping fundraising costs low. The reason that low fundraising costs should be encouraged in general involves the 'what would have happened otherwise' consideration. When one charity raises money, in part it's creating new philanthropic money, and in part it's merely causing donors to donate to it rather than to other charities. This is the same as all other marketing: when Coca-Cola runs a marketing campaign, in part it will get people to buy more fizzy drinks than they otherwise would have, but in part it will just get people to buy Coke rather than Pepsi. Adrian Sargeant, Professor of Fundraising at the University of Plymouth, commented to me, 'On the issue of charities and whether expenditure grows the pie, I think the answer there is no – it doesn't' (private communication, August 2014). This creates a risk: if charities keep spending more and more on fundraising, battling against each other, then they'll reduce the overall size of the charitable pie, because a larger amount of money will have been squandered on negative-sum fundraising. If we have a social norm against charities spending too much of their budget on fundraising, we can avoid this bad outcome to some extent.

page 132 *providing textbooks has no discernible effect on children's school performance*: For example: '[A]mong those in school, test scores are remarkably low and unresponsive to more-of-the-same inputs, such as hiring additional teachers, buying more textbooks, or providing flexible grants,' in Michael Kremer, Conner Brannen and Rachel Glennerster, 'The Challenge of Education and Learning in the Developing World', *Science*, vol. 340, no. 6130 (19 April 2013), p. 297. There was also no effect on dropout or repetition rate among students. The most important randomised controlled trial on textbook distribution is Glewwe, Kremer and Moulin, 'Many children left behind?', which found a positive effect of textbook distribution only on the most able of students. This trial was conducted in Kenya; a study to assess whether the same conclusion holds in other countries in Sub-Saharan Africa was conduced by Maria Kuecken and Anne-Marie Valfort, 'When do textbooks matter for achievement?' *Economic Letters*, 2013. Their conclusion was consistent with the conclusion of Glewwe, Kremer and Moulin. A meta-analysis has been conducted on randomized controlled trials of increases in instructional materials by Patrick McEwan, 'Improving Learning in Primary Schools of Developing Countries: A Meta-Analysis of Randomised Experiments', unpublished paper, which concludes that 'instructional materials have few effects on learning in the absence of teacher training' (p. 2). In communication, the executive director of Books for Africa, Patrick Plonski, referenced studies that seemed to support distribution of textbooks, such as Sebastian Fehrler, Katharina Michaelowa, and Annika Wechtler, 'The cost-effectiveness of inputs in primary education: insights from recent student surveys for sub-Saharan Africa,' *Journal of Development Studies*, vol. 45, no. 9 (2009), pp. 1545–78. However, the studies that seemed to support textbook distribution were retrospective analyses: showing that there's a *correlation* between increased textbook ownership and higher test scores, but not necessarily that increased textbook ownership *causes* higher test scores. Given the results of the randomised controlled trials, the best interpretation of these earlier retrospective studies is that parents are more likely to purchase books for their children the more academically able they are: higher ability causing greater textbook ownership, rather than the other way round. For this argument in depth, see Paul Glewwe and Michael Kremer, 'Schools, teachers, and education outcomes in developing countries', in Eric A. Hanushek and F. Welch (eds.), *Handbook of the Economics of Education*, vol. 2, New York: Elsevier, 2006, pp. 945–1017.

page 134 *The American Cancer Society spends*: American Cancer Society, 'Stewardship report', 2013, p. 44. www.cancer.org/acs/groups/content/@corporatecommunications/documents/document/acspc-041227.pdf.

page 134 *The ALS Association (of ice bucket challenge fame) spends*: ALS Association, 'Annual report', 2014, p. 3, www.alsa.org/assets/pdfs/annual_report_fy2014.pdf. The figures have been recalculated to exclude administration and fundraising costs.

page 135 *it costs DMI between 40¢ and 80¢ per listener per year*: Private conversation with Will Snell, December 2014. For example its programme in DR Congo costs $1 million per year, and through that they will reach 2.5 million people.

page 135 *what the recipients of these cash transfers do with the money*: Private conversation with Paul Niehaus, August 2014; Johannes Haushofer and Jeremy Shapiro, 'Policy brief: impacts of unconditional cash transfers', unpublished paper, 24 October 2013, pp. 16–17, www.princeton.edu/~joha/publications/Haushofer_Shapiro_Policy_Brief_2013.pdf.

page 136 *Diarrhoea is a major problem*: WHO factsheet, Diarrhoeal disease, www.who.int/mediacentre/factsheets/fs330/en/. Diarrhoea is also a leading cause of malnutrition.

page 136 *a significant number*. 'The pooled relative risk of diarrhoeal disease associated with not washing hands from the intervention trials was 1.88 (95% CI 1.31–2.68), implying that hand washing could reduce diarrhoea risk by 47%,' Val Curtis, and Sandy Cairncross, 'Effect of washing hands with soap on diarrhoea risk in the community: a systematic review', *Lancet Infectious Diseases*, vol. 3, no. 5 (May 2003), pp. 275–81.

page 137 *The ads that DMI run are terribly corny*: 'Audio: Burkina Faso breastfeedingspotA', DevelopmentMediaInternational, www.developmentmedia.net/audio-burkina-faso-breastfeeding-spot-2013.

page 138 *'one $10 bed net can mean the difference between life and death'*:

'Saving lives', Nothing But Nets, www.nothingbutnets.net/new/saving-lives/.

page 140 *But when high-quality studies were conducted*: See, for example, David Roodman, *Due Diligence: An Impertinent Inquiry into Microfinance*, Washington, D.C.: Center for Global Development, 2012. Roodman comments: 'On current evidence, the best estimate of the average impact of microcredit on poverty is zero . . . The commonsense idea that credit is a useful tool that sometimes helps and sometimes hurts appears close to the truth.' (www.cgdev.org/doc/full_text/DueDiligence/Roodman_Due_Diligence.html). Initially, there were academic studies conducted on microfinance that did seem to show strong impact, summarised in Nathanael Goldberg, 'Measuring the impact of microfinance: taking stock of what we know', Grameen Foundation, December 2005, http://files.givewell.org/files/Cause1-2/Independent%20research%20on%20microfinance/GFUSA-MicrofinanceImpactWhitepaper-1.pdf. However, these studies weren't randomised: when randomised controlled trials came out, they changed the picture dramatically. This example illustrates just how important getting high-quality evidence is: low-quality evidence can include highly cited academic studies, not just anecdotes. For an overview of the 'hierarchy of evidence' see Trisha Greenhalgh, 'How to read a paper: getting your bearings (deciding what the paper is about)', *BMJ*, vol. 315, no. 7102 (26 July 1997), pp. 243–6. Note that microcredit is only one form of microfinance; other forms of microfinance such as 'microsavings' (providing secure places for the very poor to save money) have shown promise.

page 140 *Rather than starting new companies*: In an interview with *Time*, David Roodman from the Center for Global Development commented, 'There are a fair number of stories where women cannot pay back their loans but they're in [community borrowing groups]. So people come and take their roofs, flashlights, everything.' For this and the other problems listed, see 'Why we don't recommend microfinance', Giving What We Can blog, 29 November 2012, https://www.givingwhatwecan.org/blog/2012-11-29/why-we-don%E2%80%99t-recommend-microfinance; Sam Donald, 'Why we (still) don't recommend microfinance', Giving What We Can blog, 12 March 2014, https://www.givingwhatwecan.org/blog/2014-03-12/why-we-still-dont-recommend-microfinance; Holden Karnofsky, '6 myths about microfinance charity that donors can do without', The GiveWell blog, 23 October 2009, http://blog.givewell.org/2009/10/23/6-myths-about-microfinance-charity-that-donors-can-do-without/.

page 140 *The latest evidence suggests*: Abhijit Banerjee, Dean Karlan and Jonathan Zinman, 'Six randomised evaluations of microcredit: introduction and further steps', 6 September 2014, http://karlan. yale.edu/p/AEJ%20Intro.pdf.

page 140 *Cash transfers are one of the most well-studied development programmes*: See the list of studies in 'Cash transfers in the developing world: program track record', GiveWell, November 2014, www.givewell.org/international/technical/programs/cash-transfers #ProgramTrackRecord.

page 141 *Innovations for Poverty Action has run a randomised controlled trial on GiveDirectly*: Johannes Haushofer and Jeremy Shapiro, 'Household response to income changes: evidence from an unconditional cash transfer program in Kenya', 15 November 2013, www.princeton.edu/~joha/publications/Haushofer_Shapiro_ UCT_2013.pdf.

page 142 *may be optimistic*: It's very difficult to know how to adjust one's estimates of cost-effectiveness in order to take this into account. GiveWell has tried to make adjustments to the estimate in order to take into account the facts that the programme may not work as well in countries other than Burkina Faso, and that self-reporting may overstate the benefits of the programme. According to GiveWell's revised estimate, the cost per child life saved is $5,200 (this figure doesn't include non-lifesaving health benefits). DMI, however, thinks these adjustments are inappropriate and stands by an estimate of approximately $1,100 per life saved (again not including non-lifesaving health benefits, which the $10/QALY figure does include). 'Development Media International (DMI): what do you get for your dollar?', GiveWell, December 2014, www.givewell.org/international/top-charities/ DMI#cea.

page 143 *a study of bed nets distributed by the Kenyan government*: Noboru Minakawa, Gabriel O. Dida, Gorge O. Sonye, Kyoko Futami and Satoshi Kaneko, 'Unforeseen misuses of bed nets in fishing villages along Lake Victoria', *Malaria Journal*, vol. 7 (2008), p. 165.

page 144 *figure is 0.4%*. https://www.givedirectly.org/quality-of-service. html, accessed January 2015.

page 145 *These programs also receive substantial support from Gavi*: 'Gavi pledging conference June 2011', www.gavi.org/funding/ resource-mobilisation/process/gavi-pledging-conference-june-2011/.

page 145 *GiveDirectly could productively use an additional $25–$30 million*: 'GiveDirectly', GiveWell, December 2014, www.givewell.org/

international/top-charities/give-directly.

page 145 *DMI could productively use $10 million*: 'Development Media International', GiveWell, December 2014, www.givewell.org/ international/top-charities/DMI.

page 148 *such as polio, measles, diarrheal disease and guinea worm*: See Levine, *Case Studies in Global Health*, pp. 33–40, 57–64, 81–8, 127–34.

page 148 *the link between aid and economic growth is less clear*: For a nontechnical overview, see David Roodman, 'Macro aid effectiveness research: a guide for the perplexed', working paper 135, Center for Global Development, December 2007, www.cgdev.org/ files/15003_file_Guide_Perplexed.pdf.

page 150 *GiveDirectly*: https://www.givedirectly.org/; 'GiveDirectly', GiveWell December 2014, www.givewell.org/international/ top-charities/give-directly..

page 151 *Development Media International*: http://developmentmedia. net/;'Development Media International', GiveWell, December 2014, www.givewell.org/international/top-charities/DMI.

page 152 *Deworm the World Initiative*: www.evidenceaction.org/; 'Deworm the World Initiative (DtWI), led by Evidence Action', GiveWell, December 2014, www.givewell.org/international/ top-charities/deworm-world-initiative.

page 153 *Schistosomiasis Control Initiative*: www3.imperial.ac.uk/ schisto; 'Schistosomiasis Control Initiative (SCI)', GiveWell, November 2014, www.givewell.org/international/top-charities/ schistosomiasis-control-initiative.

page 154 *Against Malaria Foundation*: https://www.againstmalaria. com/Default.aspx; 'Against Malaria Foundation (AMF)', GiveWell, November 2014, www.givewell.org/international/top-charities/ AMF.

page 154 *Living Goods*: http://livinggoods.org/; 'Living goods', GiveWell, November 2014, www.givewell.org/international/ top-charities/living-goods.

page 155 *The Iodine Global Network (IGN)*: www.ign.org; another 'standout' charity, as listed by GiveWell in December 2014, is Global Alliance for Improved Nutrition: Universal Salt Iodization (GAIN-USI) program (www.givewell.org/international/top-charities/GAIN). Like IGN, GAIN-USI focuses on increasing the coverage of salt iodisation. I didn't include them in the body text because of their similar focus to IGN and because, at the time of writing, details of how GAIN-USI would use additional funding were not available.

Another charity worthy of note is Project Healthy Children (PHC): projecthealthychildren.org. PHC works with developed world governments to fortify foods like flour, sugar, rice and oil with micronutrients such as folic acid, iodine, iron, vitamin A and zinc, at a cost of between 5¢ and 10¢ per person. This is a top-recommended charity by Giving What We Can; however PHC declined to participate in GiveWell's review process. For consistency, I only list GiveWell recommendations in this chapter.

page 156 *One estimate put the economic benefits of these programs at $27 for every $1 spent*: For an overview of the relevant estimates, see 'Micronutrients', Giving What We Can, 2013, https://www.giving-whatwecan.org/research/charities-area/micronutrients.

Chapter 8: The Moral Case for Sweatshop Goods

page 158 *its garment workers are paid up to fifty times more than the competition*: American Apparel, 'About us', www.americanapparel.net/aboutus/. I use American Apparel as an example of a supposedly 'ethical' company because of their emphasis on 'sweatshop-free' production. Independently of this, however, other aspects of the business are problematic. Dov Charney, the founder and former CEO of the company, has been the subject of numerous allegations of misconduct and sexual harassment, which in part led to his dismissal in early 2014 (see www.buzzfeed.com/sapna/exclusive-read-ousted-american-apparel-ceo-dov-charneys-term#.lgZarE7Wz). American Apparel's advertising campaigns have also come under criticism for sexualising minors (see www.independent.co.uk/life-style/fashion/features/american-apparels-most-controversial-moments-following-ban-on-back-to-school-ad-9712735.html).

page 159 *under pretty horrific working conditions*: Lucy Ash, 'Inside China's sweatshops', BBC News, 20 July 2002.

page 160 *columnist Nicholas D. Kristof illustrated this well*: Nicholas D. Kristof, 'Where sweatshops are a dream', *New York Times*, 15 January 2009, p. A35.

page 160 *nearly four million people from Laos, Cambodia, and Burma immigrated to Thailand*: Marc Margolis, 'Roads to nowhere: more and more migrants from poor countries are heading to other former backwaters for work', *Newsweek*, 11 September 2006.

page 161 *Bolivians risk deportation by illegally entering Brazil*: Jack Chang, 'Bolivians fail to find better life in Brazil', *Miami Herald*, 28 December 2007. Cited in Benjamin Powell, *Out of Poverty: Sweatshops in the Global Economy*, New York: Cambridge University Press, 2014, p. 60.

page 161 *The average earnings of a sweatshop worker in Brazil are $2,000 per year*: Powell, *Out of poverty*, pp. 60–1. Other daily figures ibid.

page 161 *'The overwhelming mainstream view among economists'*: Quoted in Allen R. Myerson, 'In principle, a case for more "sweatshops"', *New York Times*, 22 June 1997, p. E5.

page 161 *'My concern is not that there are too many sweatshops but that there are too few'*: ibid.

page 161 *low wage, labour-intensive manufacturing is a stepping stone*: Powell, *Out of poverty*, pp. 120–1.

page 162 *'it is widely thought that most of them'*: Bureau of International Labor Affairs, *By the Sweat and Toil of Children: The Use of Child Labor in American Imports: A Report to the Committees on Appropriations*, Washington, D.C.: US Dept of Labor, 1994, p. 30.

page 163 *an investigation by UNICEF*: UNICEF, *The State of the World's Children*, Oxford University Press, 1997, p. 60.

page 163 *We should certainly feel outrage and horror at the conditions sweatshop labourers toil under*: Note that none of the arguments I've given apply to the use of forced labour: there is no argument that non-voluntary work benefits the workers. (Though chattel slavery, where people are bought and sold as if they were commodities, is thankfully now very rare, debt bondage, where a person pledges their labour in return for a loan, and where that debt can be passed down through generations, still exists.) If a company contracts with factories that use involuntary workers, we should utterly condemn this, and demand that the situation is rectified.

page 163 *in favour of domestically produced goods*. Nor is the solution to buy second-hand clothes, as is advised by, for example, the Institute for Humane Education (http://humaneeducation. org/blog/2013/04/03/5-tips-keeping-sweatshop-free-closet/) and Labour Behind the Label (www.labourbehindthelabel.org/jobs/item/980). This would have the same effect of reducing employment opportunities for the very badly off in poor countries.

page 164 *$6.9 billion was spent on Fairtrade certified products worldwide*: Rebecca Smithers, 'Global fairtrade sales reach £4.4bn following 15% growth during 2013', *Guardian*, 3 September 2014.

page 165 *Fairtrade coffee production comes from comparatively rich countries*: Paul Griffiths, 'Ethical objections to fair trade', *Journal of Business Ethics*, vol. 105, no. 3 (February 2012), p. 364.

page 165 *less than 1% of the additional price of their Fairtrade coffee reached coffee exporters*: Ibid., pp. 359–60.

page 165 *only 11% of the additional price reached the coffee-producing countries*: Joni Valkila, Pertti Haaparanta and Niina Niemi, 'Empowering coffee traders? The coffee value chain from Nicaraguan fair trade farmers to Finnish consumers', *Journal of Business Ethics*, vol. 97, no. 2 (December 2010), pp. 257–70.

page 165 *coffee producers would receive only 40¢ per pound*: Bernard Kilian, Connie Jones, Lawrence Pratt and Andrés Villalobos, 'Is sustainable agriculture a viable strategy to improve farm income in Central America? A case study on coffee', *Journal of Business Research*, vol. 59, no. 3 (March 2006), pp. 322–30. For further discussion of these estimates, see Griffiths, 'Ethical objections to fair trade', pp. 359–60.

page 166 *a four-year study on earnings of Fairtrade workers in Ethiopia and Uganda*: Fair Trade, Employment and Poverty Reduction project, *Fairtrade, Employment and Poverty Reduction in Ethiopia, and Uganda*, April 2014, http://ftepr.org/wp-content/uploads/FTEPR-Final-Report-19-May-2014-FINAL.pdf.

page 166 *'The British public has been led to believe'*: Carl Mortished, 'Fairtrade coffee fails to help the poor, British report finds', *Globe and Mail* (Toronto), 26 May 2014.

page 166 *Fairtrade certification does not improve the lives of agricultural workers*: Fair Trade, Employment and Poverty Reduction project, 'Response to Fairtrade Statement on FTEPR Final Report 31st May 2014', http://ftepr.org/wp-content/uploads/Response-to-Fairtrade-Statement-on-FTEPR-Final-Report-Posted.pdf.

page 167 *'there is limited evidence of the impact on workers of participation in Fairtrade'*: Valerie Nelson and Barry Pound, 'The last ten years: a comprehensive review of the literature on the impact of Fairtrade', September 2009, p. 35, www.fairtrade.net/fileadmin/user_upload/content/2009/about_us/2010_03_NRI_Full_Literature_Review.pdf.

page 167 *nine metric tons of carbon dioxide equivalent every year*: Department of Energy and Climate Change, *2013 UK Greenhouse Gas Emissions, Final Figures*, 2015, https://www.gov.uk/government/statistics/final-uk-emissions-estimates.

page 167 *one metric ton of methane produces as much warming as twenty-one metric tons of carbon dioxide*: 'Overview of greenhouse gases', United States Environmental Protection Agency, http://epa.gov/climatechange/ghgemissions/gases/ch4.html.

page 167 *many popular ways of reducing your greenhouse gas emissions*: These facts come from David MacKay, *Sustainable Energy – Without the Hot Air*, Cambridge: UIT, 2009, ch. 11.

page 168 *you would save only a fraction of a metric ton of carbon emissions*: US domestic energy use has been estimated at thirteen metric tons of CO_{2eq} (Christopher M. Jones and Daniel M. Kammen, 'Quantifying carbon footprint reduction opportunities for U.S. households and communities', *Environmental Science Technologies*, vol. 45, no. 9 (2011), pp. 4088–95). UK domestic energy use is approximately five metric tons per year per household. Great Britain's housing energy fact file, UK Government Department for Energy and Climate Change, 2011, https://www.gov.uk/government/uploads/system/uploads/attachment_data/file/48195/3224-great-britains-housing-energy-fact-file-2011.pdf.

page 168 *if you stopped using plastic bags entirely you'd cut out 100kg CO_{2eq} per year*: 'Plastic bags and plastic bottles – CO_2 emissions during their lifetime', Time for change, April 2009, http://time-forchange.org/plastic-bags-and-plastic-bottles-CO2-emissions; 'Facts about the plastic bag pandemic', Reuseit, www.reuseit.com/facts-and-myths/facts-about-the-plastic-bag-pandemic.htm. What about other reasons to reduce the use of plastic bags, such as cutting down on landfill? In reality, plastic bags account for only a tiny amount of the trash that we produce (Joseph Stromberg, 'Why our environmental obsession with plastic bags makes no sense', Vox, 4 October 2014, www.vox.com/2014/10/4/6901299/plastic-bags-environment).

page 168 *only 10% of the carbon footprint of food comes from transportation whereas 80% comes from production*: Sarah DeWeerdt, 'Is local food better?', *World Watch Magazine*, vol. 22, no. 3 (May/June 2009), pp. 6–10, www.worldwatch.org/node/6064; 'The tricky truth about food miles', Shrink that Footprint, http://shrinkthat-footprint.com/food-miles.

page 168 *Cutting out red meat*: Christopher Weber and Scott Matthews, 'Food-miles and the relative climate impacts of food choices in the United States', *Environmental Science and Technology*, vol. 42, no. 10 (2008), pp. 3508–13.

page 168 *Locally grown tomatoes*: Annika Carlsson-Kanyama, 'Food consumption patterns and their influence on climate change', *Ambio*, vol. 27, no. 7 (1998), pp. 528–34.

page 169 *beef, which can cut out about a metric ton of CO_{2eq} per year*: Gidon Eshel and Pamela A. Martin, 'Diet, energy, and global warming', *Earth Interactions*, vol. 10, no. 9 (April 2006), pp. 1–17.

page 169 *driving half as much would cut out two metric tons of CO2eq per year*: 'Greenhouse gas emissions from a typical passenger vehicle', United States Environmental Protection Agency, May 2014, www.epa.gov/otaq/climate/documents/420f14040.pdf.

page 169 *forgoing a round trip flight between London and New York would* *eliminate a metric ton of CO$_{2eq}$*: Christian N. Jardine, 'Calculating the carbon dioxide emissions of flights', Environmental Change Institute, University of Oxford, February 2009, www.eci.ox.ac.uk/research/energy/downloads/jardine09-carboninflights.pdf.

page 169 *loft insulation, which would save a metric ton of CO$_{2eq}$ for a detached house*: 'Our calculations', Energy Saving Trust, 2014, www.energysavingtrust.org.uk/content/our-calculations.

page 169 *'While the carbon we release by flying or driving is certain and verifiable'*: George Monbiot, 'Selling indulgences', *Guardian*, 18 October 2006.

page 171 *Cool Earth was founded in 2007 in the United Kingdom by businessman Johan Eliasch and MP Frank Field*: 'The team', Cool Earth, www.coolearth.org/the-team/.

page 171 *improves the lives of those living in the rainforest*: In the late 2000s there was some criticism of Cool Earth as 'neo-colonialism' or of engaging in a 'land grab' via buying up significant chunks of the rainforest (e.g. Juliette Jowit, 'Amazon tribe hits back at green "colonialism"', *Guardian*, 14 October 2007; Conor Foley, 'Not cool', Comment is Free, *Guardian*, 12 June 2008, www.theguardian.com/commentisfree/2008/jun/12/brazil.climatechange). These critics, however, seem to misunderstand what the organisation is doing: Cool Earth doesn't own any land in the Amazon rainforest; it simply works with locals to provide them with better economic opportunities so that they aren't forced to sell their land to loggers.

page 171 *with far less deforestation in Cool Earth areas than the surroundings*: Katja Grace, 'Less burn for your buck', Giving What We Can blog, 14 November 2013, https://www.givingwhatwecan.org/blog/2013-11-14/less-burn-for-your-buck-part-ii.

page 172 *it costs them about $100 to prevent an acre of rainforest from being cut down*: 'Save an acre', Cool Earth, www.coolearth.org/save-an-acre.

page 172 *each acre locks in 260 metric tons of CO$_2$*: 'Rainforest facts', Cool Earth, 12 July 2013, www.coolearth.org/rainforest-facts/rainforest-fact-22-260-tonnes-of-co2.

page 172 *suggesting that they were protecting an acre of rainforest for $103*: $154 to protect five acres from 30% logging = $154/(5 x 0.3) = $103.

page 173 *Monbiot claimed that carbon offsetting*: Monbiot, 'Selling indulgences'.

page 173 *'When you cheat on your partner'*: Cheatneutral, www.cheatneutral.com/.

page 174 *I will spare you the grim details here*: If you're interested in further reading, I recommend picking up a copy Peter Singer and

Jim Mason, *The Way We Eat: Why Our Food Choices Matter*, New York: Holtzbrinck, 2006.

page 175 *Of all the animals raised for food*: In this discussion, I don't talk about fish, for two reasons. First, the data on both the number of fish used for human consumption and their quality of life is much more limited than the corresponding data for land animals. Second, there's more uncertainty about the sentience of fish relative to that of land animals than there is about the sentience of different land animals. Still, from the data that does exist I suspect that cutting out fish is of comparable importance to cutting out chicken: the fish people eat have often been fed other fish, so the total number of fish deaths indirectly resulting from human consumption is very high, and it appears that the lives of factory farmed fish are very bad, too.

page 175 *The only quantitative estimates of farmed animal welfare*: Norwood and Lusk, *Compassion, By the Pound*, pp. 227–9. Although the book is co-written by Norwood and Lusk, the estimates are only Norwood's.

page 177 *According to Animal Charity Evaluators*: This uses the 'lower bound' estimate for the effectiveness of leafleting given in the 'Leafleting impact calculator' provided by Animal Charity Evaluators (www.animalcharityevaluators.org/research/interventions/leafleting/leafleting-calculator/). Even though I've used the 'lower bound' estimate in the spirit of being conservative, it should be borne in mind that the evidence on leafleting is of considerably lower quality than the evidence on other programmes discussed elsewhere in this book. The true cost to change someone's dietary habits through leafleting may therefore be quite different from this estimate. Further studies on this issue are currently underway.

page 178 *a phenomenon that they call 'moral licensing'*: For an overview, see Anna C. Merritt, Daniel A. Effron and Benoît Monin, 'Moral self-licensing: when being good frees us to be bad', *Social and Personality Psychology Compass*, vol. 4, no. 5 (May 2010), pp. 344–57.

page 179 *in a recent experiment*: Nina Mazar and Chen-Bo Zhong, 'Do green products make us better people?', *Psychological Science*, vol. 21, no. 4 (April 2010), pp. 494–8.

page 180 *the moral licensing effect may not occur*: For discussion of when the licensing effect does and doesn't occur, see Merritt, Effron and Monin, 'Moral self-licensing'.

Chapter 9: Don't 'Follow Your Passion'

page 181 *As Peter Hurford entered his final year at Denison University*: 'My careers plan', Everyday Utilitarian blog, 19 June 2013, http:// everydayutilitarian.com/essays/my-careers-plan/; private conversation with author, June 2014.

page 183 *if you're not happy at work, you'll be less productive*: For the link between happiness and productivity, see Ivan Robertson and Cary L. Cooper (eds.), *Well-being: Productivity and Happiness at Work*, New York: Palgrave Macmillan, 2011 and Andrew J. Oswald, Eugenio Proto and Daniel Sgroi, 'Happiness and productivity', IZA discussion papers, no. 4645, 2009, www.econstor.eu/ handle/10419/35451.

page 183 *'You have to trust in something'*: '"You've got to find what you love," Jobs says', *Stanford Report*, 14 June 2005. For criticism, see Cal Newport, *So Good They Can't Ignore You: Why Skills Trump Passion in the Quest for Work You Love*, New York: Business Plus, 2012, ch. 1.

page 184 *'You owe it to yourself to do work that you love'*: Jenny Ungless and Rowan Davies, *Career Ahead: The Complete Career Handbook*, London: Raleo, 2008.

page 184 *A popular YouTube video*: 'What if money was no object?', https://vimeo.com/63961985. The video, which reached 2 million views on YouTube before it was taken down for copyright infringement, consists of a brief excerpt, with added background music, from a lecture delivered by Alan Watts and later published on CD as *Do You Do It or Does It Do You?: How to Let the Universe Meditate You* (Sounds True, 2005).

page 185 *In one study of Canadian college students*: Robert J. Vallerand et al., 'Les passions de l'âme: On obsessive and harmonious passion', *Journal of Personality and Social Psychology*, vol. 85, no. 4 (October 2003), p. 759, table 1.

page 185 *fewer than 1 in 1,000 high school athletes will make it into professional sports*: 'Estimated probability of competing in athletics beyond the high school interscholastic level', NCAA, 24 September 2013, www.ncaa.org/about/resources/research/ probability-competing-beyond-high-school.

page 185 *Psychologists Jordi Quoidbach, Daniel T. Gilbert and Timothy Wilson*: Jordi Quoidbach, Daniel T. Gilbert and Timothy D. Wilson, 'The end of history illusion', *Science*, vol. 339, no. 6115 (4 January 2013), pp. 96–8.

page 186 *this is known in psychology as the 'job characteristics theory'*: These are probably the most widely accepted and solid predictors of job satisfaction in current psychology. For discussion, see Thomas A. Judge and Ryan Klinger, 'Promote job satisfaction through mental challenge', in Edward Locke (ed.), *Handbook of Principles of Organisational Behavior: Indispensable Knowledge for Evidence-Based Management*, 2nd edn, Chichester: John Wiley, 2009, pp. 107–21 and Stephen E. Humphrey, Jennifer D. Nahrgang and Frederick P. Morgeson, 'Integrating motivational, social, and contextual work design features: A meta-analytic summary and theoretical extension of the work design literature', *Journal of Applied Psychology*, vol. 92, no. 5 (September 2007), pp. 1332–56.

page 187 *each of these factors also correlates with motivation, productivity and commitment to your employer*: Benjamin Todd, 'How to find a job you'll love', 80,000 Hours blog, 16 August 2012, https://80000hours.org/2012/08/how-to-find-a-job-you-ll-love/.

page 187 *some psychologists have argued is the key to having genuinely satisfying experiences*: Mihaly Csikszentmihalyi, *Flow: The Psychology of Optimal Experience*, New York: Harper & Row, 1990.

page 187 *There are other factors that also matter to your job satisfaction*: See the information and references cited in 'Predictors of job satisfaction', 80,000 Hours, 28 August 2014, https://80000hours.org/career-guide/framework/job-satisfaction/job-satisfaction-research/#predictors-of-job-satisfaction and references cited there.

page 187 *He travelled in India*: See Walter Isaacson, *Steve Jobs*, New York: Simon & Schuster, 2011, pp. 39–50.

page 188 *while Jobs and Wozniak were trying to sell circuit boards to hobbyists*: Jeffrey Young and William L. Simon, *iCon Steve Jobs: The Greatest Second Act in the History of Business*, Hoboken, New Jersey: John Wiley & Sons, 2005, pp. 35–6.

page 189 *it's been found that professors*: Daniel T. Gilbert et al., 'Immune neglect: A source of durability bias in affective forecasting', *Journal of Personality and Social Psychology*, vol. 75, no. 3 (September 1998), pp. 617–38.

page 189 *it's difficult to predict where you'll be most satisfied*: 'Don't go with your gut instinct', 80,000 Hours, 8 March 2013, https://80000hours.org/career-guide/big-picture/dont-go-with-your-gut-instinct/.

page 189 *it's hard for anyone to know which job you'll be best at*: For a general overview, see Frank L. Schmidt and John E. Hunter, 'The validity and utility of selection methods in personnel psychology: practical and theoretical implications of eighty-five years of research findings', *Psychological Bulletin*, vol. 124, no. 2 (September 1998), pp. 262–74.

page 193 *there are many ways of boosting your potential for influence later*: Benjamin Todd, 'Should you do a degree?', 80,000 Hours blog, 18 February 2014, https://80000hours.org/2014/02/should-you-do-a-degree/.

page 196 *think of career decisions like an entrepreneur would think about starting a company*: Jess Whittlestone, 'Your career is like a startup', 80,000 Hours blog, https://80000hours.org/2013/07/your-career-is-like-a-startup/. This idea was independently proposed by LinkedIn co-founder Reid Hoffman and entrepreneur Ben Casnocha in their book *The Start-Up of You: Adapt to the Future, Invest in Yourself, and Transform Your Career*, New York, Crown Business, 2012.

page 197 *the popular Lean Startup movement*: Eric Ries, *The Lean Startup: How Today's Entrepreneurs Use Continuous Innovation to Create Radically Successful Businesses*, New York: Crown Business, 2011.

page 203 *entrepreneurs have less than a 10% chance of ever selling their shares in the company at profit*: Ryan Carey, 'The payoff and probability of obtaining venture capital', 80,000 Hours blog, 25 June 2014, https://80000hours.org/2014/06/the-payoff-and-probability-of-obtaining-venture-capital/.

page 203 *Chris Hallquist, for example*: Private conversation with author, July 2014.

page 204 *App Academy, a three-month intensive programming school*: Marcus Wohlsen, 'Tuition at learn-to-code boot camp is free – until you get a job', *Wired*, 15 March 2013.

page 204 *whether a job will be around in the future*: For an in-depth analysis, see Carl B. Frey and Michael A. Osborne, 'The future of employment: how susceptible are jobs to computerisation?', Oxford Martin School, University of Oxford, 17 September 2013, www.oxfordmartin.ox.ac.uk/downloads/academic/The_Future_of_Employment.pdf.

page 205 *David Brooks, writing in the* New York Times: Brooks, David, 'The way to produce a person', *New York Times*, 3 June 2013.

page 207 *Habiba Islam graduated from Oxford University*: Private communication with author, May 2014.

page 207 *This is what Jess Whittlestone did*: Private communication with author, October 2014.

page 209 *GiveDirectly has raised more than $20 million*: https://www.givedirectly.org/financials.html.

page 210 *Professor William Nordhaus at Yale University has estimated*: William D. Nordhaus, 'Schumpeterian profits in the American economy: theory and measurement', NBER working paper no.

10433, April 2004, p. 22.

page 211 *Annual global remittances are over $400 billion*: 'Migration and development brief', World Bank, October 2014, http://siteresources. worldbank.org/INTPROSPECTS/Resources/334934-1288990760745/ MigrationandDevelopmentBrief23.pdf. Official development assistance was $135 billion in 2013 ('Net official development assistance from DAC and other donors in 2013: preliminary data for 2013', OECD, www.oecd.org/dac/stats/documentupload/ ODA%202013%20Tables%20and%20Charts%20En.pdf).

page 211 *Wave could therefore increase the amount going to Kenya every year by $24 million*: Note that even if Wave transfers only a fraction of global remittances, they might also have an impact by eventually driving down the prices of competitor such as PayPal.

page 213 *a large proportion of scientific achievement comes from a very small number of scientists*: Alfred J. Lotka, 'The frequency distribution of scientific productivity', *Journal of the Washington Academy of Sciences*, vol. 16, no. 12 (1926), pp. 317–24.

page 213 *the difficulty of finding jobs outside of academia*: Jordan Weissmann, 'How many Ph.D.'s actually get to become college professors?', *The Atlantic*, 23 February 2013, www.theatlantic. com/business/archive/2013/02/how-many-phds-actually-get-to-become-college-professors/273434/.

page 213 *Within philosophy, for example, there are about four times as many doctoral candidates as there are tenure-track positions*: Carolyn Dicey Jennings, quoted in 'To get a job in philosophy', The Philosophy Smoker, 18 April 2012, http://philosophysmoker.blog-spot.com.ar/2012/04/to-get-job-in-philosophy.html

page 214 *within economics the number of people who seek academic employment more closely matches the number of academic jobs*: Richard B. Freeman, 'It's better being an economist (but don't tell anyone)', *Journal of Economic Perspectives*, vol. 13, no. 3 (summer 1999), pp. 139–45.

page 214 *Daniel Kahneman and Amos Tversky were psychologists who caused a revolution within economics*: For an excellent overview of this path-breaking research, see Daniel Kahneman, *Thinking, Fast and Slow*, New York: Farrar, Straus and Giroux, 2011.

page 215 *this field has improved our ability to cause desirable behaviour change*: For examples, see 'Poor behaviour: behavioural economics meets development policy', *The Economist*, 4 December 2014, and Dean S. Karlan and Jacob Appel, *More Than Good Intentions: How a New Economics Is Helping to Solve Global Poverty*, New York: Dutton, 2011.

NOTES

page 216 *the distribution of book sales*: Newman, 'Power laws, Pareto distributions and Zipf's law', p. 5.

page 216 *as is the distribution of Twitter follower counts*: *State of the Twittersphere*, HubSpot, January 2010, https://web.archive.org/web/20111112131058/www.hubspot.com/Portals/53/docs/01.10.sot.report.pdf.

page 217 *the main reason they use volunteers*: See Holden Karnofsky, 'Is volunteering just a show?', The GiveWell Blog, 12 November 2008, http://blog.givewell.org/2008/11/12/is-volunteering-just-a-show/.

page 219 *'There are many things that I'd like to see done in the world'*: Private conversation with author, December 2014.

page 220 *has distributed more than 10 million long-lasting insecticide-treated bed nets*: Against Malaria Foundation, https://www.againstmalaria.com/.

Chapter 10: Poverty vs Climate Change vs . . .

page 222 *In the summer of 2013:* Barack Obama, Pariser Platz, Brandenburg Gate, Berlin, Germany, June 19, 2013, www.whitehouse.gov/the-press-office/2013/06/19/remarks-president-o-bama-brandenburg-gate-berlin-germany; John Kerry, 'Remarks on climate change', Jakarta, Indonesia, 16 February 2014, www.state.gov/secretary/remarks/2014/02/221704.htm; Kate Sheppard, 'Harry Reid: "Climate change is the worst problem facing the world today"', *Huffington Post*, 3 June 2014, www.huffington-post.com/2014/03/06/harry-reid-climate-change_n_4914683.html; Justin Gillis, 'U.N. climate panel endorses ceiling on global emissions', *New York Times*, 27 September 2013, www.nytimes.com/2013/09/28/science/global-climate-change-report.html.

page 223 *a framework for thinking about the question*: This 'three-factor model' of cause evaluation was first proposed by GiveWell as part of the Open Philanthropy Project. It was later expanded by 80,000 Hours to cover career decisions, and made mathematically precise by Owen Cotton-Barratt. Note that sometimes the term 'importance' is used instead of 'scale', and 'crowdedness' is used instead of 'tractability'. See Holden Karnofsky, 'Narrowing down U.S. policy areas', 22 May 2014, http://blog.givewell.org/2014/05/22/narrowing-down-u-s-policy-areas/; Benjamin Todd, 'A framework for strategically selecting a cause', 80,000 Hours, 19 December 2013, https://80000hours.org/2013/12/a-framework-for-strategically-selecting-a-cause/; and Owen Cotton-Barratt, 'Estimating cost-effectiveness for problems of unknown difficulty', Future of Humanity Institute, 4 December 2014, www.fhi.ox.ac.uk/estimating-cost-effectiveness/.

page 226 *Preventing the aging process is just a very difficult problem to solve*: A minority of experts would disagree with this assessment. British researcher Aubrey de Grey, for instance, has proposed an approach to the problem of aging that requires no understanding of the intricacies of human metabolism. On this approach, aging is a relatively tractable problem, constrained by public funding rather than human ignorance. See Aubrey de Grey and Michael Rae, *Ending Aging: The Rejuvenation Breakthroughs that Could Reverse Human Aging in Our Lifetime*, New York: St Martin's Press, 2007.

page 229 *defined as living on less than $11,000 per year*: Again, I'm inflation-adjusting, so I'm using a '$1.50/day' poverty line, using US2014 dollars.

page 230 *US criminal justice reform*: For an overview, see 'Criminal justice reform', GiveWell, May 2014, www.givewell.org/labs/causes/criminal-justice-reform.

page 231 *Incarceration also costs the government about $25,000*: John Schmitt, Kris Warner and Sarika Gupta, 'The high budgetary cost of incarceration', Center for Economic and Policy Research, June 2010, www.cepr.net/documents/publications/incarceration-2010-06.pdf.

page 232 *A further $40 million per year*: 'Criminal justice reform', GiveWell.

page 232 *the cost per year of life in prison averted would be as low as $29*: 'Pew Public Safety Performance Project', GiveWell, July 2014, www.givewell.org/labs/causes/criminal-justice-reform/Pew-Public-Safety-Performance-Project.

page 233 *Location rather than other factors accounts for 85% of the global variation in earnings*: For an overview, see Bryan Caplan and Vipul Naik, 'A radical case for open borders', www.depts.ttu.edu/freemarketinstitute/docs/ARadicalCaseforOpenBorders.pdf.

page 233 *Economists Michael Clemens, Claudio Montenegro and Lant Pritchett have estimated*: 'The place premium: wage differences for identical workers across the U.S. border', Center for Global Development, working paper 148, 3 July 2008, www.cgdev.org/sites/default/files/16352_file_CMP_place_premium_148.pdf.

page 234 *greater than a 50% increase in world GDP*: For a comprehensive list of these estimates, see 'Double world GDP', Open Borders: The Case, http://openborders.info/double-world-gdp/. Readers interested in open borders are encouraged to explore this excellent resource.

You might have some concerns about this idea. Won't mass immigration be politically disruptive? Won't it cause a 'brain drain', resulting in all the best talent from poor countries leaving, making those left behind worse off than before? Won't it harm the native workers of the rich country, depressing wages and increasing unemployment?

There are good responses to each of these worries. Let's take the objections in turn. Regarding political disruption, it would improve politics in poor countries: dictators and corrupt governments would have far less power over their people, because those people would have a much easier opportunity to leave the country. For the rich countries, the evidence is ambiguous. For example most social scientists detect little effect of immigration on the size of government, even though immigrants are more in favour of the welfare state: there is a delay before they are eligible to vote, and even when they do have the vote, their turnout at elections is very low.

Regarding the 'brain drain', immigration from poor countries to rich countries would significantly benefit those who choose to remain in the poorer country. Immigrants send substantial remittances back to their home countries – where total global remittances are several times larger than total foreign aid spending, and can be as much as a third of a poor country's GDP. A larger diaspora increases trade between the home country and the country to which immigrants move. Immigrants often return to their home countries, and when they do, they bring back valuable skills. Puerto Rico provides a good illustration of this. More than half of Puerto Ricans live abroad, but the very fact that Puerto Ricans have been able to emigrate to the US means that the standard of living of those who still live in Puerto Rico has increased sixfold since 1980, and is now comparable with countries like the UK and Italy.

Regarding effects on natives' wages and employment, the evidence is ambiguous as to whether immigration would help or harm: a recent survey by David Roodman, commissioned by GiveWell, suggests that immigration would either help or be only mildly harmful. ('The domestic economic impacts of immigration', David Roodman (blog), 3 September 2014, http://davidroodman.com/blog/2014/09/03/the-domestic-economic-impacts-of-immigration/). Immigrants 'take' jobs, but they often take jobs that natives are unwilling to do (such as fruit picking), and they also create jobs, because they demand services in the economy. Moreover, they need to be managed and supervised, and these positions usually go to natives, who often have better education and a better grasp of English. In areas in the US where immigration is higher more women enter the workforce because childcare is cheaper. Among those who estimate that immigration would have a negative effect on the incomes of natives, the effect is very small. A review by Professors Rachel Friedberg and Jennifer Hunt, for example, found that a 10% increase in the fraction of immigrants in the population reduces native wages by about 1%, and found no evidence of significant reductions in native employment: 'The impact of immigrants on host country wages, employment and growth', *Journal of Economic Perspectives*, vol. 9, no. 2 (spring 1995), pp. 23–44.

page 234 *Canada is most sympathetic to increased levels of immigration*: Lant Pritchett, *Let Their People Come: Breaking the Gridlock on International Labor Mobility*, Washington, D.C.: Center for Global Development, 2006, p. 74.

page 235 *'bringing America's annual legal intake of foreign workers'*: 'Principles', ImmigrationWorks USA, www.immigrationworksusa. org/index.php?p=50.

page 236 *amounting to 14.5% of global greenhouse gas emissions*: 'Key facts and findings', Food and Agriculture Organisation of the United Nations, www.fao.org/news/story/en/item/197623/ icode/.

page 236 *Total expenditure from non-profits on factory farming practices is less than $20 million per year*: 'Treatment of animals in industrial agriculture', GiveWell, September 2013, www.givewell.org/labs/ causes/treatment-animals-industrial-agriculture.

page 237 *a 2–4 °C rise in temperature would cause a reduction in GDP by about 2%*: Tol and Yohe, 'A review of the Stern Review'.

page 237 *according to the second most pessimistic model in the Stern Review*: Nebojša Nakićenović and Rob Swart (eds.), *Special Report on Emissions Scenarios: A Special Report of Working Group III of the Intergovernmental Panel on Climate Change*, Cambridge University Press, 2000, sect. 4.4.4, table 4-6.

Page 238 *the UK spends about £1 billion per year*: HM Treasury, 'Spending Round 2013', 26 June 2013, p. 46, https://www.gov.uk/government/ uploads/system/uploads/attachment_data/file/209036/spending-round-2013-complete.pdf

page 240 *Geoengineering itself may pose significant risks*: One potential bad consequence of extreme climate change is that a single country that was going to be particularly harmed by the changing climate may unilaterally attempt geoengineering. (Geoengineering strategies would probably cost only a few billion dollars, easily enough for a small country to pay for.) If this were attempted without sufficient preparation and risk-assessment, and it went wrong, the consequences could be catastrophic.

page 241 *Other global catastrophic risks*: For an overview, see 'Global catastrophic risks', GiveWell, February 2014, www.givewell.org/labs/causes/global-catastrophic-risks.

SELECTED SOURCES AND RESOURCES

Books, articles etc.

Adelman, Carol, Jeremiah Norris, and Kacie Marano, *The Index of Global Philanthropy and Remittances: 2010*, Washington, D.C.: Hudson Institute, 2010

Aos, Steve, Roxanne Lieb, Jim Mayfield, Marna Miller and Annie Pennucci, 'Benefits and costs of prevention and early intervention programs for youth', Washington State Institute for Public Policy, 17 September 2004, www.wsipp.wa.gov/ReportFile/881/Wsipp_Benefits-and-Costs-of-Prevention-and-Early-Intervention-Programs-for-Youth_Summary-Report.pdf

Baird, Sarah, Joan Hamory Hicks and Edward Miguel, 'Worms at work: long-run impacts of child health gains', working paper, Harvard University, 2012, http://scholar.harvard.edu/files/kremer/files/klps-labor_2012-03-23_clean.pdf

Banerjee, Abhijit and Esther Duflo 'The economic lives of the poor', *Journal of Economic Perspectives*, vol. 21, no. 1 (winter 2007), pp. 141–67

Banerjee, Abhijit and Michael Kremer, 'Teacher–student ratios and school performance in Udaipur, India: a prospective evaluation', mimeo, Brookings Institution, Washington, D.C., 2002

Berger, Ken and Robert M. Penna, 'The elitist philanthropy of so-called effective altruism', *Stanford Social Innovation Review* blog, 2013, www.ssireview.org/blog/entry/the_elitist_philanthropy_of_so_called_effective_altruism

Borland, Ralph, 'Radical plumbers and PlayPumps: objects in development', PhD thesis, Trinity College Dublin, 2011

Broome, John, *Weighing Lives*, Oxford University Press, 2004

Bunker, John, 'The role of medical care in contributing to health improvements within societies', *International Journal of Epidemiology*, vol. 30, no. 6 (December 2001), pp. 1260–3

Bureau of International Labor Affairs, *By the Sweat and Toil of Children: The Use of Child Labor in American Imports: A Report to the Committees on Appropriations*, Washington, D.C.: US Dept of Labor, 1994

Carlsson-Kanyama, Annika, 'Food consumption patterns and their influence on climate change', *Ambio*, vol. 27, no. 7 (1998), pp. 528–34

Central Intelligence Agency, *The CIA World Factbook 2014*, https://www.cia.gov/library/publications/the-world-factbook/geos/xx.html

Channing, Arndt, Sam Jones and Finn Tarp, 'Aid, growth, and development: have we come full circle?', *Journal of Globalization and Development*, vol. 1, no. 2 (December 2010), pp. 1–29

Clark, Gregory, *A Farewell to Alms: A Brief Economic History of the World*, Princeton University Press, 2007

Clemens, Michael, Claudio Montenegro and Lant Pritchett, 'The place premium: wage differences for identical workers across the U.S. border', Center for Global Development, working paper 148, 3 July 2008, www.cgdev.org/sites/default/files/16352_file_CMP_place_premium_148.pdf

Congressional Budget Office, 'Trends in the distribution of household income between 1979 and 2007', October 2011, www.cbo.gov/sites/default/files/10-25-HouseholdIncome_0.pdf

Cook, John et al., 'Quantifying the consensus on anthropogenic global warming', *Environmental Research Letters*, vol. 8, no. 2 (April–June 2013)

Csikszentmihalyi, Mihaly, *Flow: The Psychology of Optimal Experience*, New York: Harper & Row, 1990

Curtis, Val and Sandy Cairncross, 'Effect of washing hands with soap on diarrhoea risk in the community: a systematic review', *Lancet Infectious Diseases*, vol. 3, no. 5 (May 2003), pp. 275–81

de Grey, Aubrey and Michael Rae, *Ending Aging: The Rejuvenation Breakthroughs that Could Reverse Human Aging in Our Lifetime*, New York: St Martin's Press, 2007

de Ville de Goyet, Claude, Ricardo Zapata Marti and Claudio Osorio, 'Natural disaster mitigation and relief', in Dean T. Jamison et al., *Disease Control Priorities in Developing Countries*, 2nd. edn, Washington, D.C.: World Bank, 2006, ch. 61

Dishion, Thomas, Joan McCord and François Poulin, 'When interventions harm. Peer groups and problem behavior', *American Psychologist*, vol. 54, no. 9 (September 1999), pp. 755–64

Dunn, Elizabeth, Lara Aknin and Michael Norton, 'Spending money on others promotes happiness', *Science*, vol. 319, no. 5870 (21 March 2008), pp. 1687–8

Easterly, William, 'Can the West save Africa?', *Journal of Economic Literature*, vol. 47, no. 2 (June 2009), pp. 406–7

—— *The White Man's Burden: Why the West's Efforts to Aid the Rest Have Done so Much Ill and so Little Good*, New York: Penguin, 2006

Edlin, Aaron S., Andrew Gelman and Noah Kaplan, 'Vote for charity's sake', *Economists' Voice*, vol. 5, no. 6 (October 2008), pp. 1–4

Eshel, Gidon and Pamela A. Martin, 'Diet, energy, and global warming', *Earth Interactions*, vol. 10, no. 9 (April 2006), pp. 1–17

Fair Trade, Employment and Poverty Reduction project, *Fairtrade, Employment and Poverty Reduction in Ethiopia, and Uganda*, April 2014, http://ftepr.org/wp-content/uploads/FTEPR-Final-Report-19-May-2014-FINAL.pdf

Fredrickson, B. L. and Daniel Kahneman, 'Duration neglect in retrospective evaluations of affective episodes', *Journal of Personality and Social Psychology*, vol. 65, no. 1 (July 1993), pp. 45–55

Freeman, Richard B., 'It's better being an economist (but don't tell anyone)', *Journal of Economic Perspectives*, vol. 13, no. 3 (summer 1999), pp. 139–45

Frey, Carl B. and Michael A. Osborne, 'The future of employment: how susceptible are jobs to computerisation?', Oxford Martin School, University of Oxford, 17 September 2013, www.oxfordmartin.ox.ac.uk/downloads/academic/The_Future_of_Employment.pdf

Friedberg, Rachel and Jennifer Hunt, 'The impact of immigrants on host country wages, employment and growth', *Journal of Economic Perspectives*, vol. 9, no. 2 (spring 1995), pp. 23–44

Galárraga, Omar, M. Arantxa Colchero, Richard G. Wamai and Stefano M. Bertozzi, 'HIV prevention cost-effectiveness', *BMC Public Health*, vol. 9, sup. 1 (2009), pp. S1–S5

Gilbert, Daniel T. et al., 'Immune neglect: A source of durability bias in affective forecasting', *Journal of Personality and Social Psychology*, vol. 75, no. 3 (September 1998), pp. 617–38

GiveWell, 'Combination deworming (mass drug administration targeting both schistosomiasis and soil-transmitted helminths)', December 2014, www.givewell.org/international/technical/programs/deworming

Glewwe, Paul and Michael Kremer, 'Schools, teachers, and education outcomes in developing countries', in Eric A. Hanushek and F.

Welch (eds.), *Handbook of the Economics of Education*, vol. 2, New York: Elsevier, 2006, pp. 945–1017

Glewwe, Paul, Michael Kremer and Sylvie Moulin, 'Many children left behind? Textbooks and test scores in Kenya', *American Economic Journal: Applied Economics*, vol. 1, no. 1 (January 2009), pp. 112–35

Glewwe, Paul, Michael Kremer, Sylvie Moulin and Eric Zitzewitz, 'Retrospective vs. prospective analyses of school inputs: the case of flip charts in Kenya', *Journal of Development Economics*, vol. 74, no. 1 (June 2004), pp. 251–68

Glover, Jonathan, *Humanity: A Moral History of the Twentieth Century*, New Haven: Yale University Press, 1995

Griffiths, Paul, 'Ethical objections to fair trade', *Journal of Business Ethics*, vol. 105, no. 3 (February 2012), pp. 357–73

Groom, Ben and David Maddison, 'Non-identical quadruplets: four new estimates of the elasticity of marginal utility for the UK', working paper no. 141, Centre for Climate Change Economics and Policy, August 2013

Grosse, Scott D., 'Assessing cost-effectiveness in healthcare: history of the $50,000 per QALY threshold', *Pharmacoeconomics & Outcomes Research*, vol. 8, no. 2 (April 2008), pp. 165–78; Chris P. Lee, Glenn M. Chertow and Stefanos A. Zenios, 'An empiric estimate of the value of life: updating the renal dialysis cost-effectiveness standard', *Value in Health*, vol. 12, no. 1 (2009), pp. 80–7

Henderson, D. A., *Smallpox: The Death of a Disease – the Inside Story of Eradicating a Worldwide Killer*, New York: Prometheus Books, 2009

Hindmarsh, R. A., *Nuclear Disaster at Fukushima Daiichi: Social, Political and Environmental Issues*, New York: Routledge, 2013

Hoffman, Reid and Ben Casnocha, *The Start-Up of You: Adapt to the Future, Invest in Yourself, and Transform Your Career*, New York, Crown Business, 2012

Humphreys, Margaret, *Malaria: Poverty, Race, and Public Health in the United States*, Baltimore: Johns Hopkins University Press, 2001, ch. 7

IPCC, *Climate Change 2013: The Physical Science Basis*, Cambridge University Press, 2013

———— *Climate Change 2014: Impacts, Adaptation, and Vulnerability*, Cambridge University Press, 2014

Isaacson, Walter, *Steve Jobs*, New York: Simon & Schuster, 2011

Johnston, Louis and Samuel H. Williamson, 'What was the U.S. GDP then?' MeasuringWorth, 2014, www.measuringworth.com

Jones, Christopher M. and Daniel M. Kammen, 'Quantifying carbon footprint reduction opportunities for U.S. households and communities', *Environmental Science Technologies*, vol. 45, no. 9 (2011), pp. 4088–95

Judge, Thomas A. and Ryan Klinger, 'Promote job satisfaction through mental challenge', in Edward Locke (ed.), *Handbook of Principles of Organisational Behavior: Indispensable Knowledge for Evidence-Based Management*, 2nd edn, Chichester: John Wiley, 2009, pp. 107–21

Kahneman, Daniel, *Thinking, Fast and Slow*, New York: Farrar, Straus and Giroux, 2011

Kamm, F. M., *Morality, Mortality*, vol. I: *Death and Whom to Save from It*, Oxford University Press, 1993

Karlan, Dean S. and Jacob Appel, *More Than Good Intentions: How a New Economics Is Helping to Solve Global Poverty*, New York: Dutton, 2011

Kavanagh, Dennis, David Richards, Andrew Geddes and Martin Smith, *British Politics: Continuities and Change*, 5th edn, Oxford University Press, 2006

Kilian, Bernard, Connie Jones, Lawrence Pratt and Andrés Villalobos, 'Is sustainable agriculture a viable strategy to improve farm income in Central America? A case study on coffee', *Journal of Business Research*, vol. 59, no. 3 (March 2006), pp. 322–30

Koplow, David, *Smallpox: The Fight to Eradicate a Global Scourge*, Berkeley: University of California Press, 2003

Kremer, Michael, 'Randomised evaluations of educational programs in developing countries: some lessons', *American Economic Review*, vol. 93, no. 2 (May 2003), pp. 102–6

Kremer, Michael, Conner Brannen and Rachel Glennerster, 'The Challenge of Education and Learning in the Developing World', *Science*, vol. 340, no. 6130 (19 April 2013), pp. 297–300

Krueger, Alan B. and David A. Schkade, 'The reliability of subjective well-being measures', *Journal of Public Economics*, vol. 92, nos. 8–9 (August 2008), pp. 1833–45

Larson, Reed and Mihaly Csikszentmihalyi, 'The experience sampling method', *New Directions for Methodology of Social & Behavioral Science*, vol. 15 (March 1983), pp. 41–56

Laxminarayan, Ramanan, Jeffrey Chow and Sonbol A. Shahid-Salles, 'Intervention cost-effectiveness: overview of main messages', in Dean Jamison et al. (eds.), *Disease Control Priorities in Developing Countries*, 2nd edn, Oxford University Press, 2006, pp. 41–2

Lee, Chris P., Glenn M. Chertow and Stefanos A. Zenios, 'An empiric estimate of the value of life: updating the renal dialysis cost-effectiveness standard', *Value in Health*, vol. 12, no. 1 (2009), pp. 80–7

Levine, Ruth, *Case Studies in Global Health: Millions Saved*, Sudbury, Mass.: Jones and Bartlett, 2007

Locke, Thomas P., Glenn M. Johnson, Kathryn Kirigin-Ramp, Jay D. Atwater and Meg Gerrard, 'An evaluation of a juvenile education program in a state penitentiary', *Evaluation Review*, vol. 10, no. 3 (June 1986), pp. 281–98

Loewenstein, George F., Eike U. Weber, Christopher K. Hsee and Ned Welch, 'Risk as feelings', *Psychological Bulletin*, vol. 127, no. 2 (March 2001), pp. 267–86

Lomborg, Bjørn, *The Skeptical Environmentalist: Measuring the Real State of the World*, Cambridge University Press, 2001

Lotka, Alfred J., 'The frequency distribution of scientific productivity', *Journal of the Washington Academy of Sciences*, vol. 16, no. 12 (1926), pp. 317–24

MacKay, David, *Sustainable Energy – Without the Hot Air*, Cambridge: UIT, 2009

Maddison, Angus, *Contours of the World Economy 1–2030 AD*, Oxford University Press, 2007

Madestam, Andreas, Daniel Shoag, Stan Veuger and David Yanagizawa-Drott, 'Do political protests matter? Evidence from the Tea Party Movement', *Quarterly Journal of Economics*, vol. 128, no. 4 (2013), pp. 1633–85

Mazar, Nina and Chen-Bo Zhong, 'Do green products make us better people?', *Psychological Science*, vol. 21, no. 4 (April 2010), pp. 494–8

Melman, Mark, 'The making of a "philanthropreneur"', *Journal of Values Based Leadership*, 15 March 2008, www.valuesbasedleadershipjournal.com/issues/vol1issue2/field_melman.php

Merritt, Anna C., Daniel A. Effron and Benoît Monin, 'Moral self-licensing: when being good frees us to be bad', *Social and Personality Psychology Compass*, vol. 4, no. 5 (May 2010), pp. 344–57

Miguel, Edward and Michael Kremer, 'Worms: identifying impacts on education and health in the presence of treatment externalities', *Econometrica*, vol. 72, no. 1 (January 2004), pp. 159–217

Milanovic, Branko, *The Haves and the Have-Nots: A Brief and Idiosyncratic History of Global Inequality*, New York: Basic Books, 2011

Minakawa, Noboru, Gabriel O. Dida, Gorge O. Sonye, Kyoko Futami and Satoshi Kaneko, 'Unforeseen misuses of bed nets in fishing villages along Lake Victoria', *Malaria Journal*, vol. 7 (2008), p. 165

Minoiu, Camelia and Sanjay G. Reddy, 'Development aid and

economic growth: a positive long-run relation', *Quarterly Review of Economics and Finance*, vol. 50, no. 1 (2010), pp. 27–39

Mogensen, Andreas, 'Giving without sacrifice? The relationship between income, happiness, and giving', www.givingwhatwecan. org/sites/givingwhatwecan.org/files/attachments/giving-without-sacrifice.pdf

Morgeson, Frederick P., 'Integrating motivational, social, and contextual work design features: A meta-analytic summary and theoretical extension of the work design literature', *Journal of Applied Psychology*, vol. 92, no. 5 (September 2007), pp. 1332–56

Moyo, Dambisa, *Dead Aid: Why Aid Is Not Working and How There Is a Better Way for Africa*, New York: Farrar, Straus and Giroux, 2009

Nakićenović, Nebojša and Rob Swart (eds.), *Special Report on Emissions Scenarios: A Special Report of Working Group III of the Intergovernmental Panel on Climate Change*, Cambridge University Press, 2000

Newman, Mark, 'Power laws, Pareto distributions and Zipf's law', *Contemporary Physics*, vol. 46, no. 5 (2005), pp. 323–51

Newport, Cal, *So Good They Can't Ignore You: Why Skills Trump Passion in the Quest for Work You Love*, New York: Business Plus, 2012

Norwood, F. Bailey and Jayson Lusk, *Compassion, by the Pound: The Economics of Farm Animal Welfare*, New York: Oxford University Press, 2011

Obiols, Ana Lucía and Karl Erpf, 'Mission report on the evaluation of the PlayPumps installed in Mozambique', The Swiss Resource Centre and Consultancies for Development, April 2008, www-tc. pbs.org/frontlineworld/stories/southernafrica904/flash/pdf/mozambique_report.pdf

Orbinski, James, *An Imperfect Offering: Humanitarian Action for the Twenty-First Century*, New York: Walker, 2008

Oswald, Andrew J., Eugenio Proto and Daniel Sgroi, 'Happiness and productivity', IZA discussion paper no. 4645, 2009, www.cconstor. eu/handle/10419/35451

Pallotta, Dan, *Uncharitable: How Restraints on Nonprofits Undermine Their Potential*, Medford, Mass.: Tufts University Press, 2008

Parfit, Derek, 'Innumerate Ethics', *Philosophy and Public Affairs*, vol. 7, no. 4 (summer 1978), pp. 285–301

Peele, Gillian, *Governing the UK: British Politics in the Twenty-First Century*, 4th edn, Malden, Mass./Oxford: Wiley/Blackwell, 2004

Petrosino, Anthony, Carolyn Turpin-Petrosino, Meghan E. Hollis-Peel and Julia G. Lavenberg, 'Scared Straight and other juvenile awareness programs for preventing juvenile delinquency: a systematic review', *Campbell Systematic Reviews*, vol. 9, no. 5 (2013)

Piketty, Thomas, *Capital in the Twenty-First Century*, Cambridge, Mass.: Harvard University Press, 2014

Pinker, Steven, *The Better Angels of Our Nature: Why Violence Has Declined*, New York: Viking, 2011

Powell, Benjamin, *Out of Poverty: Sweatshops in the Global Economy*, New York: Cambridge University Press, 2014

Pritchett, Lant, *Let Their People Come: Breaking the Gridlock on International Labor Mobility*, Washington, D.C.: Center for Global Development, 2006

Prunier, Gérard, *The Rwanda Crisis: History of a Genocide*, New York: Columbia University Press, 1995

Quoidbach, Jordi, Daniel T. Gilbert and Timothy D. Wilson, 'The end of history illusion', *Science*, vol. 339, no. 6115 (4 January 2013), pp. 96–8

Ravallion, Martin, Shaohua Chen and Prem Sangraula, 'Dollar a day revisited', policy research working paper 4620, World Bank, May 2008

Riddell, Roger, *Does Foreign Aid Really Work?*, Oxford University Press, 2007

Ries, Eric, *The Lean Startup: How Today's Entrepreneurs Use Continuous Innovation to Create Radically Successful Businesses*, New York: Crown Business, 2011

Robertson, Ivan and Cary L. Cooper (eds.), *Well-being: Productivity and Happiness at Work*, New York: Palgrave Macmillan, 2011

Roodman, David, *Due Diligence: An Impertinent Inquiry into Microfinance*, Washington, D.C.: Center for Global Development, 2012

————— 'Macro aid effectiveness research: a guide for the perplexed', working paper 135, Center for Global Development, December 2007, www.cgdev.org/files/15003_file_Guide_Perplexed.pdf

Salomon, Joshua A. et al., 'Common values in assessing health outcomes from disease and injury: disability weights measurement study for the Global Burden of Disease Study 2010', *Lancet*, vol. 380 (15, 22 and 29 December 2012), table 2; available at www.jefftk.com/gbdweights2010.pdf

Schmidt, Frank L. and John E. Hunter, 'The validity and utility of selection methods in personnel psychology: practical and theoretical implications of eighty-five years of research findings', *Psychological Bulletin*, vol. 124, no. 2 (September 1998), pp. 262–74

Simon, William L., *iCon Steve Jobs: The Greatest Second Act in the History of Business*, Hoboken, New Jersey: John Wiley & Sons, 2005

Singer, Peter, 'Famine, affluence and morality', *Philosophy and Pubic Affairs*, vol. 1, no. 1 (spring 1972), pp. 229–43

—— *The Life You Can Save*, New York: Random House, 2009

—— *The Most Good You Can Do*, New Haven: Yale University Press, 2015

Singer, Peter and Jim Mason, *The Way We Eat: Why Our Food Choices Matter*, New York: Holtzbrinck, 2006

Smith, Martin, *The Core Executive in Britain*, Basingstoke: Palgrave Macmillan, 1999

Spiegelhalter, David and Michael Blastland, *The Norm Chronicles*, New York: Basic Books, 2014

Stern, Nicolas et al., *The Economics of Climate Change: The Stern Review*, Cambridge University Press, 2007

Stevenson, Betsey and Justin Wolfers, 'Subjective well-being and income: is there any evidence of satiation?', *American Economic Review*, vol. 103, no. 3 (May 2013), pp. 598–604

Tabutin, Dominique and Bruno Schoumaker, 'The demography of Sub-Saharan Africa from the 1950s to the 2000s [A survey of changes and a statistical assessment]', *Population*, vol. 59, nos. 3–4 (2004), pp. 457–556

Taleb, Nassim Nicholas, *The Black Swan: The Impact of the Highly Improbable*, New York: Random House, 2007

Taurek, John, 'Should the numbers count?', *Philosophy and Public Affairs*, vol. 6, no. 4 (summer 1977), pp. 293–316

Tol, Richard and Gary Yohe, 'A review of the Stern Review', *World Economics*, vol. 7, no. 4 (December 2006), pp. 233–50

UN, 'Millennium Development Goal Indicators', http://mdgs.un.org/unsd/mdg/Metadata.aspx?IndicatorId=0&SeriesId=580

Ungless, Jenny and Rowan Davies, *Career Ahead: The Complete Career Handbook*, London: Raleo, 2008

UNICEF, 'An evaluation of the PlayPump water system as an appropriate technology for water, sanitation and hygiene programmes', October 2007, www-tc.pbs.org/frontlineworld/stories/southernafrica904/flash/pdf/unicef_pp_report.pdf

—— *The State of the World's Children*, Oxford University Press, 1997

Valkila, Joni, Pertti Haaparanta and Niina Niemi, 'Empowering coffee traders? The coffee value chain from Nicaraguan fair trade farmers to Finnish consumers', *Journal of Business Ethics*, vol. 97, no. 2 (December 2010), pp. 257–70

Vallerand, Robert J. et al., 'Les passions de l'âme: On obsessive and harmonious passion', *Journal of Personality and Social Psychology*, vol. 85, no. 4 (October 2003), pp. 756–67

Weber, Christopher and Scott Matthews, 'Food-miles and the relative climate impacts of food choices in the United States', *Environmental Science and Technology*, vol. 42, no. 10 (2008), pp. 3508–13

Weinstein, Milton C., 'How much are Americans willing to pay for a quality-adjusted life year?', *Medical Care*, vol. 46, no. 4, (April 2008), pp. 343–5

Weinstein, Milton C., George Torrance and Alistair McGuire, 'QALYs: the basics', *Value in Health*, vol. 12, sup. s1 (March–April 2009), pp. S5–S9

Wilson, Richard, 'Analyzing the daily risks of life', *Technology Review*, vol. 81, no. 4 (February 1979), pp. 41–6

World Bank, 'Life expectancy at birth, total (years)', http://data.worldbank.org/indicator/SP.DYN.LE00.IN/countries/LS-ZF-XN?display=graph&hootPostID=cc8d300b9308f8acab94418eff2132ac

———— 'Poverty overview', www.worldbank.org/en/topic/poverty/overview

———— World Bank Development Marketplace, http://wbi.worldbank.org/wbi/content/development-marketplace-1

World Health Organization, 'Global burden of disease 2004 update: disability weights for diseases and conditions', www.who.int/healthinfo/global_burden_disease/GBD2004_DisabilityWeights.pdf

———— 'Soil-transmitted helminth infections', fact sheet no. 366, WHO, www.who.int/mediacentre/factsheets/fs366/en/

———— *World Health Statistics 2013*, Geneva: WHO, 2013

Young, Aaron, Humayun J. Chaudhry, Jon V. Thomas and Michael Dugan, 'A census of actively licensed physicians in the United States, 2012', *Journal of Medical Regulation*, vol. 99, no. 2 (2013), pp. 11–24

Websites

Against Malaria Foundation: www.againstmalaria.com
Animal Charity Evaluators: www.animalcharityevaluators.org
CauseVox: www.causevox.com
Center for Global Development: www.cgdev.org
Centre for the Study of Existential Risk: http://cser.org
Charity Science: www.charityscience.com
ClimateWorks: www.climateworks.org
Cool Earth: www.coolearth.org
Development Media International: www.developmentmedia.net
Deworm the World Initiative: www.evidenceaction.org/#deworm-the-world
Effective Altruism: www.effectivealtruism.org

80:000 Hours: https://80000hours.org
Future of Humanity Institute: www.fhi.ox.ac.uk
GiveDirectly: https://www.givedirectly.org
GiveWell: www.givewell.org
Giving What We Can: https://www.givingwhatwecan.org
Global Alliance for Improved Nutrition – Universal Salt Iodization: www.gainhealth.org
ImmigrationWorks USA: www.immigrationworksusa.org/ Institute for Humane Education: http://humaneeducation.org
Iodine Global Network: www.ign.org
Living Goods: http://livinggoods.org
Mercy for Animals: www.mercyforanimals.org
Nuclear Threat Initiative: www/nti.org
Open Borders: http://openborders.info
Oxford Geoengineering Programme: www.geoengineering.ox.ac.uk
Pew Charitable Trusts: www.pewtrusts.org
Project Healthy Children (PHC): projecthealthychildren.org
Schistosomiasis Control Initiative: www3.imperial.ac.uk/schisto
Skoll Global Threats Fund: www.skollglobalthreats.org
Solar Radiation Management Governance Initiative: www.srmgi.org
The Humane League: www.thehumaneleague.com
The Humane Society of the United States: www.humanesociety.org
University of Chicago Crime Lab: http://crimelab.uchicago.edu

INDEX

(Page numbers in italics refer to graphs and tables)

nitrous oxide 119, 167
  see also carbon dioxide equivalent;
    climate change; methane
No Sweat Apparel 159
  see also ethical consumption;
    sweatshops
Noda, Yoshihiko 97
Nordhous, Prof. William 210
Norwood, Bailey 175
Nothing But Nets 138–9
Nuclear Threat Initiative 242

Obama, Barack 221
obstetric fistula 47–8
Occupy Wall Street 19
offsetting emissions 169–74
  likened to indulgences 173–4
  see also climate change; green
    living
One Foundation 3
100x Multiplier 28, 74, 79
One Water 3
Orbinski, James 33, 34–5, 36, 39
Ord, Toby 16
Oxfam 145
Oxford University, and career
  politics 110–11, 112
Oxford University Geoengineering
  Programme 240

peanut butter 100–1
Penna, Robert M. 46–7
People Tree 163
pertussis 144
Pew Charitable Trust 232–3
Piketty, Thomas 19–20
Pim Srey Rath 160
plastic bags 168
PlayPump 1–6, 12
  first sponsor for 2
  as Roundabout Water Solutions 6
  shortcomings of 4–6

PlayPumps International 2, 4, 6, 192
polio 144
politics and advocacy:
  and career choice, high-potential
    long shot 215–16
  see also careers
politics as career 109–14
poverty, global versus domestic
  228–9
Poverty Action Lab 11
Pritchett, Lant 233

quality-adjusted life-year (QALI)
  40, 41
  and Development Media
    International 137
  explained and discussed 39–44
  and health 61–2, 73–4, 75–6,
    78, 92, 137
  see also wellbeing-adjusted life-
    year
Quirk, Lincoln 211
Quoidbach, Jordi 185

rainforest 171–3
  see also green living
regression to the mean 88–9
Reid, Harry 222
remittances, international 211
research:
  and career choice, high-potential
    long shot 212–15
    see also careers
  combining fields in 214–15
Ries, Eric 197
ring vaccination 81
Roundabout Water Solutions 6
Rumsfeld, Donald 53
Rwanda 33–5
  genocide in 33, 34–5, 54
  see also Hutu; Tutsi
Rwandan Patriotic Front 34

see also causes, selection of
voting 102–6
Vox.com 216

Washington Post 216
Washington State Institute for
 Public Policy 87
water–diamonds paradox 67–8
Watts, Alan 184
Wave 211
wellbeing:
    and level of income 25–8, *26*
        see also income distribution
wellbeing-adjusted life-year (WALY)
 45–6
    see also quality-adjusted life-year
wheat, disease-resistant 212
White Man's Burden, The (Easterly)
 51–2

Whittlestone, Jess 207–8
Wikipedia 216
Wilson, Timothy 185
Winfrey, Oprah 66
women's height 57, *57*
World Bank 71
World Bank Development
 Marketplace Award 3
World Health Assembly 82
World Health Organization 71
    smallpox campaign of 80, 83
        see also smallpox
WorldVision 145
Wozniak, Steve 187–8

YouTube 184

Zhdanov, Viktor 82–3